DATE DUE

Slipping Through the Cracks:
The Status of Black Women

Edited by

Margaret C. Simms and Julianne Malveaux

Transaction Books
New Brunswick (U.S.A.) and Oxford (U.K.)

Second printing, 1987

Copyright © 1986 by Transaction, Inc.
New Brunswick, New Jersey 08903

ISSN: 0034-6446
ISBN: 0-88738-662-8 (paper)
Printed in the United States of America

Contents

Continued

Health Issues

Development Issues

Research and Policy Implications

Preface

This publication was developed as a written record of a symposium on the economic status of black women that was co-sponsored by *The Review of Black Political Economy* and the Congressional Black Caucus Foundation. We focused on the problems and needs of black women because they have not been given adequate attention. As Julianne Malveaux indicates in her introduction to the Research and Policy Implications section at the end of this volume, black women have too often slipped through the cracks when the focus is on blacks (mostly male) or women (mostly white). Our intention was not to ignore black men or black children nor was it to create artificial divisions within the black community. Because black women have made such a valuable economic contribution to the black family and the black community as a whole, it is impossible to propose solutions to the problems affecting the community without examining the status of its women.

The term "economic status" has been broadly defined. It includes employment—labor force participation, occupational status, and earnings—and there is a section on education and training because they provide black women with access to better employment opportunities. Because of the prevalence of single parenting among black women, their position is given separate attention. We also examined health conditions because of the impact that health problems have on household income and budgets, as well as the effect of the mother's health on the well-being of her children. Many of the problems of black women are not unique to the United States. Since our symposium was held at the end of the United Nations Decade for Women, there is also a section on the role of black women in two developing countries.

Several of the articles included in this volume present findings from doctoral dissertations and this represents their first distribution to a wider audience. Other essays include data recently made available by government sources or from research studies. However, it is clear that much remains to be done in terms of research and in terms of policy formulation and implementation. The legislative agenda that was developed at the end of the symposium was distributed at a meeting of Congresswoman Cardiss Collins' braintrust on black women. It is our hope that readers of this volume will have the same interest in policy action as the individuals who were present at that time.

A tremendous amount of time and effort went into the symposium and the completion of this publication. I would like to thank staff members at the Congressional Black Caucus Foundation, especially Sherille Ismail and Frank Morris, for handling all the logistics for the symposium. The cooperation of all authors and discussants was essential for getting this volume published in a short period of time. We appreciate the support of the Rockefeller Foundation, which provided a grant to cover symposium costs, and would like to thank the Ford Foundation for their support in the publication of this volume. A special thanks goes to my co-editor Julianne Malveaux. Her hard work was vital to putting this publication together.

Margaret C. Simms

Section Introduction

Julianne Malveaux

Work has been so major a part of black women's legacy that it is frequently jested that black women are born with a broom in hand. The jest is light humor to cover up the slave legacy and the Reconstruction rigors that made work a permanent part of black women's experience.

Soujourner Truth's asked, "Ain't I A Woman?" at a women's conference in Akron, Ohio, in 1851. Her words detailed what black women meant by "work" in slavery:

> I ploughed and planted and gathered into barns and no man could head me! And ain't I a woman? I could work as much and eat as much as a man—when I could get it—and bear the lash as well! And ain't I a woman? I have bourne thirteen children and seen them all sold off to slavery, and when I cried out with my mother's grief, none but Jesus heard me! And ain't I a woman?

From Sojourner Truth's day to this, the burden of black women has been a heavy one. Black girls were denied their childhoods; in 1890, 20% of them worked. In the late nineteenth century, black women mostly worked in private households and in agriculture, and Cecelia Conrad's review of Paula Giddings' *When and Where I Enter* and Jacqueline Jones' *Labor of Love, Labor of Sorrow* details this early postslavery phase of black women's history.

Both Giddings and Jones fill a critical gap in describing the history of black women in the social-political-economic sphere. Giddings' book is precious for the way it holds black women who are historical figures up to the light like multifaceted jewels and examines them and the forces that they shaped. Jones writes without the Giddings fascination but integrates secondary sources not readily available to present a picture of black women's coping strategies in the face of adversity.

But Jacqueline Jones may have written two books. The first is useful original research on the status of black women from slavery until 1940. The second is a set of random thoughts about black women's development from 1940 to 1985. In fact, the second half of Jones' book might well be called "Labor of Stereotypes, Labor of Misinterpretation," for there Jones departs from work history to present a surface examination of organizations like the Student Nonviolent Coordinating Committee (SNCC), a biased discussion of the purview of *Ebony*, and a churlish lecture to black women on feminism and the Jesse Jackson campaign.

Jones' subjectivity in the second half of her book might be less a tragedy if there were a larger literature on black women. But with the exception of Phyllis Wallace's *Black Women in the Labor Force*, little has been written on the unique status of black women in the workplace, either historically or from a contemporary persepctive. Discussions of black women in the workplace have usually been buried between discussions of blacks (usually men) and women (usually white).

Karen Fulbright focuses on the upper end of the distribution of black women in the workplace in her study of managerial black women. She has written her article, based on her doctoral dissertation, to refute Cynthia Epstein's myth of the "double negative" or, more popularly stated, the "twofer." Although Fulbright uses a small sample in her article, the research directions she points to with her theory should be examined by researchers in the future.

Fulbright's work touches only the tip of the iceberg. Just as she examines the status of black managers, so, too, should the status of black female scientists, business owners, and others in nontraditional jobs be examined. Work remains as much a part of the history of black women as it was in 1890, but the work that black women now do is very different from the work we have done in the past. Fulbright's work points out the mistake of considering black women a monolith. Instead, her work recognizes the upper tier of a multitiered system of black female employment: (1) those black women who work in nontraditional jobs, (2) those who work in typically female professional jobs (teachers, nurses, and social workers), (3) those who work in typically female clerical jobs, (4) those who are marginally employed in service and private household jobs, and (5) those who revolve between work and welfare.

Although black women are not monolithic, their aggregate status differs significantly from the status of white women. A number of researchers have argued that these differences are blurring as the labor force participation rates of black and white women begin to converge. Barbara Jones poses the opposite hypothesis: she argues that convergence in black and white women's participation rates is the result of barriers that face black women who attempt to participate in the labor market. Even though black women's participation rates remain higher than those of white women, the increase in black women's participation rates has been slower than the increase in white women's participation rates. Most alarming are the declines in the labor force participation rates of young black women and the implications that these low rates have for the future status of black women.

What do status differences between black and white women mean for public policy initiatives focused on women? The Malveaux article on comparable worth provides one answer, but similar analysis of other aspects of employment policy is necessary. For example, how do federal layoff policies affect black women? How will changing tax policies affect black women? What impact will various employment and training programs have on black women? As Charles Betsey's review of the articles in this section indicates, there is no unanimity of opinion on the wisdom, or the impact, of some policies targeted toward women or toward black women. Betsey's review makes it clear that we need to know more about the status of black women in employment. The articles in this section are steps in this direction.

Though black women's history has been a history of steady labor force participation, black women's work legacy has been low-paid, unstable work in the service sector. Though the status of black women has changed, the inequity that has tinged the work experience of black women remains the fruit of this legacy. Despite the fact that black women's work experiences can currently be described as multitiered, the employment experiences of black women must remain a central concern of those policymakers who strive for equity for black women in the labor market. And as some of the articles in this section show, policies directed toward "women" may not always have a positive impact on black women. Whereas black women's legacy is heavy participation in the marketplace, the policy challenge is to make this participation as equitable, and as rewarding, as possible.

BLACK WOMEN AND LABOR FORCE PARTICIPATION: AN ANALYSIS OF SLUGGISH GROWTH RATES

Barbara A.P. Jones

The labor force participation rate of black women has not increased as fast as that of white women in spite of the fact that black females have the characteristics economists have found most encourage participation. Also black women at all socioeconomic levels have more positive attitudes towards labor market activity. The explanation for the failure for their work rates to grow as fast as those of white women appears to be inadequate employment opportunities for black women from lower socioeconomic groups. Education in or of itself, however, is not the solution to the problem because education yields lower returns to black women with limited schooling than is true for comparable whites. Any strategy devised to solve these employment inequities must address the low relative demand for these workers.

Traditionally, black female earnings have made significant contributions to the incomes of black families. This has been the case for husband-wife families as well as for households with female heads. Recently, however, the growth in the labor force participation rate of black women has not kept pace with that of the total female population. Thus, the relative economic advantages of more earners in all black families is dissipating and a more serious problem of no earners exists in many of the rapidly growing number of black families with female heads.

This article examines patterns and trends in black female labor force activity in an attempt to discover possible explanations for the relative declines in work rates. Alternative strategies for increasing the labor market returns to black women are then assessed.

TRENDS IN LABOR FORCE PARTICIPATION[1]

Historically, black women have participated in the labor force at much higher rates than their white counterparts. This has been particularly true for married women with young children. The past two decades have witnessed significant increases in work rates for both black and white women, but the rate for black women has not increased as rapidly as the rate for white women, in spite of the fact that black women possess more of the characteristics researchers have found to have positive influences on the decision for women, particularly wives, to seek employment outside the home.

In 1962, 46.6% of black women 16 years of age and older were either employed or looking for a job. The comparable figure for white women was only 38.1%. Thus, there was a 8.5 percentage point gap between the two. By 1983, the gap had narrowed to 1.5 points when 54.2% of black women were in the labor force (see Table 1).

In order to understand these trends, we need to examine existing information on the determinants of labor force participation among women. What do we know about the decision of black women to enter the labor force? Most economic studies of female labor force participation rates have been done for married women living with their spouses. Results from studies utilizing a household decision-making model in which a wife selects from the alternatives, market work and homework or leisure, in an effort to maximize the family utility, indicate that one set of variables encourages labor force participation while another group has the opposite effect.[2]

Women are encouraged to enter or remain in the labor force: (1) if they have high earnings or potential earnings which are highly correlated with education; (2) if a large proportion of family income is accounted for by their earnings; (3) if they are in good health; (4) by the presence of older children in the household; and (5) if they have prior work experience. Thus, we would expect, other things being equal, for healthy, better educated women who can command higher salaries, whose earnings potential is high relative to the other sources of family income, and who have older children and previous work experience to be in the labor force in larger proportions than women without these characteristics. On the other hand, high earnings of other family members including the husband, and the presence of small children discourage participation. In an earlier study of factors affecting black wives' labor force participation rate which used National Longitudinal Survey (NLS) data, this author found earn-

TABLE 1
Civilian Labor Force Participation Rates for Women
by Race and Age, 1972-83

	Total 16 and over		16 to 19		20 to 24		25 to 34	
	Black	White	Black	White	Black	White	Black	White
1983	54.2	52.7	33.0	54.5	59.1	72.1	72.3	68.7
1982	53.7	52.4	33.5	55.0	60.1	71.8	70.2	17.8
1981	53.5	51.9	34.0	55.4	61.1	71.5	70.0	66.4
1980	53.1	51.2	34.9	56.2	60.2	70.6	70.0	66.4
1979	53.1	50.5	36.8	57.4	61.5	70.5	70.1	63.1
1978	53.1	49.4	37.3	56.7	62.7	69.3	70.6	61.2
1977	50.8	48.0	32.9	54.5	59.3	67.8	68.5	58.5
1976	49.8	46.9	32.9	52.8	56.9	66.3	66.7	56.0
1975	48.8	45.9	34.2	51.5	55.9	65.5	62.8	53.8
1974	49.0	45.2	33.4	51.7	58.8	63.9	62.4	51.3
1973	49.3	44.1	34.2	50.1	58.0	61.7	62.7	48.7
1972	48.7	43.2	32.2	48.1	57.0	49.4	60.8	46.0

	35 to 44		45 to 54		55 to 64		65 and over	
	Black	White	Black	White	Black	White	Black	White
1983	72.6	68.2	62.3	61.9	44.8	41.1	8.2	7.8
1982	71.7	67.5	62.4	61.4	44.8	41.5	8.5	7.8
1981	69.8	66.4	62.0	60.9	45.4	40.9	9.3	7.9
1980	68.1	65.0	61.4	59.6	44.8	40.9	10.2	7.9
1979	68.0	63.0	59.6	58.1	44.0	41.5	10.9	8.1
1978	67.2	60.7	59.4	56.7	43.8	41.1	11.1	8.1
1977	64.1	58.9	57.9	55.3	43.7	40.7	10.5	7.9
1976	63.0	57.1	56.8	54.7	43.7	40.7	11.3	7.9
1975	62.0	54.9	56.6	54.3	43.1	41.6	10.7	8.0
1974	62.2	53.6	56.4	54.3	42.8	40.4	10.4	8.0
1973	61.7	52.2	56.1	53.4	44.7	40.7	11.4	8.7
1972	61.4	57.7	57.2	53.4	44.0	41.9	12.6	9.0

Source: U.S. Department of Labor, Handbook of Labor Statistics, (June 1985) p. 21.

---

ings and other family income to be the most influential variables. The negative effect of young children was offset by the positive influence of older ones.

Although these earlier studies of labor force participation rates of wives are cross-sectional analyses, i.e., an attempt to explain variations in participation patterns among women at a given point in time, the findings do suggest changes in work rates of black and white wives that we might expect to find over time. The positive relationship between labor force participation rates and the earnings variables—size of earnings and wife's earnings as a percent of total family income—suggest faster growth in work rates for wives whose earnings are growing faster and for wives whose earnings as a percent to total family income have increased faster. Since average earnings for black women have increased more rapidly than those for whites, and earnings of black women relative to those of black men have increased more than white female earnings relative to those of white males, we would expect to see faster growth in black female work rates.

Other family income has the strongest negative influence on wives' decisions to work outside the home. Thus, the fact that black males' earnings have increased somewhat faster than the earnings of white males since the late 1960s would support the sluggish growth in black female work rates. However, because the increase in relative black male earnings was small, about 20%, the influence of the variable was basically offset at the national level by the fact that husband-wife families (the family type where male earnings have the greatest impact) as a proportion of all black families declined by over 25 percent and were replaced by families headed by separated and divorced women who have the highest labor force participation rates among women.

The other variable which could have encouraged faster growth in labor force participation rates for white women has been number of children since, on average, black women have more children than white women. But while the mean size of of both black and white families has declined since the late 1960s, so has the relative size of black families. The faster drop in the number of children in black families should have encouraged black women to enter the labor force at higher rates.

All in all, findings from economic studies of factors which influence work rates of wives would lead us to expect increases in labor force participation rates among black wives that are at least comparable to those of whites. However, one study, by a sociologist, Valerie Kincade Oppenheimer,[3] introduces another variable, the demand for women's labor, which she found strongly influences female labor force participation rates. She explains the increase in female work rates during and after World War II by looking at the increase in the number of positions available to women generally and at the number of "female jobs." During this period there was a rapid expansion in the number of clerical jobs, elementary and secondary teaching positions, etc. She argues that it was these increased employment opportunities, i.e., the increased demand for female labor, that lured women into the labor force.

If, indeed, women respond to increased employment opportunities by entering the labor force, then perhaps they leave or fail to enter the labor force when employment opportunities are limited. This line of reasoning suggests that the demand for the labor of black women has not increased as rapidly as the demand for white women workers. This argument would explain the uneven growth in black female work rates—increasing rates among better educated women and declining rates among the less well trained.

Another characteristic of black women that influences labor force participation rates is marital status. Although we do not have the systematic analysis of labor force participation rates among nonmarried women that exist for married ones, we know that, generally, never-married (single), divorced, and separated women have higher work rates than married women probably due to their lower other family income. Thus, the increasing proportion of black women who are not married (as indicated in Table 2) should increase their overall labor force participation rates. However, in recent years work rates among black women have not been following the traditional pattern. Work rates among black never-married women were lower than rates among married women living with their husbands and the rate among black divorced women has fluctuated over time rather than displaying an upward trend like that of white divorcees. Likewise, the labor force participation rates for white never-married women are higher than for white married women. The lower rates for never-married black women and the fact that such women are increasing as a proportion of all black women helps explain the relative decline in black female labor force participation rates.

A final personal characteristic which affects labor force participation is age. As Table 1 indicates, the labor force participation rate of black women, aged 16 to 19 is lower than for any other pre-retirement age group and the rates have fluctuated showing no upward trend in the past decade. After the teenage years the rates for black women increase and peak with the 25 to 44 year olds. This basic pattern holds for white women as well, but there are racial differences that are significant. While the labor force participation rate for black teenage women has held steady, the rate for comparable whites, already 16 points higher than for blacks in 1972, has increased. In 1983, the gap reached 21 percentage points. The pattern for 20 to 24 year olds is quite similar, but more exaggerated. Here white women were eight percentage points below blacks in 1972 and 13 points

TABLE 2
**Female Labor Force Participation Rate by Marital Status, Race, and Sex,
1972-81**

Black

	Never Married	Married Husb pres	Married Husb abs	Widowed	Divorced
1981	50.3	59.5	59.9	26.6	68.8
1980	49.4	59.0	58.0	24.3	68.8
1979	50.7	59.7	58.9	25.0	66.8
1977	43.0	56.7	53.1	26.6	67.5
1976	46.5	56.7	54.6	27.4	68.5
1975	43.2	54.1	53.3	28.0	69.0
1974	41.8	52.4	54.1	28.5	73.4
1973	46.6	54.0	48.7	28.6	70.9
1972	44.1	51.9	50.9	33.7	65.8

White

	Never Married	Married Husb pres	Married Husb abs	Widowed	Divorced
1981	65.0	50.3	61.8	21.7	76.0
1980	64.2	49.3	60.4	22.3	75.6
1979	65.2	48.5	58.9	22.0	75.3
1977	61.9	45.8	56.3	21.9	74.4
1976	61.2	44.1	58.9	21.7	72.0
1975	59.1	43.6	55.7	23.8	72.7
1974	59.7	42.2	55.8	24.2	73.2
1973	55.8	42.2	53.1	25.2	71.4
1972	54.9	41.5	52.7	26.8	70.1

Source of data: U.S. Department of Labor, "Marital and Family
Characteristic of Workers," various issues, 1972-1983.

above them in 1983. Among all age groups over 25, the rates for blacks
and whites have been increasing and except for 25 to 34 year olds the
percentage point gap between the two groups has remained constant.
Thus, we can pinpoint the relative decline in labor force participation

rates among black women as a whole to the experiences among women 16 to 24, and to a lesser extent to those 25 to 34 years of age. Because female work rates are in a state of transition, we do not know whether these younger women will experience higher work rates as they get older or whether these cohorts will continue to participate in the labor force at relatively low levels.

UNEMPLOYMENT

A comparison of unemployment rates between black and white women, two groups that now have similar labor force participation rates, provides some insight into the relative demand for workers from the two groups. Assuming Oppenheimer is correct in her finding about the impact of demand for labor on labor force participation rates, an analysis of unemployment rates may help us understand the relative decline in labor force participation rates of black women.

In 1983, and throughout the previous decade, black female unemployment rates were twice those for white females, and among black females unemployment rates declined with each progressive age group. The highest unemployment rate was among 16 to 19 year olds and the lowest, among those 65 and over. Also, the ratio of black to white rates shows the same age pattern. The highest relative rates were also among the young.

A variable that reflects more accurately success in the labor market, employment-to-population ratios, shows a slight absolute decline between 1972 and 1983 in the proportion of the black female population with jobs and considerable decline relative to white women. By the end of the period the employment-to-population ratio for white women exceeded that of blacks by four percentage points. In 1983, only 17% of black teenage women were employed (see Table 4). This was the lowest percent for any group other than those 65 years of age and older. The high unemployment and low labor force participation rates among young women, the group with the highest proportion of never-married women, explains the low work rates for this marital group.

It is interesting to note that the unemployment rate for young black women has been rising and the employment-to-population ratio falling both absolutely and relative to whites during a period when median years of schooling for young black women have risen faster than those of young whites. It should also be noted that the greatest employment differences among black and white women are found in those age groups with the

TABLE 3
Unemployment Rates of Women by Race and Age,
1972-83

	Total 16 and over		16 to 19		20 to 24		25 to 34	
	Black	White	Black	White	Black	White	Black	White
1983	18.6	7.9	48.2	18.3	31.8	10.3	18.6	7.6
1982	17.6	8.3	47.1	19.0	29.6	10.9	17.8	8.0
1981	15.6	6.9	42.2	16.6	26.4	9.1	14.9	6.6
1980	14.0	6.5	39.8	14.8	23.5	8.5	13.2	6.3
1979	13.3	5.9	39.1	14.0	22.6	7.8	12.1	5.6
1978	13.8	6.2	40.8	14.4	22.7	8.3	11.9	5.8
1977	14.9	7.3	43.4	15.9	25.5	9.3	13.6	6.7
1976	14.3	7.9	41.6	16.4	22.8	10.4	13.6	7.6
1975	14.8	8.6	41.0	17.4	24.3	11.2	13.4	8.4
1974	11.3	6.1	37.4	14.5	19.0	8.2	9.0	5.8
1973	11.1	5.3	36.1	13.0	18.4	7.1	10.3	5.1
1972	11.8	5.9	40.5	14.2	17.9	8.2	10.5	5.5

	35 to 44		45 to 54		55 to 64		65 and over	
	Black	White	Black	White	Black	White	Black	White
1983	11.4	6.2	9.9	5.5	7.3	4.7	6.3	3.1
1982	10.7	6.4	8.5	5.5	6.1	5.0	4.5	3.1
1981	9.8	5.1	6.9	4.2	4.7	3.7	6.0	3.4
1980	8.2	4.9	6.4	4.3	4.5	3.1	4.9	3.0
1979	7.2	4.2	5.2	3.7	4.7	3.0	3.9	3.1
1978	7.8	4.5	5.6	3.8	5.2	3.0	4.7	3.7
1977	8.7	5.3	5.8	5.0	4.8	4.4	3.4	4.9
1976	8.5	5.8	5.9	5.0	5.4	4.8	2.4	5.3
1975	9.0	6.5	7.0	5.8	5.3	5.0	3.6	5.3
1974	6.6	4.3	4.4	3.6	3.6	3.2	1.9	3.9
1973	5.6	3.7	3.9	3.2	3.3	2.7	3.7	2.8
1972	7.6	4.4	4.6	3.5	3.7	3.3	2.6	3.7

Source: U.S. Department of Labor, Handbook of Labor Statistics, (June 1985) pp. 72-73.

smallest differences in educational attainment. (Educational attainment is a subject that is discussed in greater detail later.)

There is evidence to support the notion that the extraordinarily high unemployment rates among black women, particularly young ones, have discouraged black women from entering the labor force and encouraged others to leave. Wallace reports a 1975 study which found that of the black

TABLE 4
Employment-to-Population Ratios of Women by Race and Age,
1972-83

	Total 16 and over		16 to 19		20 to 24		25 to 34	
	Black	White	Black	White	Black	White	Black	White
1983	44.1	48.5	17.0	44.5	40.3	64.7	58.8	63.5
1982	44.2	48.1	17.7	44.6	42.3	63.9	59.7	62.4
1981	45.1	48.3	19.7	46.2	44.9	65.0	59.6	62.1
1980	45.7	47.8	21.0	47.9	46.2	64.6	61.3	60.7
1979	46.0	47.5	22.4	49.4	47.7	65.0	61.7	59.5
1978	45.8	46.3	22.1	48.5	48.6	63.6	62.2	57.6
1977	43.3	44.5	18.5	45.9	44.3	61.5	59.2	54.6
1976	42.8	43.2	19.2	44.2	44.1	59.4	57.8	51.8
1975	41.6	42.0	20.2	42.5	42.5	58.1	54.6	49.2
1974	43.5	42.4	20.9	44.3	47.6	58.7	57.0	48.3
1973	43.8	41.8	22.0	43.6	47.4	57.4	56.4	46.2
1972	43.0	40.7	19.2	41.3	46.9	54.6	54.6	43.5

	35 to 44		45 to 54		55 to 64		65 and over	
	Black	White	Black	White	Black	White	Black	White
1983	64.4	64.0	56.5	58.4	44.6	39.2	7.7	7.5
1982	64.0	63.1	57.1	58.1	42.0	39.4	8.1	7.6
1981	63.0	63.0	57.7	58.3	43.2	39.4	8.8	7.6
1980	62.6	61.8	57.4	57.0	42.8	39.6	9.4	7.7
1979	63.1	60.3	56.5	55.9	41.9	40.2	10.2	7.8
1978	62.0	58.0	56.1	54.5	41.6	39.8	10.3	7.8
1977	58.5	55.8	54.6	52.6	41.7	38.9	9.3	7.5
1976	57.6	53.8	53.5	51.9	41.4	38.8	10.7	7.5
1975	56.4	51.3	52.6	51.2	40.8	38.6	10.2	7.6
1974	58.0	51.4	53.8	52.4	41.4	39.1	10.0	7.7
1973	58.3	48.4	53.9	51.6	43.3	36.9	10.7	8.4
1972	56.8	50.3	54.5	51.7	42.3	40.5	12.2	8.7

Source: U.S. Department of Labor, Handbook of Labor Statistics, (June 1985) p. 47.

women leaving the ranks of the unemployed, 66% withdrew from the labor force while only 33% secured employment.[4]

Despite these high unemployment rates, black women display a tenacious commitment to the labor force. Stevans et al.[5] found that white women faced with unemployment are more likely than men to withdraw from the labor force, but patterns for black women were more like those for men, showing long-run responses to cyclical swings, but "only modest response to short-run fluctuations." In other words, black women continue to seek employment in spite of initial failure to find jobs.

Our somewhat brief perusal of the percentage distribution of total and long term unemployment rates presented in Table 5 shows the same commitment to the labor force. The percent of long-term unemployment, 15 weeks and over as well as 27 weeks and over, accounted for by black women is only 12% (1.2 percentage points) less than their portion of total unemployment. This means that when faced with prolonged joblessness, black women continue to seek employment at about the same rate as the total group of unemployed workers, which is predominately male. On the other hand, white women's proportion of those unemployed 15 weeks and over was 21% (6.3 percentage points) lower than their proportion of overall unemployment, and at 27 weeks or more their proportion had fallen 30% (9 percentage points). There are two possible explanations for this phenomenon: (1) unemployed white women are more likely than black women (or males) to find employment quickly, and (2) white women are more likely to leave the labor force when they are unable to find jobs. Both explanations are probably applicable.

EDUCATIONAL ATTAINMENT

During the two decades preceding 1980, increases in educational attainment for black women were nothing less than phenomenal. In 1960 the median years of schooling for black women aged 25 and over was 8.6, 2.6 years less than the median for white women. By 1980 the median had risen to 12.0 years, only half a year behind white women (see Table 6).

Since there is a positive relationship between years of schooling and labor force participation rates, women in the labor force have slightly higher educational levels than the total population. This holds for both black and white women; however, the gap between educational attainment for black women in the labor force and the total population is greater than the gap for the two groups of white women. This racial difference suggests that a larger percentage of black women are excluded from the labor force because of inadequate education.

This is consistent with Mott's findings for women 35-44 years of age between 1967 and 1972. He found that black women who left the labor force "were, on average, of lower socioeconomic status and had been less 'successful' in terms of wages when they were working." Those who re-

TABLE 5
Percent Distribution of Total and Long-Term Unemployment
by Sex, Age, and Race, 1972-83

| | Total Unemployment | | | | Unemployed 15 Weeks and Over | | | |
| | Females | | Males | | Females | | Males | |
	Black	White	Black	White	Black	White	Black	White
1983	9.9	30.5	9.1	45.3	8.7	24.2	14.2	50.5
1982	9.1	31.8	9.0	45.4	9.2	25.6	13.6	49.3
1981	10.2	33.4	9.5	43.3	10.4	25.9	14.0	47.3
1980	9.3	33.6	9.3	44.2	9.1	26.2	13.0	49.2
1979	11.1	37.3	9.3	39.5	11.5	30.0	13.9	42.9
1978	11.1	37.3	9.9	39.1	11.0	30.0	14.4	42.1
1977	9.9	36.9	10.2	41.5	8.6	32.1	12.5	45.3
1976	8.5	36.1	10.2	44.2	7.2	31.6	10.9	48.6
1975	7.9	35.4	10.3	45.9	7.1	30.7	11.0	49.7
1974	9.0	37.6	10.8	42.3	8.5	30.7	12.7	46.9
1973	10.3	37.0	10.9	42.2	10.1	30.2	11.7	46.9
1972	9.3	35.6	11.3	44.6	7.7	30.1	10.0	50.5

| | Unemployment 27 Weeks and Over | | | |
| | Females | | Males | |
	Black	White	Black	White
1983	8.7	21.5	15.6	51.5
1982	13.9	23.5	24.1	49.2
1981	10.1	23.0	16.4	48.0
1980	9.8	24.3	14.6	48.6
1979	12.4	27.2	16.6	42.1
1978	12.2	27.6	15.6	42.2
1977	9.0	29.7	13.0	47.1
1976	7.4	30.4	11.5	49.1
1975	6.7	29.8	11.7	50.5
1974	8.8	27.9	13.1	49.3
1973	10.1	28.1	11.9	49.1
1972	6.9	30.1	10.1	51.3

Source: U.S. Department of Labor, Handbook of Labor Statistics, (June 1985) pp. 82-83.

mained in the labor force were working more hours and had increases in real incomes greater than those experienced by whites. Mott went on to note that those black women who continued in the labor force were the result of "a selection process whereby the blacks with the least job skills are the ones most likely to have left the labor force." This labor force

TABLE 6
Median Years of Schooling of Women
in the Population and Labor Force, 1960-80

	Population		Labor Force	
	Black	White	Black	White
1960	8.6	11.2	9.4	12.2
1970	10.2	12.2	12.1	12.5
1975	11.1	12.3	12.8	12.5
1980	12.0	12.5	12.4	12.7

Source of data: U.S. Department of Commerce, Bureau of the Census,
Statistical Abstract of the United States (1981), p. 42;
U.S. Department of Labor, Handbook of Labor Statistics,
(June 1985) pp. 166-168.

withdrawal by low earners and potential earners which Mott observed could in part explain the convergence of black and white female earnings.[6]

One would expect for women with lower levels of education to be plagued with extremely high rates of unemployment, but the reality is that, for the most part, they are not in the labor force and, thus, are not counted among the unemployed. However, for them, joblessness is high. In 1983 only 21% of black women with five to seven years of schooling were employed along with only 27% of black women who were high school dropouts. These low employment levels must be coupled with the fact these black women workers are most likely to be employed part-time.[7] At the other end of the education ladder, 82% of black women with five or more years of college were employed.

Data such as these are often cited as evidence of the need for more education for black women. Although few would argue against this proposition, not even education comes with guarantees, nor does it provide the same returns to black women as it does to white men or white women.

Education is not an effective shield against unemployment. Although education improves black women's absolute chances of employment, it does not improve their position relative to white women. For black women with high school diplomas and beyond, a group with 67 to 84% labor force participation rates in 1983, unemployment rates declined as years of schooling increased. However, as shown in Table 7, the ratio of black to white unemployment rates increased as education increased and reached a peak of 2.96 for women with one to three years of college, falling only slightly for those with college degrees.[8] Only black women with five or more years of college had unemployment rates which were below those of similarly educated white women. Since unemployment rates are higher for white women than for white men, the disadvantage suffered by black women relative to white men is even greater.

Returns to education can also be measured by the type of employment available to workers. Economists long ago recognized that certain jobs, independent of earnings, are more desirable than others, and contrary to the prescription in principles textbooks, seldom is a wage premium paid for the less desirable jobs. Equal education, however, does not give black women equal access to the more preferred occupations.

The occupational distribution of employed women by educational attainment shows the expected pattern: women with more education are found in managerial and professional jobs and those with the least education are in service occupations. On the surface, the patterns appear to be quite similar for both black and white women. In fact the median years of schooling for women and men, black and white, are very nearly the same for each occupational category. However, when the data are turned around we see that black women suffer a more severe penalty for limited schooling and only with four or more years of college does their distribution look like that of white women.

White women are able to move into more desirable jobs with fewer years of schooling than black women and black women with increased education have more trouble moving out of the undesirable jobs. Among employed black women with less than an eighth grade education in 1983, three-fourths were employed in the lowest paying, least prestigious occupational category—service work. This was true for fewer than half of similarly educated white women. Poorly educated white women fared better than poorly educated black women. A higher proportion of white women with limited education held the better paying operative and craft positions, and one-third of employed white female high school dropouts held technical, sales and administrative support postions compared to one-fifth of comparably educated black women. As we move up the education ladder, the proportion of black women in service occupations remained 25 to 45 percent higher than that for white women. Finally, the proportion of white women in the most prestigous occupational category, managerial and professional, at each educational level other than the

TABLE 7
Unemployment Rates by Race and Educational Attainment
for Selected Years

	1983			1981			1979			1977		
	Black	White	B/W Ratio	Black	White	B/W Ratio	Black	White	B/W Ratio	Black	White	B/W Ratio
Elementary												
Less than 5	(b)	13.5	----	(b)	9.6	----	6.8	10.4	.65	5.2	11.8	.44
5 to 7 years	16.2	16.1	1.00	7.2	13.2	.54	12.3	8.1	1.51	12.5	11.5	1.08
8 years	17.0	15.4	1.10	17.6	13.0	1.35	10.4	9.3	1.11	16.7	2.8	1.63
High School												
1–3 years	27.6	18.0	1.53	25.7	12.8	2.00	18.0	11.7	1.53	20.1	13.2	1.52
4 years	20.8	8.1	2.56	16.6	6.2	2.67	12.0	5.4	2.22	13.6	7.2	1.88
College												
1 to 3 years	16.0	5.4	2.96	11.5	4.1	2.80	8.5	3.7	2.29	12.9	6.3	2.04
4 years	9.4	3.8	2.47	4.7	3.1	1.51	3.7	3.1	1.19	7.0	4.6	1.52
5 years or more	2.9	3.2	.90	1.9	2.2	.86	4.8	2.7	1.77	2.8	3.2	.87

(b) Data not shown where base is less than 75,000.

Source of data: U.S. Department of Labor, "Educational Attainment of Workers," various issues, 1972-1981.

TABLE 8
Occupational Distribution of Employed Women by Race and Educational Attainment, 1983

| | Elementary | | | | High School | | | | College | | | |
| | Less than 8 | | 8 years | | 1 to 3 years | | 4 years | | 1 to 3 years | | 4 years or more | |
	Black	White	Black	White	Black	White	Black	White	Black	White	Black	White
Total	100.0	100.0	100.0	100.0	100.0	100.0	100.0	100.0	100.0	100.0	100.0	100.0
Managerial and Professional	2.3	2.3	3.7	5.1	2.4	5.0	6.6	10.2	17.1	23.3	65.6	68.6
Technical, Sales, and Administrative support	3.2	9.5	9.1	16.4	19.8	33.5	41.0	58.0	54.4	58.7	26.8	25.5
Service occupations	75.3	42.6	67.7	37.7	50.1	36.3	29.9	18.2	18.3	13.1	5.1	4.1
Precision Production, Craft and Repair	1.4	5.1	(b)	4.8	1.6	3.2	2.7	2.2	2.3	1.0	1.0	0.7
Operators, fabricators, and Laborers	16.0	36.8	20.0	30.9	24.5	20.0	19.2	10.3	7.3	3.2	1.8	1.0
Farming, Forestry, and Fishing	(b)	3.3	(b)	2.3	(b)	2.1	(b)	1.2	(b)	1.0	(b)	0.3

(b) Base Less than 75,000.

Source of data: U.S. Department of Labor, Bureau of Labor Statistics, "Educational Attainment of Workers," March 1982-1983, pp. 27-28.

highest and the lowest, was at least 33% higher than for black women (see Table 8).

Jerry Dauterive and Jerry Jonish analyzed wage differences among black and white career women. They found that women who escape traditionally female jobs enjoy higher wages.[9] Unfortunately, however, Malveaux found that black women have had less success than white women in moving out of traditionally female jobs. She reports that "[A]lthough the quality of work among black women changed, it changed because black women moved from one set of stratified jobs to another, not because they left 'typically' female jobs.'"[10] Since studies of female labor force participation have consistently found wages to have a strong influence on women's decisions to enter or withdraw from the labor force, these findings make a significant contribution toward explaining the failure of the growth in black female work rates to keep pace with the growth for whites.

Dauterive and Jonish also argued, consistent with our findings, that "interpersonal differences in wages may not be simply a problem of the acquisition of human capital, but also of how this human capital is used in the labor markets." In other words, labor market structures and imperfections can also affect black-white wage, and, we add, employment differentials.

Obviously, there is much that is yet to be known about the impact of schooling on employment opportunities and earnings of black women. Black women with more education are attracted to the labor force in larger numbers and have greater success in finding employment, but while education brings *more* opportunity it does not bring *equal* opportunity.

A SUMMARY OF THE EVIDENCE

There is indeed evidence of a strong commitment to the labor force among black women, but this commitment has met limited receptivity in the market place. Although black women who enter the labor force face unemployment rates that are twice as high as those of white women and white men, they still have labor force participation rates that exceed those of white women.

Why have black female labor force rates not grown as fast as those of white women? Our understanding of factors that determine female labor force participation rates lead us to expect at the very least comparable growth in labor force participation rates among black women. The more rapid growth in the proportion of black families with female heads should provide added incentive for black women to enter the labor force. Faster growth in earnings among employed black females and more rapid improvements in educational attainment both encourage greater labor force participation. A variety of studies have shown that black women, even those not in the labor force, have more positive attitudes about employment than white women.[11] This positive attitude even prevails among AFDC mothers who have low labor force participation rates.[12] The sluggish growth in black female labor force participation rates appears to be a response to inadequate employment opportunities with reasonable wages.

The shift in production from goods to services, from central cities to suburbs, from metropolitan areas in the North Central region to the West and outside of the country all together has removed primary labor market employment opportunities from black workers, male and female. Indeed, the upward trend in overall unemployment rates indicates that the economy is not producing enough jobs to provide employment for all of those who wish to work and a disproportionate share of that unemployment has been visited upon the black community. The response has been declining work rates among black men and dampened growth rates among black women.

Any attempt to explain the economic plight of black women and the implications of their labor market experiences must consider economic conditions in the total black community and assess the economic well-being of black women in different social classes. The economic problems of black women in general and their problems as workers cannot be separated from the economic plight of the black community. The same forces which affect the employment opportunities of black women tend to affect those of black men. Because of the social and family relationships between black men and black women, the economic well-being of one group cannot be separated from the other.[13]

Labor force participation rates and unemployment vary by class as well as race and the work rates themselves exaggerate the class differences. Women from poor families, on average, have less schooling than women with more privileged backgrounds. These more poorly educated women have higher unemployment rates and lower labor force participation rates, which yield employment-to-population ratios as low as 21%. This is compounded by the fact that these women, once employed, are disproportionately relegated to service occupations which are characterized by larger proportions of part-time positions, low wage rates, and frequent unemployment. To this set of circumstances must be added that women more subject to unemployment are less likely to be married and/or living with their husbands and thus are less likely to have other sources of income. The net effect is a more unequal distribution of income within the black community than the same set of educational patterns would yield among whites.

Phyllis Wallace summed up the impact of the unequal impact of labor market outcomes by class in this statement:

A . . . highly qualified black middle class is developing at the same time a large black underclass survives in worsened economic conditions. Disadvantaged economic background is now seen by some as a more important determinant of economic attainment than racial discrimination.[14]

ASSESSMENT OF ALTERNATIVE STRATEGIES

Alternative strategies for increasing employment opportunities for black women (and men as well) have tended to fall into two categories — human capital development and antidiscrimination. To this list can be added more modest programs to lessen the cost of employment such as day care facilities and improved public transportation, and recently, the call for the elimination of social welfare programs has been discussed as a means of increasing work incentives.

The human capital argument assumes that sufficient employment opportunities exist, or via the multiplier effect will be created when more people begin to earn and then spend their new income, to provide jobs for the unemployed if they acquire appropriate job skills. Those who subscribe to this notion see the basic economic structure as adequate and view characteristics of the jobless as "the problem" to be corrected. Programs that fall under this rubric include the Work Incentive Program (WIN) and the training programs under the Comprehensive Employment Training Act (CETA) and its successor, the Job Training Partnership Act (JTPA).

Proponents of the antidiscrimination and affirmative action strategy again view the basic structure of the economy as appropriate, but object to the arbitrary placement of blacks at the bottom of the heap. A strict adherence to this strategy would accept unemployment, extreme income inequality, etc., as they exist so long as they are distributed equally across racial lines.

The provision of day-care facilities and transportation is part of a strategy designed to lessen the cost of employment, and thus is a wage subsidy. These programs recognize that the market will not provide adequate wages to allow a mother to pay the market rate for child care or privately produced transportation and have sufficient net income to induce her to enter the labor force. This type of program covers costs that otherwise she would have to meet, thereby increasing her net wage. Again, the assumption is that the basic structure of the economy is acceptable.

The final strategy on the list—the elimination of social welfare programs—starts from the assumption that the current economic institutions, which include an array of social welfare programs, interfere with the incentive systems inherent in the market economy and encourage joblessness. Proponents of this strategy argue for the elimination of the minimum wage and other support systems for those unwilling to enter the labor market and make do with the returns that the market provides. This strategy calls for a fundamental change in the contemporary American economy.

While the preceding presentations are simplistic descriptions of each of the strategies or strategy types, hopefully the description will facilitate discussion.

Each of the first three strategies, at best, provides a partial solution to limited employment among black women. The human capital argument does not resolve the problem of the secular trend in unemployment. Since millions of people go to work every day with skills, work habits, and attitudes that are similar to the jobless, most of those without jobs are obviously not unemployable. Also, for increased skill levels to eradicate unemployment, there must be a demand for skilled workers approximately equal to the number of "unskilled" unemployed. Does this unmet demand exist?

Antidiscrimination policy is not expected to eliminate unemployment, it merely shifts it to other groups. Since proponents of this policy recognize the difficulty of gaining support for a "zero-sums" policy, the approach is usually coupled with a call for macroeconomic policies designed to increase total employment and increase per capita incomes.

Subsidies are merely supplementary strategies that in and of themselves will have minor impact on joblessness. They are intended to facilitate other efforts.

The last strategy, the elimination of social welfare programs, offers little hope to black women. Since inadequate employment opportunities have driven large numbers of black women out of the labor force, withdrawal of income supplements may bring them back. But will it increase the demand for them as workers? The strategy will likely increase labor force participation rates, but wage employment, the ultimate goal, is not assured.

The workfare programs being proposed as an alternative to welfare are not designed to create new income earning opportunities. Rather they are being seen by many as likely to eliminate traditional low-skill public employment jobs. Workfare requires welfare recipients to perform services as a condition for receipt of welfare. The work performed is supposedly work that otherwise would not be performed. Since the "workers" receive income that in the absence of workfare they would receive without working, their economic well-being has not improved. Though jobs are created the effect is similar to drinking a diet soft drink. You go through the exercise of swallowing (working), but in the end there is no additional nourishment (income).

A complete solution to declining employment rates among black women will probably encompass aspects of each of the first three strategies (human capital development, antidiscrimination policies, and wage supplements), but these programs alone will not create sufficient new employment opportunities to supply the needs of the growing underclass—both male and female. Total success will require a fundamental change in the economic decisionmaking process such that priority will be given to employment needs over profits. This can come with economic planning. The unfettered market will not provide employment to all who wish to work, and only drastic cuts in real wages with resultant reductions in living standards for the working class will induce employers to voluntarily substitute labor capital.

NOTES

1. All data presented in this article unless otherwise noted are taken from various publications of the Bureau of Labor Statistics and/or the Bureau of the Census.

2. The results reported here represent a synthesis of the findings from William G. Bowen and T. Aldrich Finegan, *The Economics of Labor Force Participation* (Princeton, NJ: Princeton University Press, 1969); Jacob Mincer, "Labor Force Participation of Married Women," in *Aspects of Labor Economics* (Princeton, NJ: Princeton University Press, 1962), pp. 63-97; Thomas A, Mohaney, "Factors Determining the Labor Force Participation of Married Women," *Industrial and Labor Relations Review*, XIV, no. 44(July 1961), pp. 563-577; Glen G. Cain, *Married Women in the Labor Force* (Chicago: University of Chicago Press, 1966); Duran Bell, "Why Participation Rates of Black and White Wives Differ," *The Journal of Human Resources*, IX (1974); Phyllis A. Wallace, *Black Women in the Labor Force* (Cambridge, MA: MIT Press, 1980); and Barbara A. Jones, "Factors Which Determine the Labor Force Participation Rates of Black Wives," *Proceedings of the 29th Annual Meeting of the Industrial Relations Research Association* (1975).

3. Valerie Kincade Oppenheimer, *The Female Labor Force in the U.S.* (Berkeley: University of California Institute of International Studies, 1970).

4. Phyllis A. Wallace, *Black Womenn in the Labor Force*, p. 45.

5. Lonnie K. Stevans, Charles Register, and Paul Grimes, "Race and the Discouraged Female Worker: A Question of Labor Force Attachment," *The Review of Black Political Economy* 14, no. 1(Summer 1985).

6. Frank L. Mott, "Racial Differences in Female Labor Force Participation," *Urban and Social Science Review*, XI(1978), pp. 23-24.

7. Among black women, those with the least amount of education and the lowest family incomes are the ones most likely to work part-time, a phenomenon which may be explained by the fact that these women tend to be older and older black women are more likely to be employed as private household workers, an occupation which tends towards part-time employment.

8. The relatively low ratio of black to white unemployment rates for women at the lower end of the educational ladder cannot be explained by their limited labor force participation rates because for all educational groupings other than those women with less than five years of schooling and one to three years of high school, labor force participation rates are higher for black women than for their white counterparts.

9. Jerry W. Dauterive and James Jonish, "Wage Differences Among Black and White Career Women," *Review of Social Economy* (April 1977), pp. 79-94.

10. Julianne Malveaux, "The Economic Interests of Black and White Women: Are They Similar?" *Review of Black Political Economy*, 14, no. 1 (Summer 1985), p. 16.

11. For example, see Frank L. Mott, "Racial Differences in Female Labor-Force Participation," pp. 21-27.

12. Barbara A. P. Jones, "Labor Market Consequences of Poverty and Welfare Dependency" in *Understanding Black Poverty and Welfare Dependency* (New York: Praeger Publishers, forthcoming).

13. For a very persuasive argument of the economic interdependence of black males and black females see Julianne Malveaux, "The Economic Interests of Black and White Women: Are They Similar?" pp. 5-27.

14. Phyllis Wallace, *Black Women in the Labor Force*, p. 83.

THE MYTH OF THE DOUBLE-ADVANTAGE:
BLACK FEMALE MANAGERS

Karen Fulbright

This article reports on interviews conducted with 25 middle- and senior-level black female managers in private-sector employment. Three hypotheses were examined: (1) the processes that sociologists and psychologists assume influence the nontraditional career choices of white women are not the same as those that influence black women; (2) contrary to popular belief, black women are not being promoted more rapidly than other, better qualified workers as a result of affirmative action; and (3) black female managers are likely to encounter the same limits to their mobility that anyone, regardless of race or gender, might encounter, *and* they are likely to encounter limits to their mobility on account of their race and sex. Each of these hypotheses received some support from this admittedly narrow database.

It has been duly noted that black women, as "double minorities", are believed to have a "double advantage" over other workers.[1] In common jargon black women are referred to as "twofers"—two minorities for the price of one—who have better opportunities for entry and mobility in the workplace. This view has been popularized by the media, and at least one scholar developed a theory around this issue based on interviews with 25 black female lawyers.[2] The theory was posed as a mathematical theorem. That is, the two negative statuses of being a black person and a woman cancel each other out and enable black women to parlay their dual negative statuses into positive experiences.

Popular sentiment and the double-advantage theory give little acknowledgement to the possibility that instead of being doubly advantaged, black women may actually face a double burden as they experience sexism and racism. The double-advantage hypothesis sounds mathematically logical but is intuitively illogical. Therefore, the objective of this research was to assess the merits of this hypothesis by examining the experiences of one group—black female managers.

The analysis was focused on the experiences of this group for five reasons. First, very little research has focused on black women who work in male-dominated occupations. These occupations are characterized by generally higher wages, higher status, and greater opportunities for upward mobility. If the promotion of increased numbers of black women into the professional ranks is a serious objective of public policy, then we badly need to give the subject closer attention than it has received thus far.

Second, the educational requirements of management are highly standardized, vis-à-vis other occupations, thereby effectively removing the influence of substantial variation in human capital from racial and gender comparisons of career mobility.

Third, there is an existing and continuously growing body of literature on managers. This literature has focused on white males and females and black males; however, it does provide a context and a basis from which comparisons can be made with black female managers.

Fourth, although there are no directories of black female managers per se, there are existing professional organizations that serve as sources through which black female managers can be identified.

Finally, one of the most interesting things about the notion that black women who work in professsional occupations are a doubly advantaged group is that it is not clear what its basis of support is. The traditional sources to which we normally turn for information about perplexing issues are theoretical work and empirical studies. Black women in general, and black women who work in male-dominated professional occupations in particular, have been overlooked in most theoretical and empirical work on occupations.[3]

Six data sources were used to assess the notion of the double advantage of black women: (1) theoretical work on occupational segregation from the disciplines of anthropology, sociology, economics, and psychology; (2) secondary empirical data on managers in general; (3) a survey of 185 black female managers, 156 of whom work in the private, for-profit sector; (4) secondary survey data on white female and black male managers who were of comparable age, education, and number of years of experience as the black female managers; (5) interviews with 25 black female managers in the private, for-profit sector; (6) secondary data on the career mobility of white male managers. The third and fifth data sources were designed and conducted by the author between 1983 and 1985.

Since this study was an exploratory attempt to identify and document the status and experience of black female managers, it was not designed to meet the methodological requirements of one that is statistically representative. Surveys were mailed to 325 women who were identified through alumni associations, professional organizations, *Black Enterprise* magazine, and word of mouth. Comments and conclusions about the study participants are intended to develop a base upon which further research on the issue of the double advantage of black women could be placed, not to pertain to the general population of black female managers.

The private for-profit sector managers who were interviewed were selected from the 156 survey respondents who were working in the private sector. The selection criteria for middle-level managers were that they have an MBA or an advanced executive management degree and have a minimum of four years of management experience. The selection criteria for senior-level managers were that they have a graduate degree and a minimum of 10 years of management experience. The educational criteria were established because of the belief that any obstacles or barriers that these women encountered in their careers were likely to be less severe than those encountered by women who do not have advanced degrees. Five of the women worked for black-owned companies. In addition, half of the managers worked in functional areas central to the business of a company (core or line functions). The remaining women worked in functional areas generally not considered central to the business of a company (staff functions).

This article reports on the findings from the interview data, with a concentration on employment mobility. Three aspects of the professional experiences of the 25 black female managers are examined: (1) access to mobility—the influence on their choice of a nontraditionally female occupation, (2) rapidity of upward mobility within management, and (3) barriers to mobility. A brief summary of the findings of the other data sources provides useful background for a disscussion of the interview data.

Theoretical work on occupational segregation indicates that women who enter male-dominated occupations are likely to experience external difficulties such as resistance from co-workers and blocked opportunity structures as well as internal difficulties such as fear of success and role conflicts.

Empirical work indicates that black women in male-dominated occupations are more likely to encounter external barriers to their mobility than they are to encounter internal barriers to their mobility and are likely to experience racism and sexism simultaneously or interchangeably.

The survey data from the current study indicate the following: (1) women who work in companies owned and operated by blacks appear to experience a greater degree of upward mobility than their counterparts at white-owned companies, and (2) white female managers appear to experience a greater degree of upward mobility than black female or black male managers.

Thus, the review of these data sources indicates that contrary to popular belief, it is more likely that black professional women will be subject to the double burden of discrimination because of their race and gender than that their dual status will give them a double advantage. The interview data summarized in this article provide further support for this observation.

ACCESS TO MOBILITY: INFLUENCES ON NONTRADITIONAL CAREER CHOICE

It has been asserted by sociologists and psychologists that female role models in nontraditionally female occupations are an especially important element in correcting occupational segregation. In work in this area, sociologists and psychologists emphasize the influence of individual role models. They contend that the fact that women are underrepresented in male-dominated, higher-status, higher-paying occupations is partially attributable to the lack of role models for women in these occupations.

In accordance with this view, using a strict definition, the role models for the women in this study would be black female managers. Given the historically heavy concentration of black women in lower-paying, low-status occupations, it is doubtful that the women who participated in this study would have had role models that fit this strict definition. If we examine recent empirical work on women in management, however, there is evidence that this narrow definition should be broadened.

Studies of women in management have found that female managers typically have fathers who work in managerial positions or are employed in professional occupations and that their fathers had a strong influence on them.[4] Similar findings have been made regarding the fathers of white male managers.[5]

There have been no parallel studies conducted on black female or male managers per se. However, studies have been conducted of black women who are on nontraditionally female educational paths or who work in nontraditional occupations.[6] These studies identified characteristics of the "typical" black woman who has nontraditionally female educational or occupational status. They focused on the characteristics of the mothers of the women who chose nontraditionally female pursuits and found that the mothers of these women both tended to work in nontraditionally female fields and were likely to be employed in professional and semi-professional occupations. In addition, one study that assessed the influence of the fathers of black women who work in nontraditionally female occupations reported that the fathers had a strong influence on their daughters' career decisions.[7]

When the family status of the black female managers in my sample is considered, there is little support for the findings cited above. None of the women interviewed had mothers who worked in nontraditionally female fields, and only 8 of the 25 mothers worked in professional or semiprofessional occupations.[8] The same pattern holds true for the fathers of these women. One of the women's fathers worked in a nontraditionally black field (law) and only 6 out of 23 fathers worked in professional or semi-professional occupations.[9]

In addition, only three women cited their fathers, in particular, as having influenced their career decisions. The majority consistently reported that their parents did not encourage them to pursue any particular occupation but, rather, encouraged them to excel at whatever they chose to do. All reported that they grew up knowing that they would have to work all of their lives.

Given the absence from the lives of the women in this study of the most commonly identified factors believed to influence the nontraditional career orientation of black and white women, there must be one or more intervening factors.

One logical place to look would be high school guidance counselors, since one of their roles is to expose young people to career and educational options as well as to advise them on educational choices. Those who used guidance counseling services in their high schools reported that their counselors had low expectations for them. Rather than expose them to a broad range of educational and occupational choices, the counselors almost always guided the women to traditionally female occupations and low-status schools. This situation held true for women regardless of their age or the region of the country in which they grew up.

If the women's points of entry into the labor market are examined, a pattern emerges. First, the women can be evenly divided into two groups according to their differing paths of entry into a nontraditionally female business track. The first group consists of women who followed a straight path from college either by going to an MBA program or by going to work for a company in a professional capacity. The second group consists of women who moved into a management track after taking a detour through traditionally female jobs in the public or private sector. Both groups ended up in management track positions in the middle 1970s.

The family status of the two groups is quite similar. Within both groups the number of women whose parents work in professional or semi-professional occupations and those whose parents do not are fairly evenly split. In adition, none of the women recalled having a black female corporate or public sector manager who served as a role model.

One variable that does shed light on this issue is the average age of the two groups of managers. The average age of the "straight path" group is 33. Members of this group typically described their choice of management as a process of elimination among the fields of business, law, and medicine.

The average age of the "detour path" group is 38. Members of this group typically described their movement into management as a process that occurred after they were exposed to broader opportunities in this field through jobs that they held.

The significance of the average age of the two groups of women is related to the historical position in time along the continuum of the civil rights movement in which their ages placed them. Specifically, the women in the "detour path" group would have been completing their high school and college education and entering the job market during the early period of the civil rights movement. Thus, it is likely that their initial movement into jobs that were traditionally filled by black women represented a rational action given the societal conditions that prevailed during the period in which they were making major career decisions.

The civil rights movement changed those conditions. In a very concrete way it changed the opportunity structure for black people in this country. On a less tangible but no less important level it raised black people's expectations about what they could seek to achieve. In addition, affirmative action policy, which was a direct result of the civil rights movement, ultimately created an environment that opened opportunities for these women.

At the same time, the women in the "straight path" group would have been in high school and college during the period in which the civil rights movement was making advances and making its impact felt throughout society. In view of the time period in which they were making major career decisions, it is to be expected that these women should have been aware of opportunities for themselves in nontraditional occupations.

Given all of these factors, it would appear that the collective political movement that was led by civil rights activists, as well as its outcomes, exerted a stronger influence on the women in this study than individual role models and family status.

Indeed, without exception, all of the women spoke of how the civil rights movement influenced their lives. They stated that the movement opened doors, provided opportunities, and heightened their awareness of new opportunities. For example, comments by a woman who took a detour path and one who took a straight path (respectively) typify the sentiments that their counterparts expressed:

> Generally, that movement enabled me to feel that I could do anything. My family always told me that but I didn't have the exposure. The civil rights movement gave me the exposure because there were places where I could go to work and do what I wanted to do, and it makes you feel more credible. It improved everybody's self image and made me not embarrassed about being black or being female. I think that the bigger issue is being black.

> I think it created the opportunity for me to go out and seize—I really grew up thinking I could do anything I wanted to do and I think that's because I was told that, I was reading it, hearing it, seeing it.

One of the implications of not having a family member in management is that the women were not exposed to business culture in the way that most white male and female managers are. Therefore, they, unlike their white counterparts, had to spend time becoming generally acculturated to a business environment as well as to their specific environment.

Mentors could help ease this transition. Indeed, much has been written in recent years on the value of mentors. Studies of successful white male and female managers report that the majority have strong mentors and sponsors who follow their careers, providing guidance and creating opportunities. None of the women in this study described mentor relationships that were similar to those that successful white managers have. Rather, all of the mentor relationships described by the black female managers were short-term and informal. As a result, black female managers may be at a disadvantage relative to their white counterparts.

JOB MOBILITY

One of the underlying assumptions of the double-advantage concept is that affirmative action programs are propelling black professional women more rapidly than other, presumably more qualified, workers.

Mobility is related to a number of factors including those that are associated with one's personal competence and ability; those that are associated with formal structural factors such as company career paths and growth rates; and those that are associated with informal work relationships with mentors, colleagues, and superiors.

In the absence of data on the co-workers of each of the women in this study and other relevant firm-specific data, a complete analysis of their mobility cannot be made. However, the concept of mobility can be measured in a number of ways, including: changes in absolute or relative earnings, changes in levels of responsibility, rate of progress along defined career ladders, and movement from lower to higher levels in organizations.[10]

Because this study was designed to explore the experiences of individuals within corporations rather than of corporations per se, the examination of the mobility of the women can perhaps be best addressed by the last measure. Consequently, the focus of the summary that is presented in this section is the current achievement level of the women and likely explanatory variables regarding their status.

When an overall view of the careers of the black female managers is taken, we find that slightly more than half of the group ($N = 15$) have reached a high level or have made rapid progress in the companies for which they work. The first group, hereafter the "high achievers," have reached the level of vice-president, department head, or division director in the oil, automobile manufacturing, telecommunications, or banking industries. All of these industries are widely known for their underrepresentation of white and black women and black men, except at low-level positions. The second group, hereafter the "rapid achievers," have reached upper-middle- or senior-level management positions in the companies for which they work within four to eight years after being hired.

Close examination reveals that in all but three cases the achievements of these women could be reasonably attributed to factors other than affirmative action programs. Specifically, the mobility of the women was associated with one of three factors: (1) tenure—spending an average of 14 years in service with a particular company in a staff position; (2) relative age and growth rate of a company—working for a relatively young, rapidly growing company; or (3) company ownership—working for a company that is black owned and operated. The evidence indicates that in a clear majority of the cases that were examined the circumstances were such that any qualified person, regardless of race or gender, should at the very least have experienced a similar mobility pattern.

In addition, when the mobility of the high achiever group is compared with secondary data on a group of white males who worked in companies similar in size and industry to those of the high achievers and who ultimately achieved the level of chief executive officer (CEO) we find little evidence to support the double-advantage concept. The high achievers were a more highly educated group than the CEOs. Moreover, the former were concentrated in staff positions, whereas the CEOs were concentrated in line positions. Line positions are characterized by longer career ladders than staff positions, yet the CEOs reached the level of vice-president an average of four years earlier than the high achievers reached the same or lower level.[11]

LIMITS TO MOBILITY

In a seminal study of workers in corporations, Kanter identified three structural factors that can limit an individual's mobility.[12] These factors are: (1) the pyramid structure of corporations—that is, as one gets closer to the top of a corporation, the number of available positions decreases; (2) movement into a dead-end job, that is, a job with a short career ladder; and (3) movement through the wrong route into a job that normally has many opportunities, the result being that the person in the job lacks the necessary skills to take advantage of the job's opportunities.

When the careers of the black female managers are examined, we find that approximately half of the sample experienced limits to their mobility during the course of their careers. Within this group, the following patterns could be observed. Women who worked in staff positions, jobs typically viewed as being peripheral to the business of a company, experienced the mobility inhibitors that Kanter identified. In contrast, women who worked in line positions, jobs viewed as central to the business of a company, experienced mobility inhibitors that were related to race or gender. This was true despite the fact that they did the "right things." That is, they positioned themselves on career tracks in areas generally recognized as being the routes to the top of an organization, such as sales or product marketing in consumer goods manufacturing companies or lending in banking. In addition, they came up the ranks through their functional area without taking detours into dead-end jobs or unrelated areas.

However, they found themselves bumping into ceilings that were not inherent in the structure of the internal labor markets of the functional areas in which they worked. Rather, the ceilings were artificially created by individuals within corporations who had control over the distribution of work, promotions, and performance reviews of the women who worked for them. For example, one woman recalled a particularly painful experience in her career in which her manager deliberately erected barriers to her mobility:

> I was not prepared for the level of evil intent among the managers there. I knew the work would be difficult, but I did not expect the fact that I am a black to be a barrier. Management was very reluctant to accept blacks at any level; it was a very hostile environment for black people. . . . My manager would change deadlines on me, making it impossible for me to get assignments in on time. There was no recourse because it was management's word against yours.

Her only recourse was to seek employment with another company, which she ultimately did.

Another woman who feels that she has currently reached a ceiling in her present job noted that the next step in her career progression would have been her boss's job. When it became known that her boss was being promoted and his job was opening up, she applied for it but was passed over. The job was given to a white male whom she feels is less qualified than she:

> It [the job] was between me and this other woman. We were both interested in the position. We both wrote separately to the manager of the office, but at the same time neither one of us was going to get the position because there was going to be too much in the way of politics involved, and neither one of us was close enough to the guy making the decision because they're not really interested in being close to women on a professional basis. I know we both asked my boss, "Well, if we're not going to get the job, why not?" And he told me, "We really want someone that has more knowledge of administrative aspects of the office," which admittedly I didn't have. To me, it's something you can learn. I said, "Well, are you going to hire someone who has those skills?" He said "Yes." They wound up hiring some white male who has

no experience in this kind of lending. He has no experience in this group of the bank. He doesn't know the administrative paper work. He didn't know anything, except he's intelligent enough that he could learn the job. He's going to have to learn a whole lot more than I am. At least I know how to do the actual lending.

It is possible that problems that the core managers experienced were specific to that company. However, the core managers worked in seven different companies in five different industries. The combination of the breadth of their industry and company distribution, and the fact that all worked in core functional areas, implies that there is resistance on the part of management toward the upward mobility of black women who work in functional areas central to the business of the company. In addition, the women who worked in core functional areas who did not report experiencing limits to their mobility worked for companies that had been experiencing rapid growth or had a strong affirmative action program.

One of the implications of these observations is that apparently the informal structure of a company is at the very least as important as formal career-pathing issues, particularly for women who work in core functional areas. Indeed, in the course of the interviews, almost without exception, the managers raised a number of issues about the impact of the informal side of organizations on their professional (and personal) lives. Yet it is this aspect of organizational environments that is perhaps most difficult to regulate or alter without strong support from upper management.

CONCLUSION

Despite the limitations of the data, none of the evidence supports the notion that black professional women are doubly advantaged in the work place. On the contrary, the evidence indicates that at best they are subject to racial or gender discrimination or to constraints that any manager might encounter and at worst they may be subject to a combination of these three constraints.

Specifically, the data indicated that:

- The black female managers lacked early exposure to a general business environment and lacked corporate sponsors, unlike their white counterparts. Thus, their acculturation process was likely to be longer and more difficult and the opportunities offered to them were likely to be more limited than those of their white counterparts.

- Although there were women in the sample whose progress might, in the abstract, appear to have been unusually rapid, close examination revealed that when their mobility was evaluated within the context of their length of service or the growth rate and size of the companies for which they worked, valid conventional explanations for their achievements became apparent. They were *not* especially advantaged.
- The dual status of the black female managers made them vulnerable not only to the kinds of structural factors that can potentially effect the mobility of any worker but also to limits imposed by racism and sexism.

Because this research was a first effort at systematically assessing the popular belief that black women are a doubly advantaged group in professional occupations, it was necessarily exploratory. Therefore it raises at least as many questions as it answers. Although further research is clearly needed, this study provides evidence that the issue of the double advantage of black females appears to be based more on fiction than on fact.

NOTES

1. See, e.g., Glover, R.W., and Greenfield, P., *Minority Women Employment Project: A National Demonstration Program to Facilitate Entry of Minority Women into Managerial, Professional and Technical Occupations* (Austin: University of Texas Center for the Study of Human Resources, 1976); King, Allan, "Labor Market Discrimination Against Black Women," *Review of Black Political Economy*, Summer 1978, 8:325-335; Krieter, Nancy, and Piercy, Day, *Women and Work: The Myth of Equal Opportunity* (Chicago: Women Employed Institute, 1982); Nelson, Charmeynne D., "Myths About Black Women Workers in Modern America," *The Black Scholar*, March 1975, pp. 11-15.

    2. Epstein, Cynthia, "Black and Female: The Double Whammy," *Psychology Today*, vol. 57, August 1973; Epstein, Cynthia, "Positive Effects of the Multiple Negative: Explaining the Success of Black Professional Women," *American Journal of Sociology*, January 1973, vol. 78, no. 4, pp. 912-935; and *Time*, "Rarest Breed of Women: Black Business Women in the Executive Suites," November 8, 1972, pp. 98-102.

    3. Both empirical and theoretical works have focused on black males and white females. For a documentation of the omission of black women from these works see Wallace, Phyllis, *Black Women in the Labor Force* (Cambridge, Mass.: MIT Press, 1980); Hull, Gloria T., Scott, Patricia Bell, and Smith, Barbara, eds., *All the Women Are White, All the Blacks Are Men, but Some of Us Are Brave* (Old Westbury, N.Y.: The Feminist Press, 1981); Fulbright, Karen, *The Myth of the Double-Advantage: Black Women in Management* (Ph.D. diss., MIT, 1985).

    4. Crawford, Jacquelyn S., *Women in Middle Management* (New York: Forkner

Publishing Company, 1977); Johnson, M.L., "Women: Born to Manage," *Industry Week*, August 4, 1975, pp. 22-26; Henning, M., "Career Development for Women Executives" (Ph.D. diss., Harvard University, 1971).

5. Kotter, John P., *The General Managers* (New York: The Free Press, 1982); Sussman, John A., *Korn-Ferry International's Executive Profiles: A Survey of Corporate Leaders* (Los Angeles: Korn/Ferry International, 1979).

6. Burlew, Ann K., "The Experiences of Black Females in Traditional and Nontraditional Professions," *Psychology of Women Quarterly*, 1982, 6:312-326; and Epstein, Cynthia, "Positive Effects of the Multiple Negative."

7. Heaston, P., *An Analysis of Selected Role Perceptions Among Successful Black Women in the Professions*, Dissertation Abstracts International, 1976, 36:4352-a (University Microfilms No. 75-29651).

8. Includes one woman's mother who owns a beauty shop and works as a beautician.

9. Includes an owner of a small business and an army officer.

10. Work, John, *Race Economics and Corporate America* (Wilmington: Scholarly Resources, Inc., 1984).

11. Kotter, John P., *The General Managers*.

12. Kanter, R.M., *Men and Women of the Corporation* (New York: Basic Books, 1977).

REFERENCES

Alvarez, P., et al., eds. *Discrimination in Organizations*. San Francisco: Jossey-Bass, 1979.

Heidrick and Struggles, Inc. *Profile of a Black Executive*. New York: Heidrick and Struggles, Inc., 1979.

Kanter, R.M. "Variations in Managerial Career Structures in High Technology Firms: The Impact of Organizational Characteristics on Internal Labor Market Patterns," in *Internal Labor Markets*, Paul Osterman, ed. Cambridge, Mass.: MIT Press, 1984.

Schein, Edgar H., *Organizational Culture: A Dynamic Model*. Working Paper no. WP1412-893, Sloan School of Management, MIT, 1983.

Van Maanen, John, *Pathways to Membership: Socialization to Work*. Working Paper no. WP1082-79, Sloan School of Management, July 1979, MIT.

Wall Street Journal, "Survey of Women Executives." New York: Dow Jones, October 1984.

COMPARABLE WORTH AND ITS IMPACT
ON BLACK WOMEN

Julianne Malveaux

Comparable worth is a subset of affirmative action strategies that deal with all of the terms and conditions of employment including hiring, recruitment, promotion, transfer, and wages. This article describes the comparable worth strategy and its potential impact on black women, black men, and the black community. By viewing the representation of black women in municipal clerical jobs, the author concludes that black women will gain from comparable worth. Because black men are overrepresented in "typically female" jobs, it is further concluded that black males will gain from implementation of comparable worth. Finally, because comparable worth will examine the basis for pay scales, the author concludes that both gender and racial bias may be revealed when job evaluations are examined. This article also views limitations to the comparable worth strategy and distributional concerns of comparable worth.

Comparable worth is an issue that has maintained a high place on the "women's agenda" for social and economic equity since 1980, when then EEOC Director Eleanor Holmes Norton described it as "the civil rights issue of the 1980's."[1] Given its visibility it is amazing that little research has focused on the ramifications of comparable worth in the black community, or on the implications of comparable worth for black women. In fact, there seems to be an assumption that because comparable worth is on the "women's agenda" it will have uniform impacts on black and white women. Or, alternatively, the assumption has been that there is no reason to focus on the special needs of black women because comparable worth will "help us all."

The failure to analyze differences among women, and to note different ways policy can impact women makes the use of the term "a women's agenda" more exclusive than inclusive. This exclusion (of women who are "other") is not restricted to analysis of comparable worth. In fact, when one views the use of the word "woman" in the social science literature, one is most frequently struck with disappointment at the intellectual myopia that allows researchers to use the word "woman" globally, but at the same time to indirectly assert the "women" have similar labor force characteristics, regardless of race.

Marianne Ferber, for example, criticizes male researchers for the global use of terms, while at the same time writing about women and failing to note that all of them are not white. Cynthia Epstein similarly writes about black women in some of her work, but blatantly ignores them in her book, *Women and Law*.[2]

Maybe these women ignore the status of minority women because they think it is identical to the status of white women. After all, a growing literature on "convergence" asserts that racial biases among women have been eliminated while gender biases remain. This growing literature ignores or rejects the Darity and Myers argument that wage "convergence" is (1) not dramatic, given the historical differences between black and white women's labor force participation, and (2) the result of two very different phenomena—of white women entering the labor market, and of black women doing different jobs.[3]

The convergence argument might retire to the obscure cobwebs of theory were it not for the policy implications of the assertion that black and white women are similar. An assertion of similarity suggests that policies designed to improve the status of white women will also improve the status of black women, in the same amounts and for the same reason. But much of my own work shows that this assertion is not true.[4]

This article explores ways comparable worth affects black women. While detailed data on comparable worth cases is not presented, this article explores my assertion that there are a different set of benefits that black and white women will derive from comparable worth.

COMPARABLE WORTH: DEFINITIONS

Comparable worth is defined as "equal pay for jobs of equal value." The concept emerged from a frustration that despite the Equal Pay Act of 1963 and the Civil Rights Act of 1964, women's relative wages remained at about their 1960 level throughout the succeeding twenty year period. The most frequent male-female wage ratio quoted is that women earn 59% of what men earn. Depending on how wages are measured, the number may range from 50% to 75%. No matter how wage gaps are measured, though, researchers agree that a portion of the wage gaps can only be explained by gender (and not by differences in education, occupation, or other factors).

Comparable worth activists assert that women earn much less than men do because they work in "typically female" jobs, or jobs "crowded" by women. A number of researchers have addressed this question, noting that the majority of women work in jobs that are typically female.[5] Even though the proportion of women working in typically female jobs is dropping, the pace is slow, and the prospects of pay equity are dim if occupation switching is the only way this goal can be achieved.

This is true for several reasons. Firstly, substantial employment growth is scheduled to take place in jobs that are currently defined as "typically female."[6] Secondly, it will be difficult for some women to immediately shift their occupational affiliations, especially since their occupational choice some years ago was determined by the segregation women faced in the workplace. Finally, individual strategies to improve women's wages ignore global tendencies to devalue women's work, especially in "typically female" jobs.

Still many researchers have taken the approach that women need merely get more education, change fields, or pick new occupations to earn more money. These "supply-side" theories suggest that something is wrong with the workers who earn low wages, not with the markets that systematically generate low wages for women. Some economic theorists have, in fact, hypothesized that women "supply" their labor to segregated occupations, choosing to work for lower pay because they "protect" themselves from problems they may face by leaving the labor force for childbearing and attempting to reenter later.[7]

Others assert that pay differentials are a function of institutional distortions in the way wages are paid. In hierarchical workplaces, for example, job evaluation systems, rather than "free markets" determine the ways jobs are evaluated in a workplace. A set of compensable factors is identified and point values are assigned for each of these factors. A first set of gender biases may become part of the system when compensable factors are identified, and when points are assigned. Bergmann notes, for example, that the Hay System job evaluators equated the skill necessary to operate a mimeograph machine with the skill necessary to "operate a typewriter." A second set of gender biases may become incorporated into a job evaluation system when compensable factors are weighed.[8]

While one focus of comparable worth is to correct biases that exist in job evaluation systems, another focus is to make sure that those similarly

evaluated receive similar pay. Thus, those whose jobs are assigned 200
points will earn more money than those whose jobs are assigned 100
points. But most job evaluations do not measure *every* job, especially in a
large workplace. Instead "job clusters" are determined and one
"benchmark" job is evaluated in a cluster. The choice of clusters and
benchmark jobs is another potential source of bias in job evaluation
systems.

Sometimes "typically female" jobs and "typically male" jobs are similarly clustered, and then "typically female" jobs are compensated at a
different level than "typically male" jobs. In this case, a woman with 200
points may earn more than a woman with 100 points. It is not clear,
though, that a woman whose job is assigned 200 points will earn as much
as a man with the same point allocation. Comparable worth seeks to
remedy the gaps in pay between men and women whose jobs are assigned
the same number of points in an evaluation process.

Examples of the pay inequities found in existing job evaluation studies
are illustrative. In the State of Washington the job "Food Service Worker
I" was evaluated at 93 points. Average salary for that job was $472 per
month. A "Delivery Truck Driver I" was evaluated comparably, with 94
points, but average salary for that job was $792. A "Nurse Practitioner II"
had 385 points and average pay of $832 per month. A "Boiler Operator"
with just 144 points earned the same level of pay.[9]

Applying the results of job evaluations will not necessarily solve problems of gender bias in wage rates, although they may move toward elimination of such biases. Remick details the set of biases that are possible in
job evaluation processes. Beatty and Beatty list a set of problems with job
evaluations. McArthur details the basis of potential biases in the job
evaluation process, not the least of which is the fact that biases about the
person holding a job at present (and his or her gender) may influence an
"impersonal" evaluation. But in an attempt to develop a definition of an
ideal comparable worth system, Remick calls for "the application of a
single, bias-free point factor evaluation system within a given establishment, across job families, to both rank order jobs and to set salaries."
Fully cognizant of problems in the job evaluation process, then, Remick
insists that gender biases be removed from them. Her discussion represents the essence of the comparable worth argument—that jobs with similar point ratings receive similar wages. In the *AFSCME v. State of
Washington* case (578 F. Supp. 848), as well as in other cases, the issue has
been that male and female jobs have been evaluated differently, so that

men and women with the same number of points earn very different wages.[10]

Some policymakers have argued against comparable worth by noting that a comparable worth system compares different things, like "apples and oranges." The suggestion has been that if women want to earn "men's" wages they should work in "men's" jobs. This suggestion ignores the subjectivity inherent in job evaluation systems that currently allows faulty evaluation of "apples and oranges" and the fact that comparable worth merely asks that evaluation be more systematic and less biased.[11] The suggestion that women switch jobs ignores the labor market realities that suggest more job growth in "women's" than "men's" jobs, and further ignores the fact that "women's jobs" may be undervalued precisely because women work in them.

The "market" wage is frequently cited as the reason that "typically female" jobs have lower renumeration than "typically male" jobs. But a quarter of all workers are covered by nonmarket collective bargaining agreements. Another third or so work in hierarchical firms where job evaluation studies are used. The "market" sets wages for secondary labor market workers, and indirectly for those who use the results of the other firm's job evaluation to set their pay levels. And the market recursively justifies discriminatory wages. In other words, if one firm pays tellers less than it pays comparably evaluated couriers, another will do the same, citing the "market" as the reason these pay differentials exist. But if, in fact, two or three firms paid equitable wages, other firms would, based on "the market," follow suit.

Discussions of "market" wages also fail to differentiate between internal and external labor markets. Pay for jobs at the port of entry may well be based on certain "market" factors. But job evaluations are internal labor market evaluative tools that assess the value of workers in a given organization. Comparable worth strategies question the way value has been assigned, especially when women's jobs are consistently undervalued.

Comparable worth does not advocate a massive government wage-setting process, as some opponents have asserted. Instead, as Killingsworth notes, comparable worth would not establish uniform national wages, but would implement comparability for those workers who worked for a single employer. The implementation of comparable worth, then, would not preclude pay from varying from location to location, or even, in the same location, from employer to employer.[12]

Actually, the adherence to "market" wages is amusing when one notes that markets only work for some of the people some of the time. Research on the economics of discrimination, and on different racial returns to education and training suggests, in Bergmann's words, markets that are neither free nor competitive. As Remick and Steinberg note, markets are tampered with in a number of ways. Subsidies to Chrysler and Amtrak are examples. Choices to regulate import and export activities are others.[13] One might argue that our policy toward developing countries has been a way of tampering with the labor market. Border controls (or lack of controls), combined with restrictive immigration policies might also be considered labor market "tampering" because they keep wages for undocumented workers down. It is my assertion that the sanctity of "markets" is only raised infrequently: when the consumer or nonwhite nonmale stands to gain from "tampering," even though tampering may be remedial.

Some have argued that comparable worth hurts blue-collar workers, or blacks, or some combination thereof. But comparable worth activists have never proposed cutting the wages of some workers to provide higher wages for others. Instead, to bring women's pay up "to par" the rates of change in wages would differ by job category. In other words, once a comparable worth settlement takes place, all workers may be granted a 5% pay increase, while those workers whose jobs are undervalued may get 15% pay increases to help close the wage gap.

A final argument against comparable worth has been the cost argument. Opponents say the national costs of comparable worth range from $2 billion to $150 billion.[14] However, comparable worth is not likely to be implemented immediately, but in steps, as we have seen in those cities and states where comparable worth has been implemented. San Jose allocated $1.5 million for "pay equity adjustments" over a two year period to begin correcting for wage discrimination. In Minnesota, just 1.25% of the personnel budget was allocated for pay equity adjustments.[15] And in the *AFSCME* v. *State of Washington* case, the award amount is projected to be high because both pay adjustments *and* back pay are included.

San Francisco's mayor implicitly blamed comparable worth for changing the city's budget picture from rosy to ravaged in just one year.[16] Other legislators that oppose comparable worth paint gloomy pictures of high costs, reduced services, job layoffs, and other dire consequences if comparable worth is implemented. Some have sympathized with pay gaps but argued against comparable worth because they say municipalities cannot afford to address pay inequities (that are not their fault). But what is the price of fairness? If cost is the only consideration, the black community should certainly support comparable worth — after all, cost considerations have been used to oppose affirmative action, full employment, educational access and other issues.

COMPARABLE WORTH AND BLACK WOMEN

Can comparable worth improve the economic status of black women? To answer this question it is useful to review the occupational status of black women. Like white women, the majority of black women (more than 60%) work in typically female clerical and service occupations. Proportionately fewer black than white women work in management, sales, and professional jobs, while proportionately more black women work in service, operative (manufacturing), and private household jobs.[17]

Within occupational categories, though, there are differences in the status of black and white women. Among clerical workers, black women are more likely to be found as file clerks, typists, calculating machine operators, and social welfare clerical assistants. Except for social welfare clerical assistants, all of these occupations have wages below the median clerical wage.[18] Among service workers, black women are heavily represented as chambermaids, nurses aides, and practical nurses. Again, pay was lower in those occupations where black women were heavily represented.

Another key difference between black and white women's employment is the heavy concentration of black women in public sector employment. In 1981, 16% of all workers were employed by federal, state or local governments. In contrast, 26% of black women held government employment. Proportionately more black women than any other race-sex group were employed by governments—18% of black men, 17.5% of white women, and 12.9% of white men were so employed. Twenty percent of all clerical workers are employed by governments; but nearly a third of black female clerical workers (compared to less than 18% of white clerical workers) are so employed.[19]

Because of differences in the occupational status and employers of black and white women, one can conclude that implementation of comparable worth pay strategies will have a positive impact on the wage status of black women. Comparable worth's positive impact will come both because black women work in typically female clerical jobs that are underpaid, and because a disproportionate number of black women work for governments, where comparable worth strategies are most likely to be implemented.

There is an additional reason why black women will gain from comparable worth. Although black women work in clerical jobs similar to the clerical jobs in which white women work, they work in a set of clerical jobs that earn lower pay than the clerical jobs in which white women work. Malveaux explores the concept of "black women's crowding," which is defined as distinct from the "women's crowding" that white women experience.[20] It is noted that although black women are just 5.4% of the labor force, their representation in some jobs is as high as 35%. In this article, I suggest that this form of crowding results in lower wages for black women, and note that, in clerical occupations, black women are overrepresented in some of the lowest-paying clerical jobs. This means that black women in clerical ocupations tend to be underpaid relative to their white counterparts.

This overrepresentation among the lowest paying jobs suggests differential effects from the implementation of comparable worth. Table 1 shows the results of an exercise that illustrates this point. Pay gaps revealed by Remick in State of Washington data were supplemented by data on the percentage of black women in certain jobs.[21] Where all women were overrepresented, but black women were underrepresented, workers were paid an average of 94% of what they should have been paid based on job evaluation estimates. But in jobs where black women were overrepresented (with their representation in a job category at 15% or more), workers were paid 76% of what they should have been paid. Implementation of comparable worth, in this case, would improve the relative position of black women in "typically black female" jobs.

COMPARABLE WORTH AND BLACK COMMUNITY GAINS

The black community, as well as black women, will accrue gains when comparable worth is implemented. The first gain is an obvious one — the gain from higher black family wages when black women earn equitable pay. Given the large number of black women heading households, the need for black women to earn equitable pay cannot be overstated. But even where there is another household earner, black women's contribution to black family income frequently makes the difference between black family poverty and black family survival.[22]

Black men will also gain from comparable worth because they are more likely than white men to hold those "typically female" jobs in which pay

TABLE 1
Black Women's Pay When They are Overrepresented and Underrepresented in Occupations

JOB TITLE	ACTUAL SALARY	PREDICTED SALARY	RATIO	% FEMALE WASHINGTON STATE	%BLACK FEMALE NATIONAL
Black women are overrepresented as:					
INTERMEDIATE CLERK	921	1208	76.2	81.0	17.9
INTERMEDIATE CLERK/TYPIST	968	1269	76.3	96.7	16.3
TELEGRAPH OPERATOR	887	1239	71.6	95.7	15.5
DATA ENTRY OPERATOR	1017	1239	82.1	96.5	18.1
LICENSED PRACTICAL NURSE	1030	1367	75.3	89.5	18.5
AVERAGE			76.3	91.9	17.3
Black women are underrepresented as:					
LEGAL SECRETARY	1269	1401	90.6	98.7	5.0
WORD PROCESSOR	1082	1301	83.2	98.3	5.0
BOOKKEEPER	1122	1269	88.4	87.0	5.2
ADMINISTRATIVE ASSISTANT	1334	1472	90.6	95.1	2.6
INTERMEDIATE ACCOUNTANT	1585	1585	100.0	60.2	4.4
LAB TECHNICIAN	1208	1401	86.2	84.1	5.2
RETAIL SALES CLERK	921	1239	74.3	100.0	4.9
PHARMACIST	1980	1666	118.8	60.0	2.7
LIBRARIAN	1625	1794	90.6	84.6	5.1
COMMUNITY PROGRAM DEVELOPER	1932	1750	110.4	60.0	4.7
ADMINISTRATIVE SERVICES MANAGER	1839	1794	102.5	73.4	2.6
AVERAGE			94.1	81.9	4.3

Data Source: Remick (1981), unpublished BLS data, Malveaux (1984)

would be adjusted. Malveaux notes differences in the distribution of black and white men and speculates this may be because black men have, in the past, been excluded from the professional, managerial, and craft jobs in which white men have been concentrated. In the same vein, Giddings writes of the Moynihan suggestion that black women's jobs be "re-designed" for black men as one way to combat high levels of black male unemployment.[23]

There is another potential gain to the black community from adopting a comparable worth strategy. Comparable worth relies on the implementation of a "single, neutral" job evaluation process and uncovers systematic gender bias that results in very different rates of pay for workers whose jobs have a comparable number of evaluation points. Once flaws in the job evaluation process are uncovered, and examination of job evaluations begin, it is likely that pay inequities will be revealed in job categories where minority males are heavily concentrated. In San Francisco, job evaluation revealed that janitors, mostly minority males, received 97 evaluation points and $18,000 in pay. Truck drivers, mostly white males, had 98 evaluation points, but $27,000 in pay.[24] In Alameda County, California, a contrast of the job classifications dominated by minorities and those dominated by nonminorities revealed a 76% pay gap, a smaller gap than revealed when job classifications dominated by women, and those dominated by men are compared. (This gap was 37%).[25] Thus, because systematic racial bias is as likely to occur as systematic gender bias, the adoption of comparable strategies may have a benefit to the black community that is greater than the gain to black women.

Although there is potential for blacks to gain from comparable worth in municipalities, it is critical to note that comparable worth gains will not accrue to the black community merely because comparable worth is being considered in a community. The process of examining job evaluations merely opens the door for black activists and trade unionists to evaluate racial biases that may exist in job evaluations. Clearly, the subjectivity inherent in job evaluation processes has affected blacks (and other minorities) as much as it has affected women. But because comparable worth has been seen as a "women's issue," the inclusion of jobs that are "typically" minority in settlement processes may be one that requires political coalition building tactics.

Some researchers and activists detail ways to include the crowding of minorities into comparable worth consideration; others see the inclusion of minorities in comparable worth strategies as "muddying the waters."[26] Still others, for reasons of political pragmatism, choose not to see the connection between race and sex discrimination. But whenever one acknowledges that job evaluations have allowed the introduction of subjective biases in the way wages are paid, then it is a small step to move from correction of gender biases to correction of racial biases.

LIMITATIONS TO COMPARABLE WORTH STRATEGY

While comparable worth strategies promise clear gains for black women (and men) who are employed in the public sector, the implementation of comparable worth will not solve all of the employment problems of the black community. In fact, some have argued that comparable worth is a strategy limited to solving the problems of workers in low-paying, typically female jobs.[27] In any case, no assessment of comparable worth's impact on the black community is complete without a discussion of strategy limitations.

Comparable worth's benefits are limited to public-sector employees. Unless far-reaching national legislation is passed, which is not likely before 1989, comparable worth is likely to be implemented in cities and states, and to apply solely to those workers employed in the public sector. Private-sector employers are not likely, in the absence of legislation, to implement comparable worth.

Even as comparable worth is discussed as a strategy, however, workers who were formerly employed in the public sector have found their jobs subcontracted to private employers. These workers are employed primarily in food and cleaning service occupations, and are mostly minorities.[28]

When jobs leave the civil service structure, the question of "comparable pay" for those jobs is irrelevant. Instead, because subcontractors compete for contracts on the basis of a low bid, it is likely that the wages and working conditions of workers will decline when their jobs move from the public sector to the private sector. Strategies to ensure fair wages, hours and working conditions for these workers are not likely to include comparable worth strategies.

While this discussion is not meant to minimize the importance of comparable worth strategies, it makes it clear that a substantial segment of employed black women (more than 22% of whom hold service jobs) are likely to find comparable worth an inapplicable strategy to their situation. Strategies to limit contracting out are more appropriate strategies for improving the status of these women.

Comparable worth strategies are limited to employed workers. Black female unemployment rates are more than twice white female rates (15.4% and 6.5%, respectively, in 1984). Strategies to improve the status of employed women will, of necessity, exclude the unemployed. For these women, affirmative action strategies are likely to facilitate entry into paid employment, while comparable worth will facilitate the equitable pay process.

Comparable worth strategies may not include women who participate in "workfare" programs. Although the mechanics of employment and pay in workfare programs are in draft stage (at least in California where legislation was passed in 1985), it is clear that a disproportionate number of black women will work in these jobs because a disproportionate number of black women receive public assistance. If jobs are not available in the private sector, then workfare women will be provided with public sector, below "market" wages, and possibly "make-work" jobs. These women may be substitutes for unionized civil service workers who perform the same tasks. Given the low pay rates built into workfare legislation, the issue of comparable pay will also not be an issue for these women.

Comparable worth strategies will not affect women forced to participate in the underground economy. Women on welfare are likely to participate in underground economy employment because welfare payments are not large enough to provide for the needs of their families. Though there is little solid information on employment sources for these women, anecdotal information suggests that these women work in the service sector, in laundries and as hotel maids, and in related "typically female" service jobs.

It is important to note that discussion of welfare women's participation in the underground economy is not an attempt to "blame the victim" or put further restrictions on welfare women (many of whom are penalized for school attendance by reduction in welfare checks), but rather an attempt to point out the implicit subsidy offered those employers who hire these women and pay them minimum or below minimum wages. Reform in this area should begin with investigation of employers, not employees.

In any case, while the number of welfare women participating in the underground economy cannot be estimated, it is likely that a disproportionate number of them are black (because a disproportionate number of the women on welfare are black). Comparable worth strategies, no matter what their importance to women employed in the public sector, will not help these women.

Comparable worth will not help women who hold semiskilled and unskilled jobs. Comparable worth may improve the status of women working in jobs where their skills are undervalued, but those women who work in semiskilled and unskilled jobs will not benefit from implementation of comparable worth. Unionization is possibly the most direct way to ensure fair wages, hours, and working conditions for these women.

While comparable worth offers the opportunity for improvement of the wages of some black workers, it is a strategy that will not address the employment situation of many others. It is important to view comparable worth, then, as one of a set of strategies to improve the employment status of black workers. Other strategies include affirmation action, full employment legislation, job creation, encouragement of unionization, and legislation to limit contracting out.

DISTRIBUTIONAL ASPECTS OF COMPARABLE WORTH

Comparable worth is an activist strategy; it is one that requires activists to agitate and lobby legislators to support revising the way state or local civil service jobs are evaluated. While the thrust of this article has been to highlight the benefits accruing to black women as a result of implementation of comparable worth, this section raises questions about activist priorities and ways they may change depending on the demographics and fiscal realities in a state or municipality. Again, this discussion is not meant to detract from the real value of comparable worth strategies, but to suggest ways to evaluate the benefits from comparable worth.

How are black women distributed in a given community? If more are service workers than clerical workers, greater impact may be gained by encouraging unionization and limiting contracting out of service activities. While comparable worth will help clerical workers gain equitable pay, institutional arrangements will determine how service workers are paid.

Where will money to pay comparable worth pay adjustments come from? If it will come from educational budgets, from community service budgets, or from other budgets beneficial to the black community, then legislators opposed to comparable worth are likely to make that point. (In San Francisco, the mayor has asked all city departments to take a 5% budget cut, supposedly to pay for a $28 million comparable worth settlement.) If money will come from budget items particularly helpful to the black community, then careful evaluation of the budget process is in order. While comparable worth wage adjustments should not take the blame for budget shifts (what cost fairness?), activists should be cognizant of budget battles likely to emerge from comparable worth settlements, and be prepared to fight these battles with broad-based coalitions of black community activists, trade unionists, and feminist activists.

Will workers in subcontracted jobs be affected? This question (and its answer) is related to the previous one, but is raised separately because so many minority women are found in subcontracted service jobs. Are there ways the impact of such tradeoffs can be reduced? It may be appropriate to consider supporting the rights of workers whose jobs may be subcontracted with a coalition similar to the one described above.

Will there be a tax increase to pay for comparable worth? If so, what is the tax incidence? Tax increases may provide black taxpayers with a springboard for demanding that issues of racial crowding and bias in job evaluation processes be considered.

What is the relationship between comparable worth and affirmative action? Since affirmative action deals with all of the terms and conditions of employment, including hiring, recruitment, promotion, transfer, and wages, comparable worth should be considered a subset of an overall affirmative action strategy. However, comparable worth has too frequently been considered a self-standing strategy, and in some cases a sole strategy instead of one in a series of strategies. Black workers who support comparable worth should not lose sight of broader affirmative action tactics, and should consider brokering their support of comparable worth for stronger support of affirmative action efforts.

In general, comparable worth will have a positive impact on black women's wages. But the size of the impact will differ by community, and will depend on the proportion and distribution of black women in the public sector. Additionally, the positive impact of comparable worth on black women will depend on how legislators propose to pay for comparable worth and whether black community services or tax payments are adversely affected by comparable worth costs.

A key point for the black community to consider is the fact that questions about gender bias in job evaluation lead to related questions about racial bias. Comparable worth strategies are most likely to raise these questions when black workers are involved in defining those strategies. To the extent that comparable worth strategies raise these questions, and ultimately change these pay scales, black women and the black community are both beneficiaries.

CONCLUSION

Clearly, many aspects of this article are conjectural. But it lays out a framework for an empirical investigation of the impact of comparable worth on the black community. Preliminary investigation suggests that comparable worth is likely to have clear positive effects. A discussion of distributional issues highlights ways comparable worth concepts may be used to strengthen the entire employment position of black workers in municipalities.

When employment policies are considered for the black community, an important factor is the diversity of the black population and their employment status. From this standpoint comparable worth should be viewed as one of a series of strategies to improve the status of black women. While comparable worth will not help black women who are unemployed, who work in the private sector, who participate in underground economies or in workfare programs, it will have a positive effect on black women (and some black men) in public-sector jobs. As long as comparable strategies are developed in tandem with other strategies to improve the employment status of black women, the black community has nothing to lose and much to gain by supporting comparable worth.

NOTES

1. Eleanor Holmes Norton. Speech to Conference on Pay Equity. *Daily Labor Reporter* (Bureau of National Affairs), no. 211, October 30.

2. Marianne Ferber, "Women and Work: Issues of the 1980s." *Signs: Journal of Women in Culture and Society* 8, no. 2 (Winter 1982). p. 273-295; Cynthia Fuchs Epstein, *Women in Law* (New York: Basic Books, 1981).

3. James P. Smith "The Convergence to Racial Equality in Women's Wages," in Cynthia Lloyd, et al. (eds.), *Women in the Labor Market* (New York: Columbia University Press, 1979), pp. 173-215; William Darity and Sam Myers. "Changes in Black-White Income Inequality, 1968-78: A Decade of Progress?" *Review of Black Political Economy*, 10, (Summer, 1980), pp. 354-79.

4. Julianne Malveaux, "The Economic Interests of Black and White Women: Are They Similar?" in the *Review of Black Political Economy*, Vol 14, No 1, Summer 1985.

5. Andrea Beller, "Trends in Occupational Segregation by Sex and Race, 1960-1981 in Barbara F. Reskin, ed., *Sex Segregation in the Workplace: Trends, Explanations, and Remedies* (Washington, D.C.: National Academy Press, 1984) pp. 11-26.

6. Pamela Stone Cain, "Prospects for Pay Equity in a Changing Economy," in Heidi Hartmann (ed.), *Comparable Worth: New Directions for Research* (Washington, D.C.: National Academy Press, 1985).

7. Solomon Polachek, "Occupational Segregation Among Women: Theory, Evidence, and a Prognosis," in Cynthia Lloyd, et al. (eds.), *Women in the Labor Market* (New York: Columbia University Press, 1979), pp. 137-57.

8. Barbara Bergmann, "The Economic Case for Comparable Worth," in Heidi Hartmann (ed.), *Comparable Worth: New Directions for Research* (Washington, D.C.: National Academy Press, 1985); Helen Remick, "Major Issues in a prior Applications" in Helen Remick (ed.), *Comparable Worth and Wage Discrimination* (Philadelphia: Temple University Press, 1984).

9. Helen Remick, "Major Issues . . ." p. 103.

10. Richard Beatty and James R. Beatty "Some Problems with Contemporary Job Evaluation Systems," in Helen Remick, *Comparable Worth and Wage Discrimination* (Philadelphia: Temple University Press, 1984); Lelsie Zebrowitz McArthur, "Social Judgment Biases in Comparable Worth Analysis," in Heidi Hartmann (ed.), *Comparable Worth: New Directions for Research* (Washington, D.C.: National Academy Press, 1985); see also, Helen Remick, "The Comparable Worth Controversy," *IMPA Public Personnel Management Journal* vol 10, no. 4, December 1981, for a definition of comparable worth.

11. Mark Killingsworth, The Economics of Comparable Worth: Analytical, Empiracal, and Policy Questions," in Heidi Hartmann (ed.), *Comparable Worth: New Directions for Research* (Washington, D.C.: National Academy Press, 1985).

12. Killingsworth.

13. Barbara Bergmann, "The Economic Case for Comparable Worth" in Heidi Hartmann (ed.), *Comparable Worth: New Directions for Research* (Washington, D.C.: National Academy Press, 1985); Helen Remick and Ronnie J. Steinberg, "Technical Possibilities and Political Realities: Concluding Remarks" in Helen Remick (ed.), *Comparable Worth and Wage Descrimination* (Philadelphia: Temple University Press, 1984).

14. Remick and Steinberg, "Technical Possibilities . . ."

15. Remick and Steinberg.

16. Phillip Matier, "Feinstein Orders Hiring Freeze, Trims in Budget." San Francisco Examiner, October 8, 1985.

17. See Malveaux, "The Economic Interests . . ." for more details.

18. Julianne Malveaux, "Low Wage Black Women: Occupational Descriptions, Strategies for Change." Unpublished paper, NAACP Legal Defense and Education Fund, 1984.

18. Malveaux, "Low Wage Black Women."

19. Malveaux, "Low Wage Black Women."

20. Malveaux, "Low Wage Black Women."

21. Malveaux, "Low Wage Black Women"; see also Remick, "The Comparable Worth Controversy."

22. Phyllis A. Wallace, *Black Women in the Labor Force* (Cambridge: MIT Press, 1980).

23. Julianne Malveaux, "Recent Trends in Occupational Segregation by Race and Sex," presented May, 1982, to the Committee on Women's Employment and Related Social Issues, National Academy of Sciences; Paula Giddings, *When and Where I Enter: The Impact of Black Women on Race and Sex in America* (New York: William Morrow Company, 1984).

24. Tim Shreiner, "How Comparable Worth Plan Works." *San Francisco Chronicle*, February 13, 1985.

25. SEIU 250, 535, 616, Wage Gap and Job Classification Data, Exhibits B and G (Alameda County: SEIU), 1985.

26. Comparable Worth Project, "First Steps to Identifying Sex and Race-Based Pay Inequities in a Workplace" (Oakland: Comparable Worth Project, 1982); Julianne Malveaux, "An Activist's Guide to Comparable Worth," in *North Star* 1, no. 1, May 1985 (a), pp. 22-31.

27. Killingsworth, "The Economics of Comparable Worth."

28. Malveaux, "Low Wage Black Women . . ."

When and Where I Enter

(By Paula Giddings. New York: Morrow, 1984)

Labor of Love, Labor of Sorrow

(By Jacqueline Jones. New York: Basic Books, 1985)

Reviewed by Cecilia A. Conrad

The history of black women has been neglected.[1] Black studies has focused its attention on black men; women's studies has focused on the problems, history, and roles of white women. What research there is on black women has concentrated primarily on the economic status of contemporary black women.[2]

Now, there are two new books on black women's history—*When and Where I Enter*, by Paula Giddings, and *Labor of Love, Labor of Sorrow*, by Jacqueline Jones.[3] The two authors have very different perspectives. Giddings is a writer by training and experience. Jones is a professor of history at Wellesley College. Despite these different perspectives, the books are complementary, rather than competitive. Gidding's focus is the history of black women's political and social activism, with attention to the achievements of individual black women. Jones' book is a broader study of the economic history of black women in America.

Both books challenge the traditional theses that have been advanced regarding black women and their work. Because black women have had greater representation in the professions than black men and because their labor force participation rates are historically higher than those for white women, scholars have claimed that black women are less victimized by racism than black men; that black women are less victimized by sexism than white women; and that black families are matriarchical, with the female dominating the male. In the 1930s, E. Franklin Frazier criticized black women "for entering careers of their own and destroying the pattern of family life which the man has become accustomed to."[4] In the 1960s the now-infamous Moynihan report blamed the economic condition of blacks on the deterioration of the black family and cited the "reversed roles" of husbands and wives as one cause of this deterioration.[5] Moynihan's solution was to emphasize jobs for black men even if it meant "redesigning some women's jobs" to enable men to fill them, thereby restoring the black male to a dominant role in his household. Giddings and Jones reach different conclusions.

Giddings argues for a change in focus "toward why black women, who were fulfilling their responsibilities, were yet the most vulnerable and exploited group in the society" (p. 329). In her introduction Jones writes,

> It is a cruel historical irony that scholars and policymakers alike have taken the manifestations of black women's oppression and twisted them into the argument that a powerful black matriarchy exists. The persistent belief that any woman who fulfills a traditional male role, either as breadwinner or household head, wields some sort of all encompassing power over her spouse and children is belied by the experiences of black working women. (p. 7)

The history of black women's employment depicted in both books differs from the "norm" provided by white women. A key difference between the two groups is that black women were more likely than white women to work for wages outside the home. This does not mean that a sexual division of labor between black men and women did not exist. Both books illustrate that black women were consistently relegated to the worst of "women's" work.

Despite their high rates of participation in the labor force, black women fulfilled traditional female roles in society, both as homemakers and as workers. They were victims of racial discrimination even within the narrow confines of "women's work," since they were often stuck with the "women's work" that white women did not want to do. They were totally excluded from some occupations and relegated to the lowest-paying jobs in others.

Slavery offers a natural starting point for examining the nature of black women's work. As documented in Jones, black women worked in the fields alongside black men and performed "back-breaking labor" with the same efficiency as men. Jones concludes that in the fields "the notion of a distinctive 'women's work' vanished" because slaveholders realized that women could plow, hoe, and pick cotton as well as men. Nevertheless, women rarely served as skilled artisans or mechanics, or as overseers.

Jones explains that even this differentiation was motivated by profits. For the slaveholder, training female slaves for skilled work was less profitable than training males because the female slave's work was frequently interrupted for childbearing.

Within the slave household, women did the washing, the making of clothes, the cleaning, and the childcare. Men collected firewood and constructed furniture, animal traps, and household implements such as butter paddles. They also supplemented the family through hunting or fishing or, in the case of craftsmen, by earning money outside the plantation.

This sexual division of labor became more sharpened in sharecropping families after emancipation. Women worked in the fields when needed, but their primary obligations were domestic duties. Women's agricultural labor became more seasonal than that of their husbands.

Black women supplemented family incomes by working as laundresses (within their own homes) or by hiring themselves out as agricultural labor to a local planter. Jones reports that in 1910, 27% of all black agricultural laborers earned wages by hiring themselves out. In coastal areas, black women also worked as oyster shuckers, while black men specialized in oyster gathering.

In the urban South, black women worked as laundresses and domestic servants. Black families, like working-class white families, could also supplement income by taking in boarders. All of these occupations—laundress, servant, and landlady—represented extensions of the concept of women's work.

This pattern was repeated in the nonagricultural sector. Few black women found work in the industrial sector of the South. In 1910, 883 out of the 728,309 southern black women engaged in nonagricultural pursuits worked as cotton mill employees. Most of them were scrubwomen; jobs as spinners and weavers were reserved for white women. The tobacco industry employed more black women. Two percent of southern black women engaged in nonagricultural pursuits were employed in the manufacture of tobacco products. These women worked in one of the least desirable occupations—as "rehandlers"—sorting, stripping, stemming, and hanging tobacco leaves. Although cigar factories employed blacks both as laborers and operatives, skilled operative positions in cigarette factories were reserved for white women. This fact is particularly significant because demand for cigarettes was expanding while that for cigars was contracting.

In 1900, less than 3% of all black working women were engaged in manufacturing, whereas 21% of foreign-born and 38% of native-born white working women were. By 1930, the comparable figures were 5.5% of gainfully employed black women, 27.1% of foreign-born, and 19% of native-born white women (Jones, p. 166). The native-born white women had left manufacturing for newly available jobs as clerical and sales workers, from which black women were excluded. Jones argues that this exclusion was due to discrimination by consumers who preferred not to deal with blacks or even with foreign-born whites. Because of this discrimination, black women were not hired for clerical and sales jobs that required face-to-face contact with customers, whereas they were hired to perform similar tasks in situations where face-to-face contact was not required. For example, the largest employer of black clerical workers in the 1920s was a mail-order establishment, Montgomery Ward. Given this discrimination, black women with high school diplomas were often restricted to the same forms of menial employment available to their less-educated contemporaries.

During World War I, black women worked in the munitions industry, on the railroads and in meat-packing plants. These women worked on the lowest rungs of the occupational ladder, with low wages and little opportunity for advancement. For the most part, they replaced white women who were moved up into more desirable jobs.

As Giddings notes, "Although it was true that black women were leaving the kitchen and laundry, they did so only as fast as white women made their way up the employment ladder. Black women found jobs primarily in those places left vacant by the shifting of Hungarians, Italians, and Jewish girls to munitions plants where higher pay was available" (p. 143).

Domestic work and laundry remained the primary source of black women's employment during the early 1900s. In 1920, 80% of black female nonagricultural workers were maids, cooks, or washerwomen (Jones, p. 167).

Despite the visibility of individual black women, such as Mary McCleod Bethune in the Roosevelt administration, blacks, and black women in particular, were excluded from many of the relief programs sponsored by the federal government during the Great Depression. Public works jobs had as their principal goal the employment of men, not women. Fifty percent of the women who worked in WPA worked on sewing projects from which black women were often excluded by "sewing tests." In Fayetteville, North Carolina, a sewing group of black women was disbanded and a "cleaning project" replaced it. In Oklahoma, a black women's work project was closed upon the appearance of an abundant cotton crop. Black women who were denied public works jobs were told: "You can find work in kitchens," and "go hunt washings."

The growth in female participation in the labor force and expansion of women into nontraditional jobs during World War II has been widely discussed. Yet, especially in the early stages of the war, blacks were excluded from many wartime jobs. For example, the Ford Motor Company refused to hire blacks in establishments converted to wartime use. In August 1943, the personnel manager of a Detroit bomber plant told one black woman who had just completed a formal training program, "When a department is nice and peaceful we don't go around looking for trouble by putting colored people in the department" (Jones, p. 238). In late 1942, defense plants in the Detroit area had only 100 black female production employees out of a total female work force of 96,000 (Jones, p. 239).

The history of black women's employment suggests two important sources of conflict between black and white women. First, white women were the principal employers of black women as domestic workers. Second, black and white women were competitors for the same jobs. For black women, the white women who hired them to be domestic servants were frequently the same women with whom they competed for jobs. Because of these conflicts the resistance to hiring black women during World War II came not only from racist employers but also from fellow employees. Unfortunately, neither Jones nor Giddings provides much analysis of these economic conflicts. Although Jones mentions the "hate strikes" staged by white women to attempt to prevent the hiring of blacks, her analysis of this conflict is minimal. Giddings provides an excellent analysis of the conflicts between black and white women over political rights, but her discussion of the conflicts between black and white women over economic issues is less extensive.

White women gained from the exclusion of black women from skilled and semiskilled positions in two ways. By restricting the number of competitors for jobs, they could protect wages. At the same time, the crowding of black women into domestic service kept those wages low, ensuring white women a steady supply of cheap household labor. Indeed, Jones notes that when wartime recruitment efforts mentioned black women, they were "exhorted to enter 'war service', by taking jobs that white women most readily abandoned—laundry, cafeteria, and domestic work" (p. 232). Giddings cites a report in the *Baltimore Afro-American* that the chief source of opposition to the employment of black women in war industries was not management, "but. . . white local housewives, who feared lowering the barriers would rob them of maids, cooks and nurses" (Giddings, p. 237).

An exception to the usual pattern of exclusion was the field of teaching in colored schools in the South. By 1910, fully 17,266 black females taught in southern states. They outnumbered their male colleagues by a greater than three-to-one ratio and represented 1% of the region's black working women (Jones, p. 144). Giddings suggests that black women were more successful in occupations like teaching than in occupations like clerical and sales work because there were fewer competitors for jobs and a strong demand for teachers.

However, Giddings' suggestion is only a partial explanation of black women's "success" in teaching. There were other important factors at work. Where black women found success as teachers was in "colored" schools, not white schools. Here the discrimination against blacks on the part of consumers (who were also blacks) was less likely than in clerical and sales occupations. Instead, the desire of whites to avoid working with blacks gave blacks a competitive edge as teachers in "colored" schools.

Sex was not a limiting factor because teaching represented a natural extension of the idealized concept of women's work beyond the context of the individual family to a larger community. Black teachers were seen as missionaries whose duties were "to inspire women to have better homes and care for their bodies."[6]

A great emphasis was placed on the role of black women as educators by the black women's club movement, described by Giddings in *When and Where I Enter*. The concerns of these clubs included "how to aid some poor boy to complete a much-coveted education; how to lengthen the short school term in some impoverished school district"; and "how to instruct deficient mothers in the difficulties of child training."[7] Several of the women active in this movement founded schools whose curricula included academic subjects but emphasized industrial arts training, particularly homemaking. As Giddings notes, this emphasis of industrial arts reflected the dominance exercised by Booker T. Washington over funding for black schools. However, the emphasis on homemaking represented the influence of the "cult of domesticity" as well.[8] Under the cult of domesticity, homemaking was elevated to a profession and defined as the exclusive sphere of women. The black women in the club movement appear to have subscribed fully to this cult. The domestic arts were seen as necessary to ensure a healthy, wholesome homelife or else "women would be social and moral liabilities."[9]

Labor of Love, Labor of Sorrow is a detailed, carefully documented chronological account of black women's work, employment, and family life. Because statistics are interspersed with anecdotes throughout the book, Jones' book is enjoyable reading. However, for an economist this intermingling of statistics with anecdotes can be frustrating. There are no tables that neatly summarize changes in the occupational distribution of black women over time. To obtain this information requires flipping back and forth between the index and various sections of the text.

When and Where I Enter is less detailed and less carefully documented, but it is rich in anecdotes and quotations. Giddings' focus is not black women's work and employment, but the political and social activism of black women. Hence, her book provides less information on general patterns of black women's economic lives than *Labor of Love, Labor of Sorrow*, but it provides more information on the activities of middle-class black women.

My principal complaint is that these books were not written by economists. We need more studies that apply the methodology of economics to understanding the history of black women's work, employment, and family life. These two excellent books provide a wealth of information and ideas for further study; what is required is more explanations—and further study.

Neither of these books directly discusses contemporary public policies and their effect on black women. However, the history of black women offers several lessons for policymakers today. First, both books illustrate the contribution of black women's earnings to the economic well-being of the black community. Employment opportunities for black women is as important an issue for the black community as employment opportunities for black men. Second, the historical pattern of occupational segregation described in both books persists today. Black women tend to be concentrated in occupations where substitutes for their labor are readily available. For example, in domestic work the services of the black maid can be easily replaced by either the employer herself or other unskilled workers. This concentration in occupations with low entry requirements not only depresses wages but also increases the vulnerability of black women's earnings to general changes in economic activity. Policies, such as those during the depression, that reinforce this pattern of occupational segregation are destined to have little long-term impact on black women's earnings.

NOTES

1. This neglect of black women is discussed by Mary Berry in the foreword of a book on black women's studies with the particularly appropriate title *All the Women Are White, All the Blacks Are Men, but Some of Us Are Brave*, Gloria T. Hull, Patricia Bell Scott, and Barbara Smith, eds. (Westbury, New York: The Feminist Press, 1982).

2. See, for example, Phyllis Wallace, *Black Women in the Labor Force* (Cambridge: MIT Press, 1980). There is the research by Claudia Goldin exploring historical precedents for the racial differences in labor force participation rates, "Female Labor Force Participation: The Origin of Black and White Differences, 1870-1880," *Journal of Economic History* 16 (Summer 1983): 39-48; and Julie Matthaei in her book *An Economic History of Women in America* (New York: Schoken Books, 1982) stresses that the experiences of black women were different from those of white women.

3. Paula Giddings, *When and Where I Enter: The Impact of Black Women on Race and Sex in America* (New York: Morrow, 1984); and Jacqueline Jones, *Labor of Love, Labor of Sorrow: Black Women, Work and the Family from Slavery to the Present* (New York: Basic Books, 1985).

4. E. Franklin Frazier as quoted in Giddings, p. 253.

5. Daniel Patrick Moynihan, "The Negro Family: The Case for National Action," Office of Policy Planning and Research, United States Department of Labor, March 1965. Reprinted in Lee Rainwater and William L. Yancey, *The Moynihan Report and the Politics of Controversy* (Cambridge: MIT Press, 1967).

6. A remark made by Olivia Davidson, second wife of Booker T. Washington, to Alabama school teachers, as quoted in Giddings, p. 99.

7. Fannie Barrier Williams as quoted in Giddings, p. 97.

8. Julie Matthaei devotes a chapter of her book, op. cit., to the cult of domesticity.

9. Nannie Helen Burroughs, founder of the National Training School for Girls in Washington, D.C., as quoted in Giddings, p. 102.

DISCUSSION

Charles L. Betsey

The essays in this section presented various views of the employment situation of black women. Since both race and gender are often the focus of discriminatory treatment, each of these four essays considers the relative contribution of each and generally concludes that black women are discriminated against as blacks *and* as women. Several of the essays explicitly consider the hypothesis that because of antidiscrimination legislation and affirmative action programs black women might be more favorably treated than others (e.g., white men). What comes through in each of these essays is the nature of black women's employment disadvantage which is both similar to and distinct from that of other women or black men.

Barbara Jones' article explores the data on recent trends in black women's labor force participation and possible explanations for those trends. She notes that while the proportion of black women participating in the labor force increased from 46.6% in 1962 to 54.2% in 1983, white women's participation increased from 38.1% to 52.7% over the same time period. Thus, the large gap between black and white women's participation that previously existed had been largely eliminated during the past 20 years.

Jones explores several possible explanations for the *relative* decline in labor force participation of black women. She considers the role of variables found to affect labor force participation in cross-section studies including own earnings, husband's earnings, presence and age of children, education, work experience, marital status, and age. Jones concludes that the largest drop in labor force participation among black women is among 16 to 19 year olds and to a lesser extent among 20 to 24 year olds.

Jones also contends that demand is an important explanatory factor and goes on to consider trends in unemployment rates as measures of the "relative demand" for black and white women. The fact that unemployment rates of black females are highest in the 16 to 19 year age group "suggest that the extraordinarily high unemployment rates among black women, particularly young ones, have discouraged young black women from entering the labor force and encouraged others to leave."

Jones briefly discusses several alternative strategies for increasing employment opportunities for black women (and men), including affirmative action, employment subsidies, and the elimination of minimum wages and social welfare programs. She ultimately decides that success in arresting the declining employment of black women will require "a fundamental change in the economic decision-making process," and ultimately economic planning.

One would be more likely to agree with Jones if she had better laid the foundation for this conclusion. We are asked to consider that economic planning is necessary because black women's labor force participation no longer substantially outpaces that of white women. Apparently, Dr. Jones believes that the reason to be concerned about the *relative* decline is self-evident. It is not. On the other hand, the data indicate that there have been absolute declines in the labor force participation of certain subgroups of black women that one should be concerned about (e.g., in-school youth between 16 and 19 years old).

Finally, Jones' analysis is constrained by her attempt to generalize from cross-sectional results to long-term trends, as well as her use of tabular data that does not hold other factors constant.

The cause for concern about black women's lower *relative* labor force participation in recent years is clearly illustrated in Cecilia Conrad's reviews of *When and Where I Enter* and *Labor of Love, Labor of Sorrow*. Black women have historically been a major or the primary source of income for black families. If black women are participating less in the labor force the economic well-being of black families may have deteriorated.

Conrad's review indicates both the distance black women have come in terms of economic integration into the American labor force and the distance they have yet to go. I found particularly striking the comments concerning the types of work black women were allowed (or forced) to enter, from teaching to laundering, and the extent to which their segregation was enforced not only by white men but by white women and black men. The wartime experiences of black women are especially relevant given the shortages of personnel that existed and the "Rosie the Riveter" image that is used to depict women's involvement in the war effort. Clearly, Roosevelt's order to end segregation on the basis of race in war production had a considerably different implication for black men's employment than it had for black women's. As is true in so many other aspects of American life, the full story of black people's role has yet to be told. Much still needs to be done, in particular the exploration of black women's unique contribution.

Karen Fulbright's essay "Black Female Managers and Mobility" deals with managerial jobs, a classic "nontraditional" field for blacks as well as women. As part of her doctoral dissertation research, Fulbright surveyed 185 black female managers and conducted an in-depth study of the backgrounds and career experiences of 25 black female managers in the private sector. Given the small sample on which detailed data are available, and most of the results based, Fulbright correctly points out the necessity of treating this as an exploratory study. Still, she is able to investigate several hypotheses about the factors that affect the career choices and mobility of black female managers using this database.

Fulbright explores the hypothesis that black women, because they are "double minorities," have a "double advantage" in the job market. Since black women satisfy the hire of a woman and a minority simultaneously, might they therefore have better employment and mobility experience than otherwise comparable workers?

Fulbright found little suport for the hypothesis. Instead, mobility for the 64% of the private-sector managers who reached high-level jobs in their corporations or had made rapid progress appeared to be related to (1) their job tenure (average of 14 years with the same company), (2) the relative age and growth rate of the company, or (3) company ownership, whether or not it was black-owned and operated. Again, these results are only suggestive but imply that similarly qualified people would have done *at least* as well as did these black women managers.

Similarly, Fulbright claims little support for the hypothesis that fathers or mothers were significant role models for black female managers. At the same time, she overlooks the fact that the incidence of black women professionals and semi-professionals among the mothers of the women in her sample is much higher than in the labor force at large. While one-third of the mothers of women in her sample held such jobs, less than one-fifth of employed black women in the U.S. were professionals or managers in 1981.

I would argue that the hypothesis that female role models (mothers) exert an influence on career choice of black women in nontraditional jobs is supported by Fulbright's data. In her further explorations of whether family background affects the path that women follow in their career, Fulbright does not provide the data that support her conclusion. She argues that age at the time the civil rights movement hit full stride is more important than father's and mother's occupations (combined somehow) in accounting for the differences in career paths.

Fulbright further finds that the functional responsibility of the manager plays a role in determining the *perception* of whether women in her sample have been inhibited in their mobility. Those in "core" functions more often reported feeling limited in their mobility than those in staff functions. On the other hand, all the staff managers appear to be employed in personnel functions. It is difficult to know exactly what to make of this distinction given the relatively young ages of both groups.

Fulbright's investigation adds an important element to the thin literature dealing with blacks in management by focusing on black female managers. The small sample size limits the strength of the conclusions that can be drawn about this group and raises several issues that will need to be pursued further in subsequent research. The issue of functional responsibility and mobility is important, as is the question of informal structures, role models, and other socio-psychological determinants of career choice and progress. Finally, since Fulbright focuses her analysis on a sample of private-sector managers, we gain no insights about black female managers in public-sector jobs. Nor does Fulbright make a distinction between any of those in her sample who are managers of *nonprofit* enterprises. There is reason to believe that the experiences of managers in public sector and private nonprofit enterprises might differ substantially from those of private for-profit managers.

Malveaux's article, "Comparable Worth and Its Impact on Black Women," attempts to analyze what has become the major women's public policy issue from the unique perspective of a black woman. Malveaux essentially addresses the issue of whether "comparable worth," if it is adopted, will improve the status of black women as well as that of white women. In so doing, she does not address the conditions under which comparable worth will indeed improve white women's status. This is a point I will return to later.

Comparable worth is usually defined as equal pay for jobs of equal value. That is, jobs that require similar skill, effort, and responsibility and entail similar working conditions should be paid equally.

Thus far, the courts have been unwilling to interpret Title VII broadly to mean that sex segregation in jobs constitutes discrimination. In its 5 to

4 decision in the Gunther case, the Supreme Court concluded in 1981 that jobs do not have to be equal to form a basis for a claim of discriminatory compensation under Title VII. The Court also made it clear that its decision did not open the door to claims of "comparable worth," but was based on evaluating evidence that Washington County, Oregon, had engaged in intentional sex discrimination by setting wages of female matrons below those of male guards in the county jail and below wages found in its own survey of other employers, and its own evaluation of the worth of the jobs. The recent decision of the 9th Circuit Court in reversing Judge Tanner's decision in the historic Washington State case (*AFSCME* v. *State of Washington*, 578 F. Supp. 848, 1983) indicates that there is still considerable question about what *is* or *is not* considered sex-based pay discrimination and therefore illegal.

Although Malveaux avoids much of the rhetoric of comparable worth advocates, she ultimately embraces the idea as both feasible and likely to better white women's occupational status. She acknowledges the essentially subjective nature of job evaluation schemes since someone's values will influence both the choice of compensable factors and the weights applied to them. At the same tme, Malveaux urges the adoption of a "bias-free point factor evaluation system" that would be applied to all jobs in a given establishment to rank order jobs and to set salaries.

Malveaux spends considerable time detailing the inadequacies of the market system and its ability to transmit and validate discriminatory price (wage) signals. My own view is that while "the market" undoubtedly reflects whatever factors influence wages (be they unionism, employer power, racism, sexism, demand and supply, etc.), the market cannot be ignored altogether in the setting of wage rates. If a "bias-free" point factor evaluation scheme is used to assign points in order to rank jobs internally, what is wrong with looking to the market to determine what the "points" are worth? To do otherwise is to court disaster, or, at least, disorder.

Contrary to popular belief, public-sector employers cannot do whatever they like. They cannot knowingly violate the law. Neither can they, with impugnity, set wage rates disregarding demand and supply considerations. So long as workers are free to move from one employer to another, setting wages higher than the market-clearing wage will lead to an excess supply of workers, while setting wages below the market-clearing wage will result in an undersupply so that jobs go unfilled or have to be filled with less qualified workers.

There are certainly examples of public-sector jobs where wages are set too high to clear the market. Sanitation workers in major cities such as

New York and San Francisco, and fire protection personnel in most cities are good examples. To the extent that wages for a large number of workers are considered excessive, employers may make efforts to reduce services, raise taxes, contract-out the functions or some combination of these. Therefore, for political and economic reasons a compensation system that uses a race and gender-neutral job evaluation system to rank jobs internally and uses market data to set wages would recognize the necessity to pay women equitably and do so in the context of generally accepted methods of setting wages.

Malveaux points out that even an ideal comparable worth scheme can only benefit employed black women in public-sector jobs. It does not address the initial employment or promotion opportunities of black women directly, nor does it address the pay of those in the private sector or those in "nontraditional" jobs in the public sector.

In judging the value of the comparable worth approach in terms of its distributional implications, Malveaux suggests that factors such as where black women are employed, whether money to finance higher pay will come from tax increases or budget cuts, and so forth are relevant. Some of these are second-order effects at best. A system that would change the distribution of wages and the total wage bill (since few would approve lowering anyone's wages to bring about adjustments) will affect not only the particular jobs it is directly applied to, but through effects on relative wages, affect the demand and supply of substitute and complementary factors of production in the same enterprise. Ultimately, these changes may affect the size of the public-sector budget and the tax rate. The particular impacts would vary depending on the circumstances. Studies of the Australian experience with locally set pay rates indicate that women's employment growth and unemployment might suffer under a comparable worth scheme.[1]

Rhetoric to the contrary, comparable worth is not a civil rights issue but a compensation issue. The civil rights issues are whether job evaluation schemes are unbiased in their treatment of women and minorities, whether women and minorities have fair and equal access to employment and promotion opportunities, and whether they are paid equally for equal work.

The articles in this session have indicated in various ways that the treatment of black women in this society is based partly on gender and also partly on race. The result is generally the worst of both worlds. Black women are overwhelmingly concentrated in low-skilled, low-status jobs that pay low wages. Policy approaches that only recognize part of the problem, i.e., race or sex discrimination, only go part of the way in remedying it.

NOTE

1. Mark Killingsworth, "The Economics of Comparable Worth: Analytical, Empirical, and Policy Questions," in Heidi Hartmann (ed.), *Comparable Worth: New Directions for Research* (Washington, D.C.: National Academy Press, 1985).

Section Introduction

Margaret C. Simms

Education and training are viewed as a means of upward mobility in American society, and black women have been just as likely as black men to take advantage of educational opportunities. Yet, as the articles in this section indicate, black women are far from being favored members of the education and training system. Margaret Wilkerson, in her review of the formal education system, focuses on the recent erosion of educational gains by black women and notes in particular the impact of teenage pregnancy (at the high school level) and declining financial aid (at the college level). Just as Fulbright found in the private sector, Wilkerson finds little evidence that black women have an advantage as faculty members or administrators in the academic arena.

Black women have also suffered discrimination within the federal employment and training system. Lynn Burbridge notes in her analysis of black women's participation in programs of the Comprehensive Employment and Training Act era that black women were underrepresented in many programs (relative to their presence in the pool of eligibles), were more likely to be in the least desirable or productive program components, and were more subject to occupational segregation. As a consequence, even though black women who completed CETA programs had higher postprogram earnings gains than any other group, most still had poverty or near-poverty incomes.

The Job Training Partnership Act (JTPA) replaced CETA in 1983. The new program places more emphasis on training and private sector involvement, prohibits the use of public service employment (a component that was beneficial for black women) and limits the use of stipends. It does, however, place an emphasis on service to welfare recipients and disadvantaged youth, two groups that are disproportionately black and female. Until recently, national data on the characteristics of JTPA participants have not been available. In her article Harriett Harper presents data released by the Department of Labor in late 1985. Although black women are a significant proportion of JTPA participants, they (especially those with the most severe labor market problems) continue to participate at rates below their representation in the eligible pool.

Both the Burbridge and the Harper articles raise questions (either implicitly or explicitly) about government policy in the areas of data collection and program implementation. Proper evaluation of program impacts requires good data. Many evaluations of CETA-era programs note that the major source of data for program performance, the Continuous Longitudinal Manpower Survey (CLMS) had major flaws—a lack of geographic identifiers, limited data on welfare recipiency, the lack of appropriate comparison groups, noncomparable information on comparison groups, inadequate sample size for important subgroups, and so forth. Unfortunately, many of these flaws appear to have been repeated in the development of the new sample survey of JTPA participants. Consequently, analysts will be unable to determine how well the program is meeting many of its goals.

From the limited data currently available for JTPA, it appears that the program is not serving minority women who head families as well as it should be. The reasons for this failure cannot be determined from the available data. However, several features of the program could very well be contributing to the problem. In addition to the limits on provision of stipends and support services, the performance standards established under JTPA may be leading to underrepresentation of minority female heads of households. In order to promote efficiency in the use of program funds, service providers operate under a system of bonuses and penalties. They are required to meet standards in terms of postprogram job placement. Individuals with experience in program evaluation have observed that this incentive structure has led program operators to select applicants with the least severe problems (a process known as creaming), leaving those with the most severe labor market problems unserved. Although this approach may be optimal from the service providers' standpoint, it may well be a suboptimal strategy for society as a whole.

John Jeffries, in his comments on this section's three articles, reiterates some of their findings. He also raises several important points not discussed by the three authors. One of them is the question of educational quality, both at the high school level and in postsecondary training schools. If education and training are to be useful, they must provide students with marketable skills—basic reading, writing, and computational skills or occupation-specific skills. If educational institutions fail to do that (or if employers *think* they fail) the diploma may have little value. However, if the schools and training institutions are successful but the labor market continues to sort individuals into low-wage jobs or unemployment based on race or gender, then education is a limited policy tool. Therefore, as Jones in the preceding section and Burbridge in this one do, Jeffries calls for demand-side policies as well.

A REPORT ON THE EDUCATIONAL STATUS OF BLACK WOMEN DURING THE UN DECADE OF WOMEN, 1976-85

Margaret B. Wilkerson

By most statistical indicators, the educational gains made by black women during the past decade are rapidly being eroded: high school completion rates and college enrollment figures are declining, and dropout rates are increasing. The increase in black women earning bachelors and graduate degrees is due almost entirely to their higher participation rates in college. A higher proportion of blacks than whites are below 24 years of age; declining enrollments at a time when the black population is expanding reflects a significant loss. Important areas for policy initiatives include increases in financial aid, a critical factor in college attendance by black women—particularly at the graduate and professional degree levels—improvement in quality of primary and secondary education and counseling, and continuing education programs for teenage mothers.

Education has historically been a high priority among black-Americans. The heroic stories of slaves who risked their lives in order to learn how to read, and whites who defied the law by teaching them, are well known. The NAACP's decision in the 1950s to challenge the legality of segregated school systems in America in *Brown* vs. *Board of Education* was recognition that education was a necessary key to the race's advancement and to the future of its children.

Today, the importance of education continues to be affirmed as a means of expanding one's understanding of the world and as a way of developing the critical skills of reflection, communication, and computation that enable one to be effective and increasingly merely functional in this highly technological society. Despite disclaimers that a college or university degree is not a union card, that it is no guarantor of employment, a high school diploma and increasingly a college degree are requisite for individuals to enter many occupations. The competition even for positions not requiring a college education makes the possession of a diploma or a degree important evidence of discipline and achievement. The 1985 Carnegie Foundation report on the federal role in higher education concluded that in the future "almost everyone will need some form of post-high school education if they are to remain personally empowered, economically productive, and civically prepared."[1] Education prepares one to be socially responsible, to move beyond victimhood, and to work productively towards change and the realization of a just and humane world. So despite rhetoric to the contrary and a few books published on the declining significance of a college degree, education remains a key element in personal and economic development.

The purpose of this essay is to assess the status of black women in education using demographic and some social indicators to understand what progress has occurred during the past decade. It is a propitious moment to do so since last year, 1985, marked the end of the United Nations Decade of Women, a 10-year period during which UN member-states agreed to focus on the social, political, and economic development of their female citizens. The substance of this article was also presented at the UN Non-Governmental Organizations Forum in Nairobi, Kenya, in July of 1985.

Although this essay focuses on the status of black women in education, a review of the data reveals that the educational trends for black women are quite similar to those for black men. In fact, in some instances, the data trends for black men are even more distressing. For purposes of illustration, this essay will occasionally compare the two groups. However, the most important comparisons are between black women and white women and men because these data offer a more comprehensive picture. In the move towards educational equity, comparisons should be made with those who experience the least amount of discrimination—white males.

The data are taken from reports published by the National Center for Education Statistics, the Census Bureau, and a variety of educational organizations. In cases where the specific data on black women was not available, statistics on blacks in general were used.

EDUCATIONAL ATTAINMENT: PROGRESS OR REGRESS?

The word that characterizes best the situation for black women in education is "erosion." What gains have been made are being rapidly eroded.

At the high school level the trends for completion and dropout rates have been somewhat positive. Improvement in educational attainment was evident at the high school level between 1970 and 1982 where the increase in the proportion of blacks 25 to 34 years old who were high school graduates was twice that for whites. However, blacks still lagged behind whites. Between 1970 and 1982, the proportion of white high school graduates increased 11 percentage points, from 76% to 87%. For blacks, it increased 26 percentage points, from 53% to 79%.[2] Since 1982 it has declined to about 60%.[3] Black women are completing high school at a higher percentage than before: their high school dropout rates declined during the Decade of Women and more are receiving high school diplomas. However, in the last several years, dropout rates have been slowly rising. The improvement in high school completion rates and the decline in dropout rates are tempered by the devaluation of the high school diploma that is now viewed as a questionable indicator of functional literacy.

Even so, high school completion rates for black women remain significantly below those of whites. Although the high school dropout rate for black females had decreased by 7.2 percentage points between 1971 and 1981, the rate for black females was still 6.1 percentage points higher than that for white females and 5.1 percentage points higher than that for white males.[4] The increase in black teenage pregnancies threatens to erode further this general status as 50% of these young women drop out of high school. Teenage mothers enter into a cycle of poverty, unemployment, and undereducation that affects their achievement as well as the achievement of their children.

So while black girls are completing high school at higher rates than ever before, a disproportionately high number are dropping out of school because of teenage pregnancy. Their education is often permanently disrupted. Children raising children is an ominous prospect. It signals "early social death," as one scholar has put it; it is a ticket to permanent economic depression; and it severely limits the ability of the mother to fulfill the informal educational role historically a part of parenting. The decline in high school completion rates is a serious omen and portends a general decline in future opportunities and achievements for many black women.

In 1980, 14.1% of high school sophomores who were black females dropped out as opposed to 11.5% of white women and 13% of white men. (The dropout rate for black males was 20.3% in 1980 and has risen since then.)[5] In a survey of high school students, a sample group cited employment as one of the top five reasons for leaving school.[6] However, black female teenagers are less likely to obtain paid employment than are white students, experiencing a 48.3% unemployment rate in 1983, while white female teenagers had an unemployment rate of 18.3%.[7] (The black female rate is more than 2.5 times the white rate, equivalent to the ratio in 1955.) The false promise of employment, early motherhood, and other problems such as substance abuse take a heavy toll among black girls.

COLLEGE ENROLLMENT

Higher high school completion rates should mean a corresponding increase in blacks attending college. In fact, the opposite is true. Blacks have actually lost ground overall in college attendance and completion rates since 1975 when the economic recession set in and federal programs ceased to expand. From 1976 to 1983, the proportion of black high school graduates going on to college fell 7 percentage points.[8] Although in recent years, more black women have been enrolling in two-year institutions and enrolling at rates equal to or slightly higher than black men, the dropout rates for blacks at these colleges are higher than at four-year institutions. The two-year college or community college has become a dead-end for many black students. In fact, in California, a recent report indicated that many white students who were attending these colleges already had four-year degrees and were using the two-year institution to retool for their professions. On the other hand, with the reduction in real dollars of financial assistance, two-year colleges have become the only viable educational route for many single black women with children. It is a question of economics. Since almost half of college-bound black students come from families whose yearly incomes are below $12,000 (while only 10% of white students' families are in that category),[9] it is no wonder that black women cluster in the less expensive, more accessible two-year college. However, even this option is being threatened in places like California—which recently levied a $50 enrollment fee for community colleges. Preliminary reports indicate that in some community college districts, the loss of minority student population may be as high as 25%.

At four-year institutions, the cost of an education becomes the most critical factor. It is not only the dollar cost of tuition (in itself a major barrier), but the loss of potential income during the short term. A four-year education is increasingly a luxury for a black woman, requiring some outside support from a spouse or family, or some form of financial aid or fellowship. Many families simply cannot afford the cost, especially since most with college-bound children earn less than $12,000 and female-headed families earn well below that figure. Even the least expensive public and private institutions cost $3,000 to $6,000 per year in fees and expenses, one-quarter to one-half of a family's income. The prospect of owing thousands of dollars in loans after graduation acts as a disincentive for black students to attend college. Financial aid support, which has decreased in real dollars during recent years, is necessary in order for these students to enroll and to continue to completion. In fact, studies indicate that black students who receive financial aid and who are enrolled in four-year institutions are nearly twice as likely to stay in college as those who do not receive aid.

Before the 1970s, historically black institutions educated more than half of all black college students. They continue to be an important source of degrees awarded to black women, awarding approximately 32.8% of all degrees received by blacks in 1980-81. However, since about 1980, they have suffered substantial losses in enrollment and are now enrolling only about 25% of all black students. A court decision requiring colleges to, among other things, balance better their population of black and white students caused considerable decline in enrollments. Although a number of black institutions have complied with this requirement, no predominantly white institution has achieved its goal in black student enrollment or hiring of black faculty.[10]

Despite their lower enrollment, historically black colleges still granted disproportionately large numbers of degrees to black students in such technically oriented disciplines as agriculture, biology, computer science, mathematics, the physical sciences, and the social sciences. Although the number of black students at these institutions is lower than before, black women are often in the majority or enrolled in numbers at least equal to those of black men. The support system in these colleges, the role models available to students, the high expectations and encouragement given to young people make black colleges attractive to those who know about the isolation and alienation that often occurs at predominantly white institutions.

Thus, the historically black institutions continue to play a significant role in the production of successful black women graduates who go on in disproportionate numbers to complete graduate and professional schools. Yet at the end of the Decade of Women, many black colleges are fighting for their existence, plagued by financial and managerial problems, and facing an ever critical education establishment that questions their value and is reluctant to acknowledge or to learn from their achievements in educating black students. Then there are those colleges that have "turned black or near-black" due to changing demographics. These institutions in transition face a crisis in mission as the new population questions and challenges institutional goals. Most often this new population is comprised largely of black women.

Predominantly white institutions are experiencing some increase in black enrollment. However, that must be measured against the very low black enrollments of the early 1970s. While in many instances these institutions offer superior facilities and stronger research capabilities, the mentoring and teaching functions are often not as strong as in black colleges. These institutions, which rarely have a significant number of black faculty and administrators—and certainly not black women—offer little in terms of black female role models. It is not unusual to find only two or three black women who are tenured faculty on a large campus; one or none on smaller ones. Afro-American studies departments and programs, and special student services play a critical role in the intellectual and personal development of black women students. However, the perception that special assistance is no longer warranted combines with a more stringent fiscal climate to threaten support for these important programs.

Overall, what is happening to black women's college enrollment? Despite the fact that more black female students are graduating from high school than in previous years, they drop out with greater frequency than whites at each successive point along the educational pipeline. Black women comprise only 5% of the total student enrollment in institutions of higher education across the country; a significant number are clustered in two-year institutions where the cost of education is much lower. The number of black women enrolled in college in 1981 was nearly double the number enrolled in 1970, and their enrollment level surpassed that of black males. However, 1982 shows a decline overall in the number of blacks enrolled in colleges and universities with black women's rate of increase since 1980 half that of the period from 1978 to 1980. Between 1978 and 1980, the number of black women enrolled increased by 7% from 601,086 to 643,011, or an increase of 41,925 students. Enrollment for black women increased by only 572 students between 1980 and 1982, an increase of less than .1%.[11] The dramatic drop in percentage increase is cause for great concern.

The trends for blacks in general and black women in particular are very troubling at the graduate and professional school levels, where enrollments are in rapid decline. Applications to medical and law schools began to drop in the mid-1970s when the chilling anti-affirmative action winds became evident with the Bakke and DeFunis court cases that challenged minority admissions programs. Even before the Supreme Court decisions were handed down, discouragement spread among blacks, as shown by a sharply reduced number of applications. The disturbing decline of blacks in graduate and professional schools portends fewer serving in the critical care and legal professions, so essential for the future of blacks in this country. This also means fewer black candidates for college and university faculty and administrative positions. And this at a time when many trend-watchers predict a reopening of faculty positions in the 1990s (somewhat like the growth of the 1960s), this time due to the retirement and demise of current faculty members. If true, just as the academic market opens up, blacks are likely to be in short supply.

The general downward trend in enrollment at all levels is very disturb-ing, especially when one realizes that the black population is younger than the white: more than 50% of blacks were under the age of 24 in 1980 (14.8% of blacks were in the 18-24 age group and 35.5% were in the 18 and under group in 1980); whereas only 39% of whites were under the age of 24 (12.9% of whites were in the 18-24 age group and 26.6% were in the 18 and under group). This larger proportion of blacks should be reflected in a growing proportion of college enrollments. Declining enrollments at a time when the black population is expanding consequently reflect a sig-nificant loss.[12] The college and university community has begun to take note of this trend. In order to maintain college enrollments, they will have to look to the growing minority population.

One encouraging sign in this rather bleak picture is the fact that, in absolute numbers, more black women are earning degrees at all levels. Blacks as a whole, however, have lost ground on the proportional share of degrees awarded at the masters' and first professional degree levels. The two areas in which increases were noted—the bachelor's and the docto-rate—are due almost entirely to the increased percentage of black women participating in higher education. Between 1976 and 1981, 8% more black females earned bachelor's degrees, and increased in numbers from 33,500 to 36,200, while the number of black men earning bachelor's degrees *decreased* by 4%. At both the bachelor's and master's degree levels, black women in 1981 earned more degrees than black men. At the doctorate and first professional degree levels they experienced a 50% and 71% increase, respectively, but still remained lower than black men in actual number and substantially lower proportionately (approximately 50%) than white men and women.[13] Despite the strong performance of black women at the

undergraduate and master's levels, their numbers drop sharply at the
doctorate and first professional degree levels.

NO CRYSTAL STAIR: BLACK WOMEN'S EXPERIENCE IN THE ACADEMY

Since most graduate and professional degrees are granted through predominantly white institutions, graduate status often means operating in
an environment which, if not hostile, is cool to chilly. Graduate and, to
some extent, professional education is a kind of cloning process in which
faculty members seek to reproduce themselves or at least those who will
fill their intellectual shoes. It is often the rare mentor who can and will
extend this benefit to a black woman. In fact, one study of white male
faculty attitudes towards black students indicated that some of these men
believed that black women students are sexually attracted to them, and so
these faculty avoided contact as much as possible.[14] Although black male
students suffer under similar difficulties (the same study found that black
men posed a physical threat to these white faculty), at least as males, they
are much closer to the fantasized clone than the female. Significantly,
despite the persistence of black women in roughly equal numbers to men
through the bachelor's degree, the numbers of black women drop off
sharply at the graduate and professional school level. College and university faculties across the country are largely male whether they are black or
white, in part because of the loss of black women beyond the four-year
degree.

The cloning process or, put another way, the role of the institution in
encouraging or dissuading black women from pursuing education raises
the issue of the status of black women in the education profession. Despite
a few visible role models, in general black women are found in lower-level
positions, not in policymaking positions, and most often remain in the
primary or secondary classroom. The latest round of teacher-competency
arguments in favor of standardized tests for entry and continuation in the
teaching profession threaten many women teachers whose value may not
be fully measured by this form of evaluation.

In predominantly white colleges and universities black women are generally statistically insignificant. Across the country less than 2% of college
faculties are black, and black women are a very small percentage of that
number. Of a total of over 3,200 institutions of higher education, only 15
are headed by black women; approximately 350 black women serve as
deans, vice-presidents, associate deans, and medical school admin-

istrators.[15] Although predominantly black colleges consistently employ a higher proportion of women faculty and administrators than their white cohorts, the number remains lower than the pool of educated black women would suggest. As administrators in all institutions, they are most often in the "assistant or assistant to" position, handling the nuts and bolts of keeping the institution going, but receiving little of the salary remuneration or visibility that might lead to more responsible positions. Appointment to these ranks is very difficult, however. Recent efforts by the American Council on Education to move women into top administrative positions has resulted in some significant successes for white women, but not a corresponding change for black women, despite the establishment of a special program focusing on minority women administrators.

But what of the quality of education provided to black female students? Not only are black women generally not in the policymaking or leadership positions in educational institutions, but their history is not reflected in the curriculum, for the most part. Despite the phenomenal move to integrate women's studies into high school and college curricula during the past decade, a move that was largely successful, black women's studies, for the most part, were not included. It took a specially funded project through the Spelman College Women's Resource Center to initiate a project that would begin to consciously integrate black women's studies into the curricula even of black colleges. No corresponding effort has been made in predominantly white institutions. It is not simply a matter of including an excluded group. The history and literature of black women encompasses the phenomena of racism, sexism, and classism and provide an invaluable basis for understanding present conditions in the United States and the world. They are important components of an enlightened college curriculum.

One of the most positive developments of the past decade is the scholarship being produced by black women and the brilliant literary works being written by women of color, a long-awaited return on a long-term educational investment. These women are the result of a difficult and often painful educational process; they have survived and prevailed, and now repay the community's investment with their talents. One can no longer be considered literate without a knowledge of the works of Toni Morrison, Paula Marshall, Alice Walker, and others. Black women scholars such as Paula Giddings, Gloria Hull, Trudier Harris, Joyce Ladner, Sharon Harley, Phyllis Wallace, and a host of others, too numerous to name, have begun to fill the silences of black women's history. Now their work must be integrated into the curriculum and their numbers replenished and increased through strong educational support and incentives.

AN AGENDA FOR ACTION

Although the UN Decade of Women saw several years of improved educational attainment for U.S. black women, that progress must be mesured against the effects of past discrimination. Now even that progress is being significantly eroded. High school completion rates are dropping, college enrollment figures are declining, as are earned degrees. Black women in graduate and professional schools are still a rarity. And this at a time when the U.S. black population is younger than the white and more fertile. At the same time, it appears to some (or rather is made to appear) that black women are making tremendous strides—over the bodies of black men. The statistics show that the status of *both* black women and men is deteriorating even in the critical area of education where some progress had been discernible. When the progress of black women is measured against that of white women during this decade, the contrasts are striking. In practically every area discussed, the educational status of white women has improved measurably, although they, too, have unsolved issues on their agenda. As for comparison with white males, the data presented here should put to rest the misconception that the only free people in this society are the white male and the black female.

The seriousness of this situation was recognized eight years ago, near the beginning of the UN Decade of Women, when a group of black women prepared the Black Women's Action Plan for the U.S. National Women's Conference in Houston. Their recommendations laid the groundwork for policy initiatives.

Recognizing the political, socioeconomic and human costs of discriminatory education and educational opportunities limited by racism and sexism, we recommend that:

1. A concerted effort be made by the federal government and state governments via federal funding to broaden educational opportunities for black women on an equitable basis.
2. Federal funds be made available to implement programs for (a) adult and continuing education; (b) extension curricula in rural areas; (c) literacy; and (d) alternative schools to meet the needs of

black women aspiring to obtain basic skills or to resume their education.

3. Recognition be given the problems and possible solutions to the plight of black female heads of households with respect to educational goals, and funding be allocated for provision of training/ education opportunities, financial aid, career counseling, child care and other support services.

4. Efforts be launched to support scholarly research of black women subsequent to identification of such scholars.

5. Elimination of sex-role stereotyping in school systems be incorporated into training programs for educational administrators and decision-makers and funding be made available for special programs.[16]

Several of the recommendations called for action by the federal government. During the past five years, however, the current administration has redefined the government's role, greatly diminishing its financial support for and involvement in education. The withdrawal of federal support and advocacy for financial aid and the diminished interest in alternative educational models and educational equity has had devastating effects, contributing to the erosion of past achievements. However, black women's groups have organized to address these and other critical social and economic issues. Such commitment brought together a group of American black women activists, educators, researchers, politicans, practitioners, and communicators who had been significantly involved over the past two decades in leadership roles. They met at the Wingspread Conference Center in Racine, Wisconsin, in May of 1984 and prepared an agenda of issues that was subsequently presented to the U.S. Delegation to the 1985 UN End of the Decade of Women Conference and the 1985 UN Non-Governmental Organizations Forum commemorating the end of the UN Decade of Women. Their agenda of issues expanded the earlier 1977 Black Women's Plan of Action. Their recommendations are summarized below:

1. Reduce illiteracy.
2. Provide continuing education for teenage mothers.
3. Provide adequate training for the future as well as the present job market.
4. Improve the quality of education for black women.
5. Support effective alternative education models.

6. Improve access to education.
7. Increase the numbers of black women employed in educational institutions.
8. Increase the numbers of black women in policymaking positions in education.[17]

As policy initiatives are developed to arrest and reverse the disturbing educational trends, several points should be borne in mind. Education is a long-term investment. It takes time to realize results from interventionist strategies. Only now, 31 years after court-ordered desegregation, for example, are researchers acquiring reliable indicators of the impact of this decision on the academic performance of black youth. Policy initiatives should be conceptualized as long-term rather than short-term strategies, a particularly important point when considering the future of financial aid, one of the most critical elements in the persistence of black women students. This form of support should be long term and consistent. The average time for completion of an undergraduate degree is now five plus, not four, years. During that cycle, black women, many of whom are single parents, are particularly vulnerable to real or even threatened reductions in financial support. Limited financial aid contributes significantly to the loss of black women students beyond the undergraduate degree. The Ford Foundation has recognized the critical nature of support at this level and has reinstituted the predoctoral fellowship program for minorities which had been a major feature of graduate support in the 1970s. In shaping the type of financial aid provided, policymakers should seriously consider the incentive of direct aid and work-study grants as opposed to the disincentive of loans.

The role of community organizations in addressing educational problems should not be minimized. Policies should encourage partnership roles that will help to rebuild the infrastructure of black communities and encourage churches, fraternal and social organizations to invest their time, resources, and expertise.

More attention should be paid to the quality of education provided to black girls. The "academic apartheid" of grade schools relegates a disproportionate number of black girls to special educational programs; they are less likely to be enrolled in programs for the gifted and talented. Screening and testing measures need to be carefully examined for race, class, and gender bias; they should measure academic potential, not simply exposure to Euro-American culture. Black girls (and boys) are often directed towards programs of training for low-status and low-paying occupations. Low expectations, poor counseling, inadequate teaching, and lack of effective parental involvement, not to mention teenage pregnancy and drug abuse, are decimating the educational opportunities for black girls. As social welfare scholar Jewelle Gibbs has written, "Black adolescent youth are an endangered species."[18]

Education is a key element in economic improvement. While one generation struggles to complete formal education and to prepare itself for the challenges of a changing world, the next is being lost to that opportunity. An old African proverb asserts that when you educate a man, you educate an individual; when you educate a woman, you educate a whole community. The development of both is desperately needed. But clearly, the education of black women is fundamental to the economic empowerment of black people.

NOTES

1. Carnegie Foundation for the Advancement of Teaching, "'Sustaining the Vision': Text of Statement by Carnegie Foundation," reprinted in *Chronicle of Higher Education* 30, no. 14, June 5, 1985, p. 18.

2. *America's Black Population, 1970-1982*, Bureau of Census, 1983, p. 16.

3. Carnegie Foundation for the Advancement of Teaching, p. 18.

4. Taken from Table 59: Percent of High School Dropouts Among Persons 14 to 34 Years Old, by Age, Race and Sex: United States, October 1971 and October 1981, published in W. Vance Grant and Thomas D. Snyder, *Digest of Education Statistics, 1983-1984*, p. 71.

5. Taken from Table 9: Percentage of 1980 Sophomores Who Dropped Out Before Graduation by Sex and Selected Background Variable, published in Samuel S. Peng, Ricky T. Takai, and William B. Fetters, "High School Dropouts," reprinted in Office of Minority Concerns, *Minorities in Higher Education*, American Council on Education, 1984, p. 11.

6. Ibid., p. 11.

7. Taken from Table 658: Civilian Labor Force—Employment Status, By Sex, Race and Age: 1983, in *Statistical Abstract of the United States: 1985*, p. 394 (U.S. Bureau of Labor Statistics, *Employment and Earnings*, published monthly).

8. Taken from figures compiled by the population division of the U.S. Census Bureau cited in Gaynelle Evans, "Social, Financial Barriers Blamed for Curbing Blacks' Access to College," *Chronicle of Higher Education*, August 7, 1985.

9. Linda Darling-Hammond, *Equality and Excellence: The Educational Status of Black Americans*, College Board Publications, 1985, cited in *Chronicle of Higher Education*, April 17, 1985, p. 1.

10. Office of Minority Concerns, pp. 7-8.

11. National Center for Education Statistics, *Fall Enrollment in Higher Education*, U.S. Department of Education, 1978, 1980, 1982.

12. Office of Minority Concerns, Table 2: General Population Characteristics by Age Group, Race and Ethnicity, 1980, p. 7.

13. Office of Minority Concerns, Table 20: Change in Degrees Awarded to Blacks by Level of Degree and Sex, 1976-1981, from Susan T. Hill, "Participation of Black Stu-

dents in Higher Education: A Statistical Profile from 1970-71 to 1980-81," Washington, D.C.: U.S. Department of Education, National Center for Education Statistics, 1983, published in Office of Minority Concerns, *Op. Cit.*, p. 15 and p. 17.

14. Joseph Katz, "White Faculty Struggling with the Effects of Racism," in J.H. Cones, J.F. Noonan, and D. Janha (Eds.), *Teaching Minority Students*, New Directions for Teaching and Learning, no. 16, San Francisco: Jossey-Bass, December 1983, p. 33.

15. Gloria Scott, Unpublished study of black women administrators in higher education, Clark College, Atlanta, Georgia, 1984. Statistics also verified by Office of Women, American Council on Education, 1985.

16. *Black Women's Action Plan*, National Women's Conference, Houston, 1977.

17. Unpublished proceedings from Conference on Black Women and the Economy, Wingspread Conference Center, Racine, Wisconsin, 1984.

18. Jewelle Taylor Gibbs, "Black Adolescents and Youth: An Endangered Species," *American Journal of Orthopsychiatry* 54, no. 1, January 1984.

BLACK WOMEN IN EMPLOYMENT
AND TRAINING PROGRAMS

Lynn C. Burbridge

This article examines the past experience of women—with a focus
on black women—in employment and training programs. In spite
of the fact that women have been underrepresented in these programs and often steered toward training in "traditionally female"
occupations, they exhibit higher postprogram earnings gains than
males. Overall, however, the training provided has at best shifted
women into low-wage clerical fields with average annual earnings
barely above the poverty level. Therefore, these programs—taken
alone—can not be expected to have a major impact on an important problem facing blacks: welfare dependency.

There are four "facts" that characterize the experience of women in
employment and training programs. First, they have generally been underrepresented in these programs. Second, large percentages of female
participants have been trained for female-intensive occupations, thus
leaving patterns of occupational segregation unchallenged. Third, in spite
of underrepresentation and occupational segregation, women have done
better than men in terms of the measured earnings gains that can be
attributed to these programs. Fourth, and finally, however, postprogram
earnings of women trainees are often barely enough to keep them out of
poverty.

Although these "facts" apply equally for white and black women, they
are of particular importance to the latter. Fully 50% of black children are
in families headed by a woman. Further, it has been shown that even
among two-parent black families the contribution of the wives to total
family income is greater than is the case for whites and that the earnings
of black wives contribute more to decreasing income inequality among

black households than white wives' earnings contribute to decreasing income inequality among white households.[1]

Of course, the earnings potential of black males is a critical issue when one is looking at black family welfare. Both the rise in black female-headed households and the greater contribution of black wives' earnings to family income is often attributed to the low earnings of black males. Thus, although the focus of this article will be on black women, the impact of employment and training policy on black males cannot and will not be totally ignored. Comparisons will also be made with white males and females.

The four "facts" presented earlier are examined in detail in the following pages. The participation of blacks and women in employment and training programs, and in particular components within these programs, is analyzed first. The next section presents a discussion of measured outcomes and their meaning. An analysis of the extent to which these programs might have contributed to the self-sufficiency of black women follows. The article ends with a discussion of needed future research and implications for future policy.

PARTICIPATION

The Manpower Demonstration and Training Act (MDTA)—passed in 1962—is generally credited with producing the first employment and training program. Originally designed to retrain technologically displaced male workers, it was soon redirected to meet the more compelling needs of disadvantaged workers. MDTA provided classroom training (institutional) and on-the-job training.

The MDTA was followed by a number of other job programs as a part of the "Great Society" initiatives in the 1960s. Among them was Job Opportunities in the Business Sector (JOBS) an on-the-job training program begun in 1968. Two youth programs—the Neighborhood Youth Corps (NYC) and Job Corps were established by the Economic Opportunity Act (EOA) of 1964. Amendments to Title IV of the Social Security Act that were passed in 1967 authorized the Work Incentive (WIN) Program to provide women on Aid to Families with Dependent Children (AFDC)—and with children over the age of 6—with work and to get them off the welfare rolls.

The Comprehensive Employment and Training Act of 1973 (CETA) initiated a new era of employment and training policy. As part of the Nixon administration's program to consolidate and decentralize government programs, CETA mandated that state and local governments or other locally based prime sponsors assume responsibility for the operation of employment and training programs. Both MDTA and EOA were superseded under this new legislation. However, WIN and Job Corps continued as nationally administered programs.

There were several major demonstration programs funded by the federal government during the 1970s as well. These were "pilot" programs implemented in selected sites to study the impact of different program activities. One such program was the Supported Work Program, providing intensive training to those with severe labor market problems—school dropouts, drug addicts, ex-convicts, and the long-term welfare dependent. Another was the Youth Incentive Entitlement Pilot Projects (YIEPP), which coupled a job guarantee with mandatory school attendance.

CETA has since been superseded by the Job Training Partnership Act of 1982 (JTPA). Although a decentralized program like CETA, it is diffferent in several respects. State governors were given more authority with respect to running the program, and a system of performance standards was mandated. Public service employment (PSE)—in other words, public job creation—was outlawed. Funds available to pay stipends to participants were curtailed. More importantly, total funding was cut in half.

Table 1 presents demographic data on the participants in these employment and training programs.[2] The programs are classified into five groups: pre-CETA adult programs, CETA programs (adult and youth), youth programs, AFDC programs, and JTPA. Unfortunately, consistent participant data were not always available by race and sex, and so the percentage of participants that were black and the percentage that were female are presented separately. The percentages of those who were youths (21 or under) and of those with less than a high school education are also given. Data on the Supported Work Program are given for AFDC participants only (that portion of the program most important to women). Data are also presented on vocational education programs in secondary schools.

The percentages of blacks in all of these programs are high in comparison to their representation in the entire U.S. population. One exception is vocational education. This exception is not surprising, since these programs are not necessarily targeted on disadvantaged students. Blacks were more represented in classroom (or institutional) training and public service employment, than in on-the-job training (OJT) or adult work experience. Their percentages are particularly high in youth and welfare

TABLE 1
Characteristics of Participants in Selected Employment and Training Programs
(percentages)

	Percent Black	Percent Female	Percent Youth[1]	Percent with Less than 12 years Education
Pre-CETA Adult Programs				
JOBS (1965-1972)	61	32	46	62
MDTA (1965-1972)				
Institutional Training	39	45	42	56
On-the-job Training	28	30	35	48
CETA Programs (1980)				
Adult Programs	33	50	28	35
Classroom Training	33	57	35	39
On-the-job Training	25	37	34	33
Public Service Employment	36	45	25	32
Work Experience	27	55	--	38
Non-summer Youth Programs	41	52	100	82
Summer Youth Programs	51	50	100	83
Youth Programs				
Job Corps (1978)	55	29	100	87
Neighborhood Youth Corps	60	27	100	91
Youth Incentive Entitlement				
Pilot Projects (1978)	77	54	100	100
Vocational Education (1979)	11	31	100	100
AFDC Programs[2]				
Supported Work (1976/77)	95	100	NA	69
WIN (1974)	49	70	NA	55
JTPA (1983)	31	49	38	39

SOURCE: L. Burbridge (1983), Westat (1982), Abt Associates (1984), J. Grasso and J. Shea (1979), S. Masters and R. Maynard (1981), Pacific Consultants et al. (1976), H. Harper (1985). See footnote no. 2 for complete citations.

Note: 1. Twenty-one years old or younger.
       2. Supported Work and WIN figures are for "percent minority" rather than "percent black."

programs, as would be expected given the greater employment problems of black youth and the greater dependency of blacks on AFDC.

Women had a higher representation in CETA than they did in its antecedents, which probably reflects the greater concern for equal access for women in the 1970s in comparison to the 1960s. However, Sue Berryman et al. have pointed out that women were still underrepresented in CETA in accordance to their eligibility.[3] In other words, given their lower earnings, and the fact that CETA's eligibility requirements are targeted on those with low earnings, more than half of CETA participants should have been women (54-65% should have been, according to estimates presented in the Berryman article). Females were also underrepresented in the CETA youth programs.[4] There is no indication that this situation has been remedied under JTPA, since JTPA participation is quite similar to that in CETA. This underrepresentation relative to eligibility was not found for blacks.

The data show the categories of women and blacks to be similar in two respects: they were more represented in classroom training and less represented in OJT. Unlike blacks, women were more represented in work experience than in PSE. The high percentages of women in AFDC programs is not surprising given that the vast majority of welfare recipients are women. However, the underrepresentation of women in two important youth programs—Job Corps and vocational education—is disheartening, since it has been shown that employment problems early in life are an important predictor of labor market problems experienced as an adult. This finding is just as true for female as it is for male youth.[5]

The data on youth and those with less than a high school education indicate that overall both groups are highly represented in employment and training programs, even in so-called adult programs. Given the particular problems of youth and high school dropouts, this finding is not surprising. The decline in the percentage of youth in adult programs from the pre-CETA to the CETA period probably reflects the greater attention given to specialized programs for youth. The decline over time in the percentages without a twelfth-grade education probably reflects this decrease in the percentage of youth served in adult programs as well as overall increases in educational attainment. The slight increase under JTPA of youth and high school dropouts may reflect only a lumping together of youth and adult programs in the data.

The differences found in the distribution of women among different program components (for example, classroom training, OJT, and so on) deserve closer scrutiny. According to interviews with CETA program staff, assignment to a component depended on three factors: applicant preferences, applicant skills, and available openings.[6] And yet, Berryman et al. found that even when they controlled for different participant characteristics women were much more likely to be assigned to classroom training than to OJT and more likely to be assigned to work experience than to PSE.[7] Further, they found that in 1978, 52% of the jobs participants trained for in classroom training were "traditionally female" jobs. Less than 20% of OJT jobs were traditionally female. Crowley et al. had similar findings when focusing on youth in employment and training programs, using the National Longitudinal Survey.[8]

When Berryman et al. examined the job preferences of CETA participants and compared them to CETA jobs actually received, differences by sex and race were apparent. Women who asked for traditionally female jobs were much more likely to get them than those who asked for a "traditionally male" or "mixed" job. Similarly, males who asked for traditionally male jobs were more likely to get what they asked for than those requesting a traditionally female or mixed job. Black women requesting a traditionally female job were more likely to get their wish than white women, whereas black males requesting a traditionally female job were less likely to get their wish than white males. Thus, occupational segregation was apparently more rigid for blacks than for whites.

Of course, having been trained for or employed in a traditionally male job while in CETA does not guarantee such a job in the private sector. A study by Strecker-Seeborg et al. found that whereas women trained in a traditionally male job are more likely than women trained in a traditionally female job to gain unsubsidized employment in male-dominated jobs, they are much less likely than similarly trained men to get one of these jobs.[9] Further, Strecker-Seeborg et al. found that the wages made by women in male-dominated jobs were no different from those made by women trained in female-dominated jobs but that their wages were 20% below those of men in male-dominated jobs. Clearly, even with training, women encounter resistance in the labor market when they attempt to pursue nontraditional fields.

PROGRAM OUTCOMES

Table 2 presents program outcomes for the employment and training programs presented in Table 1[10] (since no statistically significant results were found for the Neighborhood Youth Corps program, they are not presented here). These outcomes represent the annual earnings gains that can be attributed to the program, after one controls for differences in participant characteristics. Since there is considerable debate on the best methodological procedures for estimating program impacts, a range of estimates is presented where possible. Time and space do not permit a discussion of these issues, and so the reader is asked to accept these estimates as the best ones available.[11]

Several patterns emerge. The earnings impacts for women were generally larger than those found for men. In fact, in 7 out of the 13 studies presented, there were no positive, statistically significant earnings gains found for black males. In 6 out of 13 studies, the same thing could be said for white males. White women more often exhibited larger earnings gains than black women, but the differences tended to be small.

TABLE 2
Estimates of Annual Earnings Gains from Selected Employment and Training Programs[1] (dollars per participant)

	Black Females	White Females	Black Males	White Males
Pre-CETA Adult Programs				
JOBS				
Kiefer--1970 Cohort	130-483	816-926	*	*
MDTA				
Ashenfelter--1964 Cohort	419-627	354-636	115-530	155-605
Bloom--1964 Cohort	567-1033	687-1033	465-607	542-818
Kiefer--1970 Cohort	521-591	639-824	*	*
CETA Adult Programs[2]				
Bassi--1976 Cohort	426-788	740-1145	*	*
CBO and NCEP--1976 Cohort	1,000	1,300	600	*
Westat--1976 Cohort	604-774	540-653	*	225-290
Youth Programs				
Job Corps				
Kiefer--1970 Cohort	*	*	*	*
Mathematica--1978 Cohort[3]	194	222	285	425
YIEPP				
Abt--1978 Cohort[4]	316	NA	705	NA
Vocational Education				
Grasso and Shea--NLS[5]	683	665	*	*
AFDC Programs				
Supported Work				
Masters/Maynard[6]--				
1976/1977 Cohort	924	NA	NA	NA
WIN				
Pacific/Camil/Ketron--1974				
Cohort	255	634	*	580

*Positive, statistically significant earnings gains not found.

SOURCE: Kiefer (1979), Ashenfelter (1978), Bloom (1984), Bassi (1982), Congressional Budget Office and National Commission on Employment Policy--CBO AND NCEP--(1982), Westat (1982), Mathematica Policy Research (1980), Abt Associates (1984), J. Grasso and J. Shea (1979), S. Masters and R. Maynard (1981), Pacific Consultants, et al., (1976). Complete citations in footnote no. 10.

Note: 1. Where earnings gains were calculated for different post-program years or using different methodologies, the total range of estimates are presented; 2. Results from Bassi and CBO are for minorities and nonminorities instead of blacks and whites; 3. Results for females are for those without children; 4. The final YIEPP evaluation focused on blacks only (because of small sample sizes for other groups); 5. For men not enrolled in school in 1971 and women not enrolled in school in 1972; 6. Ninety-five percent of participants were minority women so results are for this group only.

The only programs in which males performed better than females were two youth programs: Job Corps and YIEPP. A high rate of teen pregnancy was the reason given for the differences in YIEPP. Women with children also did poorly in Job Corps, but the results presented in Table 2 are only for childless females. Note also that Kiefer's earlier study of Job Corps produced no statistically significant impacts for any group. Improvements in the Job Corps program over time is often cited as the reason for these differences.

Further, some of the studies that found impacts for men also noted that these impacts "decayed" over time. In other words, the size of the earnings gains of male participants, taken relative to a nonparticipant comparison group of similar males, declines. So the program's impact loses its force, or decays, in the postprogram period. Ashenfelter's study and the WIN study both found evidence of decay for men but not for women. Bloom's study, however, did not find decay for males. This finding is significant because Bloom simply used Ashenfelter's results, with a slightly different methodology, to reestimate impacts.[12]

Table 3 presents statistically significant earnings impacts by program activity for CETA. Since males generally did not do well in CETA, the results are presented for women only. They are presented for all adult women, for disadvantaged adult women (those with family income below the poverty level), welfare recipients, and youth. This presentation allows examination of the impact of CETA on women with different characteristics. Generally women do better in PSE, OJT, or multiple activities than they do in the other program components. This is an interesting result when one considers that women are underrepresented in OJT and PSE. Minority women seem to do better in OJT than white women. White women do better in PSE than black women. Welfare recipients do not appear to benefit from OJT at all. The analysis of the WIN program by Pacific Consultants et al. did not find this result, however. Participants— all of whom were AFDC recipients—did better in OJT. The overall better performance by black women in OJT may be explained by their greater labor force experience. However, in the case of youth this explanation is unlikely to be true.

It should be noted that the Congressional Budget Office (CBO) study (not presented in Table 3) found no differences by program component for any race/sex group.[13] The authors of this report, Howard Bloom and Maureen McLaughlin, stated that the other studies did not use the appropriate methodology to adjust for the fact that OJT trainees earned more than other participants before training. This is a serious criticism since it is the "conventional wisdom" in the employment and training literature that OJT is the most effective program activity for women and perhaps the only effective program activity for men.[14]

One explanation given for the higher impacts found for OJT and PSE is the "placement effect." Those in OJT make an immediate transition into regular employment. Those in PSE are often retained in their jobs as

TABLE 3
Estimates of Annual Earnings Gains in CETA for Women[1] by Program Activity
(dollars per participant)

	Program Activity				
	Classroom Training	On-the-job Training	Public Service Employment	Work Experience	Multiple Activities
All Adult Women					
Minority	418-618	774-1072	714-950	598	1047-1557
White	437-964	554-663	1387-1936	483	890-1789
Economically Disadvantaged Adult Women					
Minority	633-811	1223-1549	815-1448	869-1023	1195-1634
White	610-752	*	614-1660	*	873-1043
Adult Women Welfare Recipients					
Minority	369-608	*	1269-1673	586-874	796-987
White	451-850	*	1558-1807	854	2190-270
Female Youth					
Black	*	1342-1856	989-1090	*	*
White	*	*	1000-1041	*	*

*Positive, statistically significant earnings gains not found.

SOURCE: L. Bassi, "Estimating the Effect of Training Programs with Nonrandom Selection," Ph.D. Dissertation, Princeton University, 1982; L. Bassi, "The Effect of CETA on the Post-program Earnings of Participants," Journal of Human Resources 18 (1983); L. Bassi, M. Simms, L. Burbridge, and C. Betsey, "Measuring the Effect of CETA on Youth and the Economically Disadvantaged," U.S. Department of Labor Contract No. 20-11-82-19 (Washington D.C.: Urban Institute, April 1984).

Note: 1. Results for all adult women and economically disadvantaged adult women are for the 1976 cohort. Results for female youth and welfare recipients are for the 1977 cohort.

regular employees. Those in classroom training or work experience, on the other hand, have to go out and look for a job after training. So although in the short run classroom trainees may not do as well, since they lose income during the time they are looking for work, they may do as well or better in the long run.

Westat found that the percentage of postprogram time employed was greater for terminees who were placed in a job at termination in comparison to those who were not (a 42% difference in the first quarter after terminations).[15] Although there is some reduction in the placement effect over time, it dominates the first two postprogram years. Of course, it is possible that CETA placed its better participants in these jobs and that a "screening" effect is being seen rather than a placement effect.

A description of CETA as merely a job referral agency has also been given to explain the better success of women within this program. In this case, however, it is CETA's stamp of approval on persons with little labor market experience that counts. Women, who because of family responsibilities have less labor market experience than men, gain by "passing through" CETA, which gives them a start or a work experience "credential." Disadvantaged males who may have considerable work experience, but chronically low wages, do not benefit from CETA. It does not give them the skills they need to increase their wages, and the "referral services" it provides are not needed.

This hypothesis is buttressed by the fact that in virtually all the studies presented in Table 2, most of the earnings gains resulted from increased employment as opposed to increased wages. In other words, those who benefited did so by increasing their hours and weeks worked—not by making more money per hour. Women are more likely to have room to expand the time they spend in the labor market. Further, the CBO study shows that prior to training, female participants' earnings were consistently lower than those of their comparison group, while male participants' earnings were the same as those in the comparison group except for a sudden drop just prior to the training year.[16] In other words, male participants entered CETA after a sudden earnings decline that more than likely was temporary and that would have disappeared even without training. This pattern was not found for women.

However, while this may be a reasonable hypothesis to explain a portion of the earnings gains by women, it has not been shown to be the entire explanation. Levy analyzed CETA data to see if being placed in a program activity had a greater impact on earnings than being directly referred to a job (without training).[17] Although he found no impact on earnings of being in a training component, suggesting that CETA's primary impact is as a referral agency, his results were not conclusive.[18] Further, this result is contradicted by the fact that many studies, of CETA and other programs, found that length of stay in the program increased earnings gains.[19] If training did not maatter, this would not be the case. Finally, the fact that women's earning gains do not appear to decay over time also suggests that there are training effects. If all these programs did was refer people to jobs, over time the effect would decay, since eventually nonreferred people would find jobs, albeit at a later date. The advantage participants might have over their comparison group, therefore, would be expected to decay over time.

Another explanation for higher earnings gains for women is the growth in demand in female-intensive occupations. In the past 30 years there has been a dramatic increase in low-wage white-collar jobs, particularly in secretarial and clerical fields. The demand for male-dominated, low-skill blue-collar jobs has declined (in the case of laborer jobs) or stagnated (as in the case of operative jobs). Further, access to the more desirable craftsman occupations often requires union approval. Training comes as a result of being accepted to an apprenticeship within a craft; it does not come from outside the craft. Although some studies have noted that demand factors may have a role to play in explaining outcomes, it has been relatively ignored in the literature.[20]

That the demand for certain kinds of skills may be important is suggested in the analysis of the Supported Work Program, one of the few successful programs for AFDC recipients. The Masters and Maynard analysis shows the differences between experimentals and controls in terms of their occupational distributions.[21] Two years after the program began, 37% of experimentals were in clerical occupations, whereas only 22% of controls were. Moreover, 30% of experimentals were in service occupations, whereas 43% of controls were. For every other occupational category listed—professional, benchwork, machine trade, and other—the differences between experimentals and controls were minimal (never more than 3.5%). The major occupational shift that occurred then was to move the disadvantaged, mostly minority women in this program from service to clerical fields. A similar shift occurred in industrial distribution. As many as 11% of experimentals were in the finance, insurance, and real estate (FIRE) industries, whereas only 2.4% of controls were. Fully 53% of controls were in service industries, whereas 45% of experimentals were.

Data of this kind were not available for the other programs. However, Table 4 presents the occupational distribution of men and women in CETA jobs (jobs held during participation in CETA) and compares it to the occupational distribution of men and women overall, and to the occupational distribution of men and women in poverty, by race. An examination of these data may give a sense of how CETA affected the occupational distribution of disadvantaged workers. The occupational distribution of poor black and white women is considerably different from the distribution of women overall and of those in CETA. The biggest differences are in the professional, clerical, and service occupations. Poor women are less likely to be in the former two occupations and more likely to be in the latter. They are also more likely to be in operative occupations than women in CETA. However, the difference between CETA women and the occupational distribution of all women is not nearly as large. Note also that even in 1978 a much larger proportion of black women worked in private households. According to Taggart, 17% of female trainees worked in a clerical job before CETA, 35% were in these jobs while in CETA, and 25% remained in these jobs after CETA.[22] This finding confirms our expectations and may help to explain the earnings gains of this group. For black women, in particular, the shift from services to clerical fields has been a major historical trend that has been occurring since the 1950s.

It is more difficult to see as clear a pattern for men. Men in CETA are more likely to be in professional occupations than poor men, particularly poor black males. There are 6% more men in CETA clerical jobs and 6% fewer men in CETA operative jobs than is the case in the occupational distribution of poor men. But CETA's job distribution indicates that it will have relatively little impact on the percentage of men in craft jobs. (This impact depends on whether CETA trains men who are already in this field). The largest occupational category for men in CETA is nonfarm laborer, which has been a declining field. (CETA had a greater percentage of jobs in this category than was found in the occupational distributions of poor black and white males.) With the exception of professional jobs, therefore, the shift in the occupational distribution that may be expected to occur under CETA for men was not nearly as dramatic as that which could be expected for women.

An analysis of occupational shifts that may have occurred as a result of employment and training programs could go a long way in explaining many other things. It can explain why women gave gained in spite of low participation rates and occupational segregation. Women were shifted from low-paying service jobs to low-paying—but slightly better—clerical jobs that were in high demand. Many of the male-dominated jobs offered—particularly the laborer and operative jobs—were not in great demand. The "good" male jobs—the craft jobs—presented obstacles (such as unions) once one left training and entered the labor market. The question whether CETA was a referral agency for those with little labor market experience can also be examined in this regard. CETA probably did provide training for women in a real sense, but it was the short-term, general training required for the clerical field. It probably also served as an important referral agency to introduce low-income women to employers

TABLE 4
Occupational Distribution of All Jobs,[1] CETA Jobs, and Jobs held by Black and White Persons in Poverty,[2] by Sex, 1978 (percentages)

	Females				Males			
	All Jobs	CETA Jobs	Black Poor	White Poor	All Jobs	CETA Jobs	Black Poor	White Poor
Occupations								
Professional, Technical, and Kindred	16.7	21.3	3.1	7.0	15.6	15.4	3.3	8.5
Managers and Administrators	6.6	3.1	1.1	5.0	14.9	4.1	2.1	10.8
Sales Workers	6.2	.7	2.5	7.8	6.0	.5	1.4	3.9
Clerical and Kindred	34.6	47.6	17.5	20.3	6.1	8.6	2.8	2.9
Craftsmen and Kindred	2.0	1.6	1.1	1.4	22.0	16.9	15.6	18.5
Operatives, Except Transport	11.5	1.2	17.1	11.7	11.5	3.6	9.2	12.7
Transport Equipment Operatives	.7	1.5	.5	5.6	6.1	4.7	10.6	6.9
Nonfarm Laborers	1.3	3.6	1.3	1.7	6.2	26.7	23.1	11.1
Farmers, Farm Managers and Laborers	1.4	.2	2.7	1.5	4.2	.4	13.7	12.8
Service Workers, Except Private Household	16.3	18.9	35.1	37.0	7.3	19.1	18.2	11.8
Private Household Workers	2.6	.2	18.2	5.9	.03	0	0	.1

SOURCE: S. Berryman, W. Chow, R. Bell, CETA: Is It Equitable for Women? (Santa Monica: RAND, 1981); U.S. Bureau of Labor Statistics, Employment and Earnings, Vol. 26, No. 10, October 1979; U.S. Bureau of the Census, Characteristics of The Population Below The Poverty Level: 1978, Series P. 60, No. 124.

Note: 1. Occupational distribution for all jobs are for men and women 20 years old or over.
2. The data on the poverty population is for household heads and unrelated individuals. Occupations for working wives in male-headed families below the poverty level was not available (12.4 and 24.1 percent of black and white working women in poverty, respectively).

for this field. For disadvantaged males, however, short-term and general training is not sufficient to improve their employability or open up the labor market in restricted fields. For them CETA was neither a training nor a referral agency.

THE LOW EARNINGS OF FEMALE PARTICIPANTS

CETA can be credited with facilitating the shift of poor women from service to clerical occupations. (The word "facilitating" is used since this process would probably have taken place to a certain extent anyway, particularly in the case of black women.) But clerical jobs are still low-wage jobs. In spite of the greater earnings gains experienced by disadvantaged women, they were still making less than disadvantaged men by the program's end. Taking the Supported Work Program again as an example, one finds that women in the experimental group *who were working* (54% after 2 years) had an average annual income of $7,152, only 138% of the poverty level for a family of 3, or 108% of the poverty level for a family of 4 in 1978 (before taxes). In fact the total annual income of experimentals (including earnings and transfers) was only $324 dollars greater than that of controls. So although they gained in earnings, experimentals barely made more than they would have, had they remained on AFDC. It is important to note, further, that Supported Work was probably the most successful program focusing on AFDC recipients.

Certainly, if a reduction in welfare dependency is a major goal of employment and training programs, the anticipated impact should be modest. A review of the literature reveals a negligible impact on the number of recipients and small impacts on the size of welfare grants.[23] Bassi et al. estimated annual decreases of only $250 a year in the welfare grants of female participants in CETA.[24] The Win II evaluation found reductions of only $106 a year for women.[25] In Supported Work, they came to a little over $200 a year. These results are not surprising when one realizes that the mean average annual before-tax earnings of a file clerk were between $10,000 and $13,600 in 1984; for a typist the range was $12,000 to $15,000 a year.[26] The poverty level for a family of 4 in that year was $10,600.

IMPLICATIONS FOR FUTURE RESEARCH AND FUTURE POLICY

Clearly one thing that can be done in the future is to examine the impact of demand factors on earnings impacts. This sort of examination is not easily done, however. The most straightforward way is to control for geographic differences in local labor markets. In the Continuous Longitudinal Manpower Survey (CLMS), the data used for CETA, geographic identifiers are withheld in order to protect the confidentiality of prime sponsors. As a result, no data on local labor markets can be added for analysis. The data set currently being compiled for JTPA will also be lacking in geographic identifiers.

Analyses relying on further disaggregations of the data might also be useful, sample sizes permitting. Such analyses will allow a closer view of what kinds of men or women do or do not benefit from training programs. Disaggregations by education and previous occupational training would be particularly useful. A closer look at the extent to which participants were shifted into different fields would also be a contribution.

Of course, of major interest will be the impact of JTPA. Although targeted on severely disadvantaged workers, it has several features that may discourage their participation; notably the elimination of stipends and a reliance on performance standards that may encourage program operators to "cream" those with the fewest labor market problems. Further, the elimination of PSE in JTPA may change the relative advantage women have had in employment and training programs, since this was a component in which they did relatively well. Finally, since the demand for clerical workers is expected to grow at a slower pace in the future, it will be interesting to see what effect this slower growth will have on women's measured earnings gains resulting from training programs.[27]

Another area of possible future research is whether the newly adopted "workfare" programs will have a more significant impact on program outcomes for women than previous AFDC programs. The Omnibus Budget Reconciliation Act of 1981 allowed states to develop Community Work Experience Programs (CWEP) which are essentially mandatory work programs for AFDC recipients. According to a report by Demetra Nightingale, at least 23 states have CWEP components, although the program is only active in 16% of all counties nationwide. This report suggests that thus far these programs have not been as punitive as the legislation intended, being very similar—in fact—to the already tested and familiar WIN program. Further, the jobs given women in this program tend to be very similar to the PSE jobs provided under CETA. Aside from the ethical and legal issues surrounding workfare (i.e., welfare rights groups consider it a form of slavery, and unions see it as a threat to worker's jobs), workfare will probably produce very little that is new in the employment and training area.[28]

In terms of policy implications several issues are relevant. First, as stated earlier, employment and training programs alone cannot be expected to have a major impact on welfare dependency. If they are to have such an impact, much more intensive training programs are necessary to allow women to upgrade their skills (or to allow their male counterparts to upgrade theirs). If intensive skills training is not in the cards, there are other supplementary policies that may help welfare-dependent women, along with short-term training. Adjustments could be made to reduce the burden of taxation on low-income families. Further, the earned income tax credit can be broadened to provide a greater incentive for the working poor to continue to work. Since the working poor are very often without insurance coverage, a government commitment to continue health coverage, even after recipients have left the welfare rolls, may encourage more of them to take a chance in the labor market. An increase in the minimum wage would also benefit low-income workers.

As mentioned earlier, performance standards required under JTPA may encourage program operators to "cream" from their applicant pool. As the preceding analysis has shown, however, workers with the least experience in the labor market have more to *gain* from training programs even if their postprogram earnings may be less than those of more experienced workers. Performance standards that emphasize changes in earnings from the preprogram to postprogram period, rather than gross earnings in the postprogram year, will encourage program operators to accept more disadvantaged workers.

There also is a need to increase the representation of women in particular programs and program components. Women do well in Job Corps and vocational education (better than men in the latter), and yet they are underrepresented in these programs. Females, particularly black females, do well in on-the-job training. Black men seem to do well only in OJT. Greater efforts should be made to include them in these programs. Further efforts should be made to expand the number of OJT slots available as well.

Finally, some assessment of the labor market picture overall, and in different regions, should be a prerequisite for program planning. There is little to be gained from training people in useless or obsolete skills. Some sense of those skills that are in demand and of projections for future skill needs should be incorporated into long-term goal setting. However, in the process of such incorporation there has to be a commitment to train people for needed skills. Again, this commitment may entail more intensive job training in the future. However, if the employment problem facing the nation as a whole—or particular regions within the nation—is an overall shortage of jobs, training may not be a useful activity regardless of its intensity. In this case, the only alternative may be public job creation. Employment and training are—or at least were—the objectives of these programs. Public job creation is currently politically unpopular. However, in the absence of jobs to be trained for, it may be the only game in town.

NOTES

1. D. Betson and J. Van Der Gaag, "Working Married Women and the Distribution of Income," *Journal of Human Resources* 19, no. 4 (1984).

2. These data come from the following sources: L. Burbridge, "Employment and Training Programs for Youth: An Interpretation and Synthesis of Measured Outcomes," Urban Institute Project Report (Washington D.C., 1983); Westat, Inc., "Characteristics of Enrollees Who Entered Adult Oriented CETA Programs During FY 1980" (Rockville, Md., 1982), and "Characteristics of Youth Enrollees Who Entered CETA During FY 1980" (Rockville, Md., 1982); Abt Associates, *Post Program Impacts of the Youth Incentive Entitlement Pilot Projects* (New York: Manpower Demonstration Research Corp., 1984); J. Grasso and J. Shea, *Vocational Education and Training: Impact on Youth* (Washington, D.C.: Carnegie Foundation for the Advancement of Teaching, 1979); S. Masters and R. Maynard, *The Impact of Supported Work on Long Term Recipients of AFDC Benefits* (New York: Manpower Demonstration Research Corporation, 1981); Pacific Consultants, Camil Associates and Ketron, Inc., *"The Impact of WIN II: A Longitudinal Evaluation of the Work Incentive Program,"* U.S. Department of Labor Contract No. 53-3-013-06 (September 1976); H. Harper, "Black Women's Participation in JTPA and Issues for the Future," in this volume.

3. S. Berryman, W. Chow, R. Bell, *CETA: Is It Equitable for Women?* (Santa Monica: Rand, 1981).

4. A. Sum, A. Hahn, P. Harrington, and P. Simpson, "Programs for Economically Disadvantaged Youth: Their Size, Operations and Impacts Upon Participants" (n.p., n.d., Mimeographed).

5. See D.T. Ellwood, "Teenage Unemployment: Permanent Scars or Temporary Blemishes?" and M. Corcoran, "The Employment and Wage Consequences of Teenage Women's Nonemployment," in R. Freeman and D. Wise, eds., *The Youth Labor Market: Its Nature, Causes and Consequences* (Chicago: University of Chicago Press, 1982).

6. See F. Levy, "The Structure of CETA Earnings Gains," Urban Institute Project Report (Washington, D.C., November 1982).

7. S. Berryman et al., *CETA: Is It Equitable for Women?*

8. J. Crowley, T. Pollard, and R. Rumberger, "Education and Training," in Michael Borus, ed., *Tomorrow's Workers* (Lexington, Mass.: Lexington Books, 1983).

9. I. Strecker-Seeborg, M. Seeborg, and A. Zegeye, "The Impact of Nontraditional Training on the Occupational Attainment of Women," *Journal of Human Resources* 19, no. 4. (1984).

10. Results from the following studies are presented: N. Kiefer, "The Economic Benefits of Four Government Training Programs," in F.E. Bloch, ed. *Evaluating Manpower Training Programs* (Greenwich, Conn.: JAI Press, Inc., 1979); O. Ashenfelter, "Estimating the Effect of Training Programs on Earnings, *Review of Economics and Statistics* 60, February 1978); H. Bloom, "Estimating the Effect of Job Training Programs, Using Longitudinal Data: Ashenfelter's Findings Reconsidered," *Journal of Human Resources* 19, no. 4 (1984); L. Bassi, "Estimating The Effect of Training Programs with Nonrandom Selection" (Ph.D. diss., Princeton University, 1982); Congressional Budget Office and National Commission for Employment Policy, *CETA Training Programs: Do They Work For Adults?* (Washington, D.C.: Government Printing Office, 1982); Westat, "The Impact of CETA on 1978 Earnings: Participants in Selected Program Activities Who Entered CETA During FY 1976," Net Impact Report No. 1, Supplement No. 1 (Rockville Maryland, 1982); Mathematica Policy Research, *The Lasting Impacts of Job Corp Participation*, Youth Knowledge Development Report 3.4 (Washington, D.C.: Government Printing Office, 1980); Abt Associates, *Post Program Impacts.*; Grasso and Shea, *Vocational Education.*; S. Masters and R. Maynard, *The Impact of Supported Work.*; Pacific Consultants, Camil Asssociates, and Ketron, Inc., "The Impact of WIN II."

11. Many of the studies cited above can be referred to for an examination of these methodological issues; particularly, Ashenfelter, Bloom, Kiefer, and Bassi.

12. Bloom criticized Ashenfelter's results because he felt the data indicated that the participant group's earnings were increasing more slowly than those of the comparison group. He reestimated Ashenfelter's results while controlling for individual earnings trends. He found larger net impacts that did not decay.

13. Congressional Budget Office and National Commission for Employment Policy, *CETA Training Programs.*

14. For example, see Robert Taggart, *A Fisherman's Guide, An Assessment of Training and Remediation Strategies* (Kalamazoo, Mich.: Upjohn Institute for Employment Research, 1981).

15. Westat, *The Impact of CETA.*

16. Congressional Budget Office and National Commission for Employment Policy, *CETA Training Programs.*

17. F. Levy, "The Structure of CETA Earnings Gains."

18. The explanatory power of Levy's regression equation was very low.

19. For example, this was found in the CBO-NCEP study for CETA, the Mathematica study for Job Corps, and Kiefer's study of MDTA and JOBS.

20. For example, Kiefer, "The Economic Benefits," mentions it, as do Russell Rumberger and Thomas Dayton in their analysis of vocational education using NLS data, "The Economic Value of Academic and Vocational Training Acquired in High School," in Michael Borus, ed., *Youth and the Labor Market: Analyses of the National Longitudinal Survey* (Kalamazoo, Mich: Upjohn Institute for Employment Research, 1984). See also J. Mitchell, M. Chadwin, and D. Nightingale, *Implementing Welfare Employment Programs: An Institutional Analysis of the Work Incentive (WIN) Program* (Washington, D.C.: Government Printing Office, 1980).

21. S. Masters and R. Maynard, *The Impact of Supported Work.*

22. R. Taggart, *A Fisherman's Guide.*

23. Such a review can be found in D. Nightingale and L. Burbridge, "Measuring the Reduction of Welfare Dependency: The Experience of Job Training Programs," Urban Institute Project Report (Washington D.C., 1984).

24. L. Bassi, M. Simms, L. Burbridge, and C. Betsey, "Measuring the Effect of CETA on Youth and the Economically Disadvantaged," U.S. Department of Labor Contract No. 20-11-82-19 (Washington, D.C.: Urban Institute, 1984).

25. Pacific Consultants, Camil Associates, and Ketron, Inc., "The Impact of WIN II."

26. C. Presser, "Occupational Salary Levels for White-Collar Workers, 1984," *Monthly Labor Review,* October 1984.

27. See G. Silvestri, J. Lukasiewicz, and M. Einstein, "Occupational Employment Projections through 1995," *Monthly Labor Review,* November 1984.

28. D. Nightingale, "Federal Employment and Training Policy Changes During the Reagan Administration: State and Local Responses," Changing Domestic Priorities Project (Washington, D.C.: Urban Institute, May 1985).

BLACK WOMEN AND THE
JOB TRAINING PARTNERSHIP ACT

Harriett Harper

Available data show that JTPA has provided some economically disadvantaged black women with employment and training services. Many black women who had suffered employment setbacks or entry problems during the recession that ended in 1982 need assistance in gaining access to the labor market. This is particularly true of young black women. At the same time, it is not clear from available evidence whether single black women who are supporting families alone and who are considered the core group of impoverishment in the black community have been—or, under the present configuration, can be—served adequately by JTPA.

The purpose of this article is to examine the provision of employment and training services to black women under the Job Training Partnership Act (JTPA). The program is administered nationally by the Employment and Training Administration (ETA) of the United States Department of Labor. Information on the programs is now being made available from two sources: The Job Training Longitudinal Survey (JTLS) and the JTPA Annual Status Report (JASR), combined with the JTPA Quarterly Status Report (JQSR).[1] The JTLS is a sampled survey of participants; it provides national estimates of participants' characteristics and program outcomes, permitting some detailed comparative analysis. It is these data, taken from the quick turnaround (QT) portion for black women, that are used in this article.

The JASR/JQSR data come from administrative reports transmitted from the Service Delivery Areas (SDAs) and include both participation information and expenditure data. A comparison of the data for the transition year, October 1983 through June 1984, has shown that there are few significant variations in overlapping information that cannot be explained by differences between coverage determined by the sampling frame for JTLS, which uses only the 50 states, and administrative information from all SDAs, which includes those in outlying trusts and territories as well.

In order to determine what the impact of JTPA has been on black women, Current Population Survey data collected by the Bureau of the Census have been examined to establish black women's eligibility (profile of need) for employment and training services. Data from 1983 were used to coincide as closely as possible with the start-up date for the programs in the transition year. Additionally, where necessary, information on the employment and unemployment status of black women has been reviewed.

The discussion starts with a description of the legislation establishing the JTPA and the characteristics of disadvantaged black women, a group in need of JTPA services. The survey of JTPA participants is then described along with estimated results of the transition year experiences of black women, based on the quick turnaround portion of the JTLS survey.

THE JOB TRAINING PARTNERSHIP ACT

The principal employment and training program for economically disadvantaged persons and those who face serious barriers to employment in the United States is operated under the Job Training Partnership Act, P. L. 97-300, of 1982. The act replaced the Comprehensive Employment and Training Act of 1973 (CETA), as amended. The primary differences in the two acts are: (1) the relative decentralization of program responsibility to the states and localities under JTPA and (2) the reliance upon private enterprise for the bulk of employment opportunities—in contrast to CETA, which had substantial federal program participation and had a large public service employment program.

The service delivery system of JTPA is the responsibility of state governments, with authority for planning and conducting programs shared by local governments and the private sector. This authority is set out in Title I of the act. The actual employment training services are described in three main parts: Title II—Training Services for the Disadvantaged, including Part A, Adult and Youth Programs, and Part B, Summer Youth Employment and Training Programs; Title III—Employment and Training Assistance for Dislocated Workers; and Title IV—Federally Administered Programs, including Part A, Employment and Training Programs for Mature Americans and Migrant and Seasonal Farmworkers, Part B, Job Corps, Part C, Veterans' Employment Programs, Part D, National Activities, Part E, Labor Market Information, Part F, National Commission for Employment Policy, and Part G, Training to Fulfill Affirmative Action Obligations. The remainder of the act, Title V—Miscellaneous Provisions, deals with amendments to other laws, such as the Wagner-Peyser and the Social Security legislation.

Since outcomes are of overriding importance, data are presented on terminees under Title IIA, Adult and Youth programs, for the transition year. Similar data for Title III terminees were not statistically valid for women and will not be discussed. Approximately 615,500 participants were enrolled in Title IIA programs during the transition year. Of these an estimated 350,300 had been terminated, of whom 52,400 were black women.

DISADVANTAGED WOMEN

Early on, it was recognized that the new JTPA legislation (like CETA but more explicit) offers opportunities for individuals and groups concerned about employment and training opportunities for women.[2] The disadvantaged status classifications established under the law include a large proportion of women. As defined in the act, the term "economically disadvantaged" means an individual who receives, or is a member of a family that receives, cash welfare payments under a federal, state, or local welfare program; has received, or is a member of a family that has received, a total family income for the six-month period prior to application to the program involved (exclusive of unemployment compensation, child support payments, and welfare payments) not higher than the poverty level or 70% of the lower living standard; is receiving food stamps; is a foster child; or is an adult handicapped individual.

Women, especially women who maintain families alone, have been identified as prime candidates for employment and training assistance because so many of them are economically disadvantaged. If they could be helped toward economic self-sufficiency, then their families also could be moved out of a life of hopeless poverty. When JTPA started operation in 1983, 57% of all persons in poverty status (35.3 million) were females of all ages; nearly 70% of the women were of working ages, 16 years or older.[3]

The unemployment rate for women averaged 9.2% in 1983; more than 4.4 million were unemployed. A little over a million, or nearly a quarter (24%), of these women were black. Their unemployment rate for 1983 was

18.6%. More than two of every five (43%) of these unemployed black women were between the ages of 16 and 24. Of all women classified as poor, 5.7 million, or 28%, were black women. Some 66%, a somewhat smaller proportion than among all women, were of working ages. Children of poor black women householders with no husband present represented 24% of all related children under 18 years old in poverty. Three-quarters of the 4.3 million related children in poor black families were in families supported by women without a husband present. There were some 1.5 million black women living under those circumstances of poverty and unemployment or underemployment. Almost three of every five woman-maintained poor black families (57%) had no family member who was employed, and fewer than one in four of the women themselves were employed. Few worked regularly. Only 11% worked 50 to 52 weeks and fewer still worked year round and full time. Child care services, some transportation assistance, and perhaps other supportive services were identified as necessary for women in these circumstances to be able to participate in employment and training activities. It is not unexpected then that although some 42% of these poor black women householders had some income from earnings, more than 65% received all or part of their income from public assistance.[4]

Educational attainment has been positively correlated with the propensity to be employed. In 1983 only a little more than 46% of poor black women ages 25 or over who maintained their own families had completed high school. Nearly a quarter (23%) had completed no more than eight years of schooling. Some 11%, however, had attended one year or more of college.[5] The median age of these women householders was well into the prime working years (34.6 years).[6] For many, even if remediation is not necessary, at least some refresher courses before entry into the labor force might seem advisable.

The pervasiveness of poverty among black families supported by women knows no geographic bounds.[7] Although more than 62% of these poor black women householders lived in central cities and accounted for 63% of all persons in poverty in such households, nearly a quarter (23%) lived in nonmetropolitan areas, largely in the south (87%).

Virtually none, however, lived on farms (less than 0.5% nationwide). In the nonmetropolitan south in 1983, nearly two of every three persons (62.7%) who lived in households maintained by black women alone were in poverty, a far higher proportion than those persons in similar urban households inside or outside central cities.

The characteristics and general circumstances of the poor black women and their families, briefly described above, are important in determining the efficacy of JTPA in helping this group of disadvantaged women to receive employment and training services that could result in their economic self-sufficiency. Only limited data are available, covering less than a full year of program operation. Without either planned control group data on the experiences of nontreated individuals with similar characteristics or required data on participants' families and life circumstances, only limited descriptions of the services provided by JTPA can be made.

THE JOB TRAINING LONGITUDINAL SURVEY (JTLS)

Two years after JTPA was put fully into effect, there is still little information available on the provision of services and the impact of those services on the economic status of participants in JTPA programs across the country. The performance standards and measures that were established for the states were broad and do not require maintenance of detailed records of participant characteristics. Performance is judged by the cost and proportion of positive outcomes such as increased employment and earnings and reduction of welfare dependence of terminees.

The Job Training Longitudinal Survey (JTLS) is the nationwide longitudinal survey of participants in programs authorized under Titles IIA and III of the Job Training Partnership Act. Data are collected on individual characteristics, program activities, and labor market experiences both from Service Delivery Area records and through interviews with the participants. The Employment and Training Administration of the U.S. Department of Labor is responsible for planning, funding, and monitoring the survey. The U.S. Bureau of the Census performs the sampling and data collection. The JTLS is similar in many respects to the Continuous Longitudinal Manpower Survey conducted under the CETA legislation. The current participant sample for the quick turnaround component of Title IIA is 12,000 persons selected from 205 areas (SDAs or Subareas).[8]

JTPA ACTIVITIES UNDER TITLE IIA

A wide variety of training activities are authorized to prepare economically disadvantaged adults and youth (under age 22) for unsubsidized employment. These training activities may include on-the-job training, institutional and classroom training, remedial education and basic skills training, job search assistance and counseling, or exemplary youth programs. At least 40% of the Title IIA funds received by each SDA must be used for disadvantaged youth, ages 16 through 21, with adjustment made in the percentage to reflect the proportion of youth in the eligible population. Furthermore, 90% of all participants (in each SDA) must be economically disadvantaged. The remaining 10% need not be economically disadvantaged if they have other labor market disadvantages. These may include handicapped individuals, offenders, displaced homemakers, older workers, teenage parents, and others.

CHARACTERISTICS OF WOMEN TERMINATED FROM JTPA

The small numbers associated with the transition year, even for the estimated 350,300 terminees, provide little basis for complicated analysis or for drawing meaningful conclusions about the impact of the program. We can see, however, whether services are being offered to those who were intended recipients. The 107,500 adult women terminees (over 21 years old) from JTPA Title IIA programs during the transition year were 49% of all terminees. More than half (55%) were white, 30% were black, 11% were Hispanic, and 4% were women of other races. Nearly 9 of every 10 (87%) were between the ages of 22 and 44, with 49% accounted for by those aged 22 to 29. Half the women were high school graduates, but a quarter were school dropouts. An equal proportion had some post-high school education. Virtually half received some income from public assistance, including Aid to Families with Dependent Children (AFDC). And 12% were displaced homemakers, women who had been out of the labor force for a long period of time or were substantially unemployed, or who had lost their principal source of support through death, divorce, abandonment, impending loss of public assistance income, or some other sudden reversal.

There were 63,100 young female terminees, representing 48% of the total terminees during the first nine months of JTPA operations. Nearly half (47%) were white, almost two-fifths (38%) were black, and about an eighth were Hispanic. The majority (54%) of the young females were young adults aged 19 through 21; the rest were teenagers, 18 or younger. Because of their youth, only 9% had post-high school education. More than a quarter (27%) were still students in school, and a nearly equal proportion (26%) had dropped out of school. Almost 40% had graduated from high school or its equivalent. Just over two-fifths (41%) received income from public assistance but only 24% received AFDC.

BLACK WOMEN'S EXPERIENCES

The 52,400 black women who completed the JTPA Title IIA programs during the transition year were 15% of all terminees nationwide. They were just about half of all black persons served and one of every three women served. Of those who completed the program, some 61% entered employment, about the same proportion as all women terminees. A somewhat greater proportion of the adult women trainees than the youth trainees eventually found a job (see Table 1).

More than half of the black women participants (55%) were over age 21, and about 45% were youth, about in line with young black women's share of black women's unemployment in 1983. The large majority (65%) of the young women served were between 19 and 21 years of age. Still, the median age of the black women who obtained jobs was about 29, whereas it was about 22 for the other racial and ethnic groups of women and black men.

Virtually all (96%) of the black women terminees of all ages were economically disadvantaged, but although more than half were receiving some form of public assistance (62% of the adults and 44% of the young women), only about one in every three was actually receiving income from AFDC. Their dependency was substantially higher, however, than that for all participants, among whom about 33% received any public assistance and 23% received AFDC, according to a General Accounting Office study.[9]

These were fairly well educated black women. Seven of every 10 of the terminees had completed high school or better, but somewhat less than a fourth (22%) were school dropouts. About one in every six of the young women was still in school at the time of application for the program. Compared with all terminees, more of these women were high school graduates, fewer were dropouts, and more were currently enrolled in school.

PROGRAM OUTCOMES

According to an assessment by the Employment and Training Administration, an estimated 64% of participants who were terminated entered employment.[10] The highest proportion entering employment was among terminees who participated in on-the-job training. In comparison, not as high a proportion of black women terminees were successful at finding

TABLE 1

Selected Characteristics of Black Terminees Who Entered Employment, by Age at Application and Sex: Terminated from JTPA Title IIA Programs During TY 1984

Selected Characteristics	Total — Male Number	Total — Male Percent	Total — Female Number	Total — Female Percent	Adult (Age > 21) — Male Number	Adult — Male Percent	Adult — Female Number	Adult — Female Percent	Youth (Age < 22) — Male Number	Youth — Male Percent	Youth — Female Number	Youth — Female Percent
Total Terminees	50,400	—	52,400	—	29,000	—	28,700	—	21,800	—	24,000	—
Total Terminees Who Entered Employment	33,900	100	32,100	100	20,900	100	18,600	100	12,900	100	13,500	100
Age at Enrollment												
Younger than 19	4,600	13	4,700	15	—	—	—	—	4,600	35	4,700	35
19-21	8,400	25	8,800	27	—	—	—	—	8,400	65	8,800	65
22-29	12,500	37	10,100	31	12,500	60	10,100	54	—	—	—	—
30-44	7,000	21	7,100	22	7,000	33	7,100	38	—	—	—	—
45-54	800	2	900	3	800	4	900	5	—	—	—	—
55 and Older	700	2	500	2	700	3	500	3	—	—	—	—
Economically Disadvantaged												
No	1,800	5	1,300	4	1,300	6	900	5	500	4	400	3
Yes	32,100	95	30,800	96	19,700	94	17,700	95	12,400	96	13,100	97
Receiving AFDC at Application												
No	31,000	91	21,100	66	19,700	94	11,700	63	11,300	87	9,400	69
Yes	2,900	9	11,000	34	1,300	6	6,800	37	1,600	13	4,200	31
Receiving Public Assistance (Including AFDC) at Application												
No	24,500	72	14,700	46	15,100	72	7,100	38	9,300	72	7,600	56
Yes	9,400	28	17,500	54	5,800	28	11,600	62	3,600	28	5,900	44
Adult Welfare 1/	2,300	7	7,800	24	2,300	11	7,800	42	—	—	—	—
Other Adult /	3,500	10	3,800	12	3,500	17	3,800	20	—	—	—	—
Youth (Age 22)	3,600	11	5,900	19	—	—	—	—	3,600	28	5,900	44
Education Status												
School Dropout	11,100	33	7,100	22	6,600	31	4,100	22	4,500	35	3,000	22
Student (HS or Less)	2,500	7	2,500	8	400	2	100	1	2,100	16	2,400	18
In School at Application (Age 22)	2,000	6	2,400	7	—	—	—	—	2,000	15	2,400	18
High School Graduate or Equivalent (No Post-HS)	15,400	46	15,900	49	10,000	48	9,500	51	5,400	42	6,300	47
Post HS Attendee	4,900	14	6,600	21	4,000	19	4,900	26	900	7	1,800	13
Reason for Termination												
Entered Employment	32,900	100	32,100	100	20,900	100	18,600	100	12,900	100	13,500	100
Returned to School	—	—	—	—	—	—	—	—	—	—	—	—
Other Positive Terminations	—	—	—	—	—	—	—	—	—	—	—	—
Non-Positive Terminations	—	—	—	—	—	—	—	—	—	—	—	—

1/ Receiving AFDC, General Assistance, and/or Refugee Assistance and at least 22 years of Age at Enrollment.

Source: Unpublished data, Job Training Longitudinal Survey, Women's Bureau, U.S. Department of Labor.

jobs, and so few were in on-the-job training programs that no meaningful conclusion can be drawn about the impact of that program activity. The only significant activity for black women was classroom training. Together just over half of all adults and young women participated in that type of activity (see Tables 2 and 3). Nearly half (48%) of those who terminated from that program found jobs.

SUPPORT NEEDS

The Women's Bureau, aware of the importance of certain marital and family circumstances in the employment status of women, arranged for cross-tabulations of JTLS data by sex, minority, and family status (see Table 4). Having reported for some years that women who maintain families without a husband present are the focus of much of women's poverty and that the growth of such families, particularly among blacks, exacerbates the economic ills in the community, the Women's Bureau arranged to obtain information on black and Hispanic single parents of school-age or younger children.

The estimates for this group should be used with caution, not only because these data are for a single transition year, but also because they are for a very small subset of the participants. With the exception of those variables associated with dependents, the estimates are, however, considered reliable. Some 60% of respondents failed to provide data on dependents. This is not, however, a federally required data element. Because of their small numbers, single black and Hispanic mothers were combined for a total of 10,200. The small numbers associated with the transition provide little basis for drawing any meaningful conclusions. On the other hand, the very small numbers of mothers without spouses who were served (10,000) at least indicate the possibility that a large group of women known to be needy are not being served. The proportions of black and Hispanic women seem about right (82% and 18%, respectively) compared with the data from the Current Population Survey (87% and 13%, respectively), and their dire economic status (99% economically disadvantaged) seems also to be about what would be expected. Without more and better data, however, it cannot be determined how well the program is serving this group.

One reason for low participation could be the limits placed on the provision of stipends and other support services to program participants. The General Accounting Office analysis of how the support cost limits required under the JTPA might affect the quality of training provided and

TABLE 2
Estimated Number of Black Title IIA Terminees by Program Activity and Sex: Adults (Age 22 and Older) Terminated from JTPA During TY 1984

Selected Characteristics	Total		CT		OJT		JSA		WE		Other	
	Male	Female	Male	Female	Male	Female	Male	Female	Male	Female	Male	Female
Total Terminees	32,500	32,300	10,400	17,000	7,200	4,800	11,500	7,800	800	600	2,600	2,000
Age at Enrollment												
22-29	19,700	18,300	6,600	9,700	4,200	3,000	7,200	4,000	500	300	1,300	1,300
30-44	10,400	11,600	3,200	6,600	2,500	1,600	3,400	2,800	400	200	1,000	600
45-54	1,400	1,600	300	700	500	300	700	700	-	-	200	500
55 and Older	900	700	300	100	200	100	300	300	-	100	200	100
Economically Disadvantaged												
No	2,100	1,200	400	500	400	300	1,100	400	100	-	100	-
Yes	30,400	31,100	9,900	16,500	6,800	4,600	10,400	7,400	700	600	2,500	2,000
Receiving AFDC at Application												
No	30,600	19,800	9,300	9,100	6,800	3,600	11,200	5,100	800	500	2,500	1,500
Yes	1,900	12,400	1,100	7,900	400	1,300	300	2,700	-	100	100	500
Receiving Public Assistance (including AFDC) at Application												
No	21,700	12,500	6,300	5,800	4,800	2,000	8,300	3,500	200	300	1,900	800
Yes	10,800	19,800	4,000	11,200	2,400	2,800	3,300	4,200	600	300	700	1,200
Adult Welfare 1/	6,500	14,200	2,600	8,900	1,100	1,500	1,900	3,200	500	100	400	500
Other Adult	4,400	5,500	1,400	2,300	1,300	1,300	1,300	1,000	100	200	300	700
Youth (Age 22)	-	-	-	-	-	-	-	-	-	-	-	-
Education Status												
School Dropout	10,400	7,800	3,000	4,500	2,300	1,000	3,900	1,900	400	100	800	300
Student (HS or Less) In School at Application (Age 22)	500	600	200	300	100	-	100	300	-	-	-	-
High School Graduate or Equivalent (No Post-HS)	-	100	-	-	-	-	-	100	-	-	-	-
	14,500	15,600	5,000	8,000	3,300	2,300	4,600	3,500	300	400	1,300	1,300
Post HS Attendee	7,100	8,300	2,200	4,200	1,500	1,500	2,900	2,100	100	100	400	400
Reason for Termination												
Entered Employment	20,900	18,600	6,100	8,000	5,400	3,300	7,600	5,100	500	500	1,400	1,500
Returned to School	300	400	200	300	100	100	-	100	-	-	-	-
Other Positive Terminations	400	400	200	200	100	100	100	100	-	-	100	100
Non-Positive Terminations	10,800	12,800	3,900	8,500	1,600	1,400	3,900	2,400	400	200	1,100	500

1/ Receiving AFDC, General Assistance, and/or Refugee Assistance and at least 22 years of Age at Enrollment.

Note: CT= Classroom Training; OJT= On-The-Job Training; JSA= Job Search Assistance; WE= Work Experience.

Source: Unpublished data, Job Training Longitudinal Survey, Women's Bureau, U.S. Department of Labor.

TABLE 3
Estimated Number of Black Title IIA Terminees by Program Activity and Sex: Youth (Ages Less Than 22) Terminated from JTPA During TY 1984

Selected Characteristics	Program Activity and Sex											
	Total		CT		OJT		JSA		WE		Other	
	Male	Female	Male	Female	Male	Female	Male	Female	Male	Female	Male	Female
Total Terminees	21,200	24,300	6,600	11,800	2,800	1,900	6,400	5,800	2,700	2,800	2,700	2,000
Age at Enrollment												
Younger Than 19	9,100	10,400	1,900	4,600	1,200	300	2,500	2,500	1,900	1,900	1,600	1,200
19-21	12,100	13,900	4,800	7,200	1,600	1,600	3,900	3,300	700	800	1,100	800
Economically Disadvantaged												
No	700	700	200	300	200	100	200	300	-	-	-	-
Yes	20,600	23,600	6,500	11,400	2,600	1,800	6,200	5,500	2,600	2,800	2,700	2,000
Receiving AFDC at Application												
No	17,900	15,900	6,000	7,600	2,500	1,300	5,400	3,800	1,900	2,800	2,100	1,300
Yes	3,400	8,400	700	2,100	300	600	1,000	2,100	800	800	600	700
Receiving Public Assistance (Including AFDC) at Application												
No	14,600	12,500	4,800	5,700	2,000	1,200	4,500	3,300	1,800	1,400	1,500	900
Yes	6,600	11,800	1,800	6,100	800	700	2,000	2,500	900	1,400	1,200	1,100
Adult Welfare 1/	-	-	-	-	-	-	-	-	-	-	-	-
Other Adult (Age 22)	-	-	-	-	-	-	-	-	-	-	-	-
Youth (Age 22)	6,600	11,800	1,800	6,100	800	700	2,000	2,500	900	1,400	1,200	1,100
Education Status												
School Dropout	7,500	5,900	3,100	3,800	1,200	300	2,300	1,200	300	300	500	200
Student (HS or Less) In-School at Application	4,900	5,700	700	1,500	200	200	2,100	1,300	1,700	1,900	1,200	800
(Age 22)	4,800	5,700	600	1,500	200	200	1,100	1,300	1,700	1,900	1,100	800
High School Graduate or Equivalent (No Post-HS)	7,500	10,300	2,300	5,100	1,100	1,100	2,700	2,600	600	500	900	900
Post HS Attendee	1,400	2,400	500	1,300	300	300	400	600	100	-	100	100
Reason for Termination												
Entered Employment	12,900	13,500	4,100	5,700	2,000	1,500	4,100	4,300	1,000	1,400	1,700	700
Returned to School	900	600	400	900	100	-	200	-	300	200	-	-
Other Positive Terminations	900	1,600	200	900	100	-	300	300	300	300	100	100
Non-Positive Terminations	6,500	8,400	1,900	4,900	700	300	1,800	1,200	1,100	900	1,100	1,200

1/ Receiving AFDC, General Assistance, and/or Refugee Assistance and at least 22 years of Age at Enrollment.

Note: CT= Classroom Training; OJT= On-The-Job-Training; JSA= Job Search Assistance; WE= Work Experience.

Source: Unpublished data, Job Training Longitudinal Survey, Women's Bureau, U.S. Department of Labor.

TABLE 4
Estimated Number of Title IIA Terminees by Minority Status, Sex, and Family Status: Program Experiences and Characteristics, JTPA Transition Year 1984

Selected Characteristics and Program Experiences	All Terminees	Minority Status, Sex, and Family Status Black and Hispanic Female Single Parents 1/	All Others
Estimated Total	350,300	10,200	340,100
Minority Status			
White (excluding Hispanic)	187,200	----	187,200
Black (excluding Hispanic)	110,300	8,400	101,900
Hispanic	40,400	1,800	38,600
Other	12,500	----	12,500
Age at Enrollment			
Younger than 16			
16-18	2,600	----	2,600
19-21	58,600	700	57,900
22-29	71,500	3,200	68,400
30-44	111,800	4,500	107,300
45-54	82,000	1,700	80,300
55 and older	16,400	300	16,100
	7,500	----	7,500
Family Status			
Single parent	75,100	10,200	64,800
Parent in two-parent family	60,400	----	60,400
Other family member	86,600	----	86,600
Nondependent individual	128,300	----	128,300
Number in Family			
1	130,600	----	130,800
2	57,500	5,500	51,800
3-5	135,800	4,500	131,300
6 or more	26,400	300	26,100
Age of Dependents			
No dependents	108,900	----	108,900
Age of youngest less than 6	23,500	8,100	15,400
Age of youngest 6-17	10,000	2,200	7,800
All others	208,000	----	208,000
Education Status			
School dropout	96,900	3,400	93,500
Student (HS or less)	38,900	700	38,300
In school at application (age less than 22)	34,100	500	33,600
High school graduate or equivalent (no post-HS)	152,300	4,000	148,300
Post HS attendee	62,100	2,200	60,000
Program Activity			
Classroom Training	127,900	5,900	122,000
On-the-Job training	76,300	1,300	75,100
Job search assistance	81,800	1,900	79,900
Work experience	25,100	200	25,000
Other	39,200	1,000	38,200
Annualized Family Income			
None	128,400	5,900	122,300
$1-2,999	85,100	2,500	82,600
$3,000-5,999	66,900	1,000	66,000
$6,000-9,999	42,600	500	42,200
$10,000-15,999	21,800	400	21,500
$16,000-19,999	2,400	----	2,400
$20,000-24,999	1,500	----	1,500
$25,000 or more	1,600	----	1,700
Economically Disadvantaged			
Yes	331,800	10,100	321,700
No	18,500	100	18,400

the type of individuals served found differences between CETA and JTPA participants but concluded that the support cost limit was not the primary factor.[11] JTPA sets a limit of 15% of total SDA expenditures on needs-based payments, supportive services, and other nontraining costs and a combined total of 30% of funds including administrative costs. GAO found that although SDAs had at least 15% of their funds available for support costs, they expended an average of only 7%; about two-thirds

TABLE 4   (cont.)

Selected Characteristics and Program Experiences	Minority Status, Sex, and Family Status		
	All Terminees	Black and Hispanic Female Single Parents 1/	All Others
Receiving Public Assistance at Application			
AFDC	61,000	6,800	54,200
General Assistance	19,300	100	19,200
Refugee Assistance	900	----	900
SSI	7,100	200	6,900
Other	82,200	4,300	77,900
No Public Assistance	219,400	2,500	216,900
Unemployment Compensation Claimant at Application			
Yes	34,600	700	34,000
No	315,700	9,600	306,100
Barriers to Employment			
Limited English	13,600	200	13,400
Handicapped	25,800	300	25,500
Offender	32,400	400	32,000
Displaced homemaker	13,100	1,100	12,000
Teenage parent	10,800	2,000	8,800
None of these	259,000	6,500	252,600
Labor Force Status at Application			
Employed full time	9,200	200	9,000
Employed part time	20,200	300	19,900
Unemployed	269,200	8,200	261,000
Not in labor force	51,700	1,500	50,200
Labor Force Activity Prior to Entry			
Worked at any time during 26 weeks and 13 weeks prior	116,300	1,900	114,400
Worked at any time during 26 weeks prior but not during 13 weeks prior	32,800	900	31,900
Did not work at all during the 26 weeks prior	201,200	7,400	193,800
Labor Force Status at Termination			
Employed full time	204,700	5,600	199,100
Employed part time	37,900	1,400	36,500
Unemployed	55,500	2,000	53,500
Not in labor force	18,700	200	18,500
Unknown	33,500	1,000	32,500
Receiving Public Assistance at Termination			
Yes	63,900	4,500	59,400
No	286,400	5,700	280,700
Placement Status (for those who entered employment or a registered apprenticeship program at termination)			
Placed in public sector	18,100	800	17,400
Placed in private sector	192,900	5,000	187,900
Placement unknown	15,400	300	15,100
Placement was training-related	148,300	3,800	144,500

1/ Parents are defined as persons with dependents younger than 18.

Source: Unpublished data, Job Training Longitudinal Survey. Transition Year October 1983 – June 1984. Women's Bureau, U.S. Department of Labor.

of 461 SDAs spent less than 10%. Transportation and child care were the principal support services provided, and 40% provided average needs-based payments of $34 weekly. No effort was made in the GAO study to ascertain whether the amount of the payments was satisfactory to recipients. It is not clear whether information on whether the level of such payments might have been a deterrent to participation by other disadvantaged people will be made when the JTLS is expanded to a matched sample of nonparticipants.[12]

JTPA was found by GAO to serve a group who were better educated than those under CETA, who required or received less financial support, and who were more likely to be enrolled in on-the-job training. A smaller proportion of women and a smaller proportion of minorities were served than under CETA. In comparison with black women's experiences as discussed, with the exception of the higher educational attainment among them, there is little available evidence (other than the fact that they completed the training program) to indicate that they were less financially needy than black women who participated in CETA. Since the majority were in classroom training, there is some suggestion that a large proportion of the black women served might have received services providing only limited skills for sustained employment, sufficient only for less-skilled entry jobs.

WOMEN'S BUREAU ACTIONS

As soon as the JTPA legislation was enacted, the Women's Bureau issued a publication summarizing and analyzing the major provisions of the law, particularly as they related to employment and training for women, and took steps to ensure that women and women's organizations were familiar with the act's provisions and the available services.

Subsequently the bureau developed and sponsored workshops using an overall theme, "JTPA: Its Implementation and Impact on Women." The workshop design proved effective in sharing information and providing opportunities for discussion of strategies that may be used in accessing the JTPA system to ensure that women are served adequately. The format focused on the responsibility for JTPA at different levels—the federal level and particularly the state and local levels, where the major decision making and implementation occur.

Among the participants at more than 20 workshops around the country were state and local officials, governors, mayors, private industry council (PIC) representatives, community college administrators, business leaders, program operators, and leaders of women's organizations, including black organizations.

Women are indeed participating in JTPA, including black women. Again, however, indicators are that black female householders maintaining families alone and other extremely needy women have not been as well served as they might be.

NOTES

1. There are two reports from the Office of Strategic Planning and Policy Development, U.S. Department of Labor: "Summary of JTPA Administrative Data from the JASR/JQSR Reporting System for the Transition Year (October 1983-June 1984)," November 1984, and "Highlights of JTPA Program Performance for Titles IIA and III During the JTPA Transition Year (October 1983-June 1984)," November 1984.

2. Women's Bureau, U.S. Department of Labor, "Summary and Analysis of the Job Training Partnership Act of 1982," November 1982. Washington, D.C.

3. Bureau of the Census, U.S. Department of Commerce. *Money Income and Poverty Status of Families and Persons in the United States: 1983*, Current Population Reports, Series P-60, No. 145 (Washington, D.C.: U.S. Government Printing Office, 1984). The poverty income thresholds for 1983 ranged from $5,061 for one person and $6,483 for two persons to $20,310 for nine persons or more. The average poverty threshold for a family of four persons was $10,178.

4. Bureau of the Census, U.S. Department of Commerce, *Characteristics of the Population Below the Poverty Level: 1983*, Current Population Reports, Series P-60, No. 147, (Washington, D.C.: U.S. Government Printing Office, 1985).

5. Bureau of the Census, *Money Income*, Series P-60, No. 145.

6. Bureau of Census, *Characteristics of the Population*, Series P-60, No. 147.

7. Ibid.

8. Employment and Training Administration, U.S. Department of Labor. JTLS Technical Paper, Job Training Longitudinal Survey, "Summary Description of JTLS Study Design," September 1984, Washington, D.C.

9. U.S. General Accounting Office, "The Job Training Partnership Act: An Analysis of Support Cost Limits and Participant Characteristics," GAO/HRD-8616, November 6, 1985, Washington, D.C.

10. Ibid.

11. Ibid.

12. Ibid.

DISCUSSION

John M. Jeffries

The Burbridge, Wilkerson, and Harper articles all highlight different aspects of black women's participation in education and training. The most sobering conclusion to be drawn from these essays is that even while participating in programs and institutions designed ostensibly to change gender- and racially-based differential labor market outcomes, black women are the victims of preferential treatment and access. The economic, social, and political forces that tie black women to low-wage jobs, crowd them into particular occupations and industries, and limit their mobility to the lower-paying stations within high-wage job categories, condition their status outside the labor market as well. More distressing than the tenacity with which this contradiction persists is our apparent inability to conceive of, not to mention implement, policies that effectively undermine those forces responsible for differential labor market outcomes. Even if it is agreed that a hierarchical labor market is unavoidable (some may even argue that such a structure is desirable), there is no reason to accept the conclusion that gender- and racially-based earnings differentials are inevitable corollaries. Moreover, a labor market hierarchy need not imply differential treatment and access within social programs outside the labor market. Nonetheless, as each author convincingly documents, black female students and employment program participants suffer disproportionately from differential treatment.

ON THE EDUCATION OF BLACK WOMEN

Wilkerson cites numerous statistics indicating that over the past decade and relative to earlier generations, more black women have been completing high school. One positive result of greater high school completion rates is the decline in the black female high school dropout rate. Wilkerson points out, however, that even with the increasing completion rates and the decreasing dropout rates, black women continue to lag behind white females.

Wilkerson also calls to the reader's attention the increasing number of jobs requiring at least a college education, which, she implies, effectively discounts the value of a high school diploma at precisely the time more black women are finishing high school. However, the devaluation of the high school diploma has little to do with the requirements of new jobs. There is a substantial body of evidence which suggests that the new jobs created in our "new technological era," as Wilkerson puts it, will require very few if any more advanced or sophisticated skills.[1] The increasing ambiguity regarding the value of a high school diploma is, however, linked in large inner-city public school systems to the quality of instruction received. Many educators are suggesting that a high school diploma is most accurately described as a "certificate of attendance"; others suggest that high school diplomas must be differentiated in order to distinguish between diligent students who have merely "hung in there" and those who have excelled academically.[2] Our justifiable preoccupation with high school dropouts and astronomically high dropout rates has overshadowed the fact that a greater percentage of the population is graduating from high school than ever before.

Oddly enough, in the youth labor market there is a positive dimension to the "certificate of attendance." Employers argue that it is precisely because "everyone" is receiving a high school diploma that the failure to do so (i.e., dropping out) indicates a level of competence and/or attitude that is totally unacceptable in the world of work. And for employers contemplating hiring young people, particularly minority youth, a positive attitude towards work and a demonstrated capacity to "hang in there" are valued more highly than a set of occupation-specific skills.

This is not to say that the quality of education within urban public high schools is of marginal importance. Clearly the ability to read and write and master a set of computational skills is critical for minority youth in their capacities as jobseekers and citizens.

Wilkerson suggests that black female high school completion rates would be even higher were it not for the fact that many black teenagers ae forced to choose between school and work. The empirical reality is that among young black females (relative to their white counterparts) the choice between school and income is often brought about by teenage motherhood. A good education while in school should better inform teenagers about the responsibilities and emotional stresses of early intimate relationships and parenthood, and should make the alternatives to early motherhood more attractive. Therefore, the quality and breadth of public inner-city education, in my view, are at least as important as the number of years of schooling completed.

Wilkerson is also quick to bring to our attention the fact that higher high school completion rates do not automatically result in increases in black enrollments in college. The author cites evidence indicating that the proportion of black college students who graduate has fallen, and black women in particular seem more likely to pursue postsecondary education in community and two-year colleges. Two interesting facts discussed in this section of Wilkerson's article are worth repeating: (1) the black dropout rate from two-year and community colleges is greater than that in four-year colleges, and (2) a higher proportion of white students attending two-year schools have already graduated from a four-year institution.

Wilkerson suggests that minority enrollment in community and two-year institutions is linked to the rising and increasingly prohibitive costs of an undergraduate education. Equally important to consider when examining trends in minority (particularly black) postsecondary education is a hypothesized hierarchy and segmentation within the U.S. higher education system. Many authors have suggested that U.S. higher education is best characterized by open-door or low-tuition community colleges forming the base on which more selective and ultimately elitist four-year colleges rest. It is argued that this institutional stratification serves two very important functions: (1) it encourages "working-class" and low-income students to attend community colleges, thereby leaving the more "prestigious" universities to members of the more affluent class, and (2) it limits the upward mobility of low-income individuals, thereby maintaining and reproducing what is seen as the larger society's inequitable economic and social status quo.[3] Although these writings are fraught with references to assumed and undocumented conspiracies among poorly identified parties, they nevertheless raise interesting questions about the extent to which there is a "tracking system" within the higher education system.

There is also a national network of postsecondary noncollegiate occupational training schools which rely heavily on low-income student enrollment. Their reliance on tuition payments to cover operating costs, coupled with low-income students' eligibility for federal student assistance, make this pool of potential enrollees most attractive to these schools. But the Federal Trade Commission (FTC) and the U.S. Government Accounting Office (GAO) have found that the schools' advertising campaigns are misleading and, in many cases, fraudulent.[4] Consequently, low-income students who attend these schools do not acquire the marketable skills promised, and many frustrated or disappointed students drop out prior to completing the required curricula. Those enrollees who complete the training programs generally find that the jobs available to them pay very low wages. Unfortunately, both dropouts and program completers have accumulated debts in the form of student loans and find it difficult to meet their financial obligations. The FTC has found that a large proportion of all defaulted federal student loans are from students who attend postsecondary noncollegiate training schools. Black low-income students are especially vulnerable to the lures of these schools.

Black women are particularly disadvantaged by this system because, within two-year colleges and noncollegiate training schools, women are concentrated in programs that lead to traditional female, low-wage jobs. Occupational segregation is therefore reinforced by the programs offered. Black women are not only being prepared for low-income clerical and service jobs, but compared to white women in the same occupations, they command relatively low wages.[5]

I read Wilkerson's policy recommendations with great interest and agree with them. Her documentation of the differential status of black women in education and her policy recommendations raise interesting questions regarding the extent to which black America can rely on educational policy to correct labor market inequities.

BLACK WOMEN IN EMPLOYMENT AND TRAINING PROGRAMS

The Burbridge and Harper articles reveal quite clearly that relative to other participants, black women are not afforded the same opportunity to take maximum advantage of their participation in federal employment and training programs. Burbridge and Harper both show that, based on the number of black women who were eligible to participate in employment and training programs, they were underrepresented in such programs; and when enrolled, black women were consistently overrepresented in specific training components. My comments will address the significance of this latter finding.

The Comprehensive Employment and Training Act (CETA) offered varying types of assistance to its economically disadvantaged population—training, pre-employment assistance, and employment-oriented assistance. Within the training component, the two dominant categories were classroom and on-the-job training (OJT). The chief components of the pre-employment services were vocational exploration and job-search assistance, and the two employment-oriented components were public service employment (PSE) and work experience. These varying employment and training activities were provided under different CETA titles, and the mix of activities presumably reflected a local prime sponsor plan approved by the U.S. Department of Labor.

The different components are self-explanatory.[6] What's most interesting, however, is the implicit heirarchical ranking of these activities within training programs, and their relation to post-program employment and earnings. Focusing on the training and the employment-oriented components, respectively, an OJT assignment is "better" than a classroom training assignment, and a PSE placement is "better" than a work experience placement. According to Robert Taggart, "the 'plums' are the on-the-job training opportunities which provide immediate earnings as well as a high probability of future employment."[7] Taggart found that women, Hispanics, persons with limited English speaking ability, and single parents had a higher probability of a classroom training assignment; while "the relative chances of OJT assignment [were] almost the inverse for those in classroom training."[8] Burbridge reaches the same conclusion and documents even further that within classroom training a majority of participants were prepared for traditional female jobs. By contrast, less than 20% of all OJT jobs were in that category.

These findings are important because, as Burbridge points out, "assignment to a component depends on . . . applicant *preferences*, applicant skills, and available openings" (author's emphasis). Taggart also reveals the importance of applicant interests and preferences. "Most CETA entrants," he writes, "want a *job* not *training* [author's emphasis]."[9] According to his findings, males (white and black) were the least likely to receive training when they requested it. However, "among those who wanted jobs rather than training, females were more likely to receive training instead."[10]

Burbridge also discusses how this within-program differentiation influenced program outcomes. In a comparison of jobs preferred with jobs actually received, it was black females who, after requesting a traditionally female job, "got their wish" more often than white female participants who requested the same jobs. Burbridge concludes "occupational segregation was apparently more rigid for blacks than whites."

Burbridge also notes several interesting findings with respect to program impacts on earnings—two of which are worth reiterating here. Burbridge cites work conducted by Bloom and McLaughlin, which suggests that "other studies [have] not adjust[ed] adequately for the fact that OJT trainees earned more than other participants before training." This provides tremendous insight as to why women are so disproportionately underrepresented in OJT—they undoubtedly earned less than their male counterparts prior to their participation in the program. Taggart makes explicit reference to "relative employability" as a factor determining whether or not one was placed in OJT.[11] However, the Bloom and McLaughlin finding suggests that there may have been some confusion over the extent to which pre-program earnings accurately reflect an economically disadvantaged person's potential employability as opposed to sex-differentiated wage systems. More importantly, the pre-program earnings proxy for employability seems to have operated in ways which adversely affects the training opportunities for women.

A second interesting finding is that those women who did participate in OJT received a much larger boost in their earnings than their male counterparts. As Burbridge notes in her concluding section, future programs should therefore include more women in OJT.

Harper's preliminary data suggest that black women participating in programs funded by the Job Training Partnership Act (JTPA) continue to be concentrated in particular components.

CONCLUDING REMARKS

In general, I am very skeptical of the extent to which education and traditional employment and training programs can, by themselves, enhance the economic status of black women and men.[12] Employment programs and schooling must be tied to federal, state, and local community economic development in order to more directly capture the presumed benefits of supply-side labor market programs. For example, a few localities are experimenting with new initiatives which link education and employment and training funds to alternative worker-owned enterprises within depressed urban communities. These interventionist initiatives must be viewed as legitimate and necessary parts of an urban economic development strategy. For individuals to simply continue to recommend more education or more training is likely to be unproductive in the absence of a set of job-generating policies.

NOTES

Work on this article was supported in part by funds granted by the Charles H. Revson Foundation. The statements made and views expressed, however, are solely those of the author.

1. For more detailed discussion of this issue, see R. Kuttner, "The Declining Middle," *Atlantic Monthly*, July 1983; R. McGahey, "High Tech, Low Hopes," op-ed section, *New York Times*, May 15, 1983; and R. Rumberger, "The Changing Skill Requirements of Jobs in the U.S. Economy," *Industrial and Labor Relations Review* 34, July 1981. For an expanded discussion of the "new jobs" and their implications for employment and training policy see R. McGahey and J. Jeffries, *Minorities and the Labor Market: Twenty Years of Misguided Policy* (Washington, D.C.: Joint Center for Political Studies, 1985), especially chap. 5.

2. See E. Yaffe, "More Sacred Than Motherhood," *Phi Delta Kappa*, v. 63, March 1982.

3. For two interesting and comprehensive reviews of this literature see F. Pincus, "The False Promises of Community Colleges: Class Conflict and Vocational Education," *Harvard Educational Review*, vol. 50, August 1980, and G. Vaughan (ed.), *New Directions for Community Colleges: Questioning the Community College Role* (San Francisco: Jossey-Bass), vol. 3, 1980.

4. Federal Trade Commission, "Proprietary Vocational and Home Study Schools," *Federal Register*, part VII, December 28, 1978; and Transcripts from "60 Minutes," broadcast by the CBS Television Network, vol. XVII, no. 36, Sunday, May 19, 1985.

5. See Julianne Malveaux, "The Economic Interests of Black and White Women: Are they Similar?" *The Review of Black Political Economy*, vol. 14, no. 1, Summer 1985.

6. For a more detailed discussion of the components, see R. Taggart, *A Fisherman's Guide: An Assessment of Training and Remediation Strategies*. (Kalamazoo: W.E. Upjohn Institute for Employment Research, 1981), pp. 18-19.

7. Taggart, p. 33.

8. Taggart, p. 33.

9. Taggart, p. 37.

10. Taggart, p. 37.

11. Taggart, p. 35.

12. For an extended discussion of my views on the efficacy of human capital-oriented employment and training programs, see J. Jeffries and H. Stanback, "The Employment and Training Policy for Black America: Beyond Placebo to Progressive Public Policy," *The Review of Black Political Economy*, vol. 13, Summer-Fall 1984; J. Jeffries and R. McGahey, "Equity, Growth and Socioeconomic Change: Anti-Discrimination Policy in an Era of Economic Transformation," *Review of Law and Social Change*, vol. XIII, 1984-85; and R. McGahey and J. Jeffries, *Minorities in the Labor Market*.

SECTION INTRODUCTION

Margaret C. Simms

This section of the volume focuses on black women who head families. There are several reasons for devoting our attention to these single-parent families. Like all single-parent families, black families headed by women are short on resources—both economic and human. There is less income to meet family expenses and fewer adults to complete household chores and help with child care. This puts a heavy burden on the householder. Black female-headed families have been the subject of attention among policy analysts, researchers, and the general public recently. Some of the discussion has been based on erroneous stereotypes—that most are on welfare, that they have children to get on welfare, that they have large numbers of children, and that they lack a "work ethic." In fact, while black families headed by women are more likely to be on welfare, less than 10% of the aggregate income of these families comes from public assistance (excluding Social Security).

The average number of children in black female-headed families is 1.89, about the same as other families, and, as Darity and Myers point out, there is little evidence that these women have children to get on welfare or that the size of welfare benefits increases the likelihood of being on welfare. Poor employment prospects are an important factor, however. As noted in the article by this author, black women who head families are less likely to be employed and have fewer other economic resources than other types of families, black or white.

Young mothers, many of whom have never been married, tend to have lower incomes and higher poverty rates than women who were formerly married. However, preliminary results from a study conducted by Michelene R. Malson indicate that many of the never-married women who head families are as successful as those who have been divorced or separated. Malson, in a presentation at the symposium, reported that never-married women in her small sample had work experiences that were very similar to those of women who had previously been married. Consequently, they were in similar economic situations.

The vast majority of black female heads of household receive no public assistance, struggling to provide both economic and emotional support for their children. Harriette McAdoo focuses on this group of women in her article. As she points out, they have very high stress levels as a result of the many, often conflicting, roles they have. Unfortunately, the coping strategies they choose are the least healthy ones, and were it not for the support provided by the extended family many more of these women would have unhealthy levels of stress.

Over the past five years the support these families have received from the federal government has declined and there is little indication that this situation will change in the near future. In fact, some conservatives have suggested that the solution to the growth in female-headed families may be to cut federal support more drastically. One proponent of this approach is Charles Murray, whose book *Losing Ground* has received a tremendous amount of public attention since its publication in late 1984. William Darity and Samuel Myers discuss the fallacies in Murray's argument in their review, which appears at the end of this section. Although they do not agree with some of his conclusions, Darity and Myers think that the debate generated by the book is healthy. There may well be serious negative long-run consequences from some of the policies that Murray discusses. These consequences are not brought up by members of the generally liberal managerial class because to do so would be detrimental to their own position. It is clear from the discussion that proper policy analysis and policy formation are more complicated than is sometimes apparent. However, the crisis in the black community brought on by the fact that the majority of black children are raised in female-headed families demands that we develop appropriate policies to deal with this problem.

BLACK WOMEN WHO HEAD FAMILIES:
AN ECONOMIC STRUGGLE

Margaret C. Simms

Black families headed by women have much lower incomes and
higher poverty rates than almost any other type of family. They are
disproportionately dependent on welfare and are less likely to receive support from absent fathers. This is a very serious problem for
the black community because of the increasing proportion of black
families headed by women alone. This article outlines the dimensions of the economic problem and reviews the likely impact of
recent policy changes on these families.

The economic position of a family is related to its composition; this is
true for all families regardless of race or ethnicity. Families that are headed
by women with no husband present have lower incomes than those
headed by men or by married couples.[1] Black families that are female-
headed have lower incomes and higher rates of poverty than any other
family type, with the exception of those headed by Hispanic females. This
fact has implications not only for these women but for their children, both
male and female. This article examines trends in family composition and
income and reviews recent changes in government policy that have affected their economic well-being.

TRENDS IN FAMILY COMPOSITION

Over the past 15 years the number and proportion of American families
headed by women have increased. In 1970, 11.5% of all families in the
United States with children under age 18 were headed by women. By 1984
that proportion had increased to 22.9%. Among black families, the proportion headed by women increased from 33.0% to 55.9% during the

same time period.[2] While the rate of increase in female headship was faster for non-black families, the much larger percentage increase for black families and the fact that a majority of black children are in families headed by a women alone makes the trend a matter of greater concern to the black community.

How do these black families come to be headed by women? In 1970, the largest proportion of black women heading families (53.6%) were separated from their husbands and an additional 16.2% were divorced. Only 16.3% were headed by black women who had never been married. The balance (13.9%) were women who were widowed. By 1980 the proportions had changed dramatically. Over 30% of all black women heading families had never been married, making out-of-wedlock births equal to separation as the leading cause of female-headedness among black families with children. Since 1980 almost all of the increase in black female-headed families has been among this group, with the number of black families headed by a never-married woman increasing at an average rate of 167,000 a year between 1980 and 1984.[3] Consequently, by 1984 just over one-half of all black families with children were headed by women who had never been married.

 · A number of theories have been set forth to explain this dramatic change—an unfavorable sex ratio, poor employment opportunities for black males, the availability of welfare. A complete discussion of these theories is beyond the scope of this article (see article by Darity and Myers for a discussion of the welfare issues). However, the trends are mentioned here because of their implicatons for the economic status of black families. About one-half of the out-of-wedlock births among blacks are to women under the age of 20. These women are least likely to have the job skills and educational attainment necessary to generate an income above poverty or near poverty levels. This brings with it restricted housing options, poorer nutrition, fewer educational resources for their children, and, possibly, poorer health care.

MONEY INCOME AND POVERTY RATES

In 1983 the median income of black families headed by women was only $7,999, an amount surpassing only that of families headed by Hispanic women.[4] This income was less than 60% that of white families headed by women, about one-half that of families headed by black males, one-third of that for families headed by white males or black couples where both parents work, and only one-fourth that for white two-earner families. As Table 1 indicates, the economic conditions of black female-headed families improves if the woman is able to work full-time, year-round. Median income for these families is more than double that for all black female-headed families and income is also higher relative to that of other family types whose household heads are employed full-time. Unfortunately, only 31% of black women who head families do work full-time compared to 38% of white females who head families, 52% of black males who head families (or share headship with their wives), and 59% of white males who are household heads. They are also less likely than other householders to have another family member who is employed.

Poverty rates are very high among families headed by black women. Over one-half of black families headed by women are in poverty and they constitute two-thirds of all black families in poverty. While poverty rates are very high among black families with an adult male present, black families headed by a woman are three times as likely to be poor or near poor. Being employed does reduce the chances of being poor, but Table 2 shows that even after controlling for employment status of the household head and the presence of other workers in the household, black female-headed families are more likely to be in poverty than other types of families with similar employment characteristics. In fact, black female-headed families with two workers are just as likely to be in poverty as white families with an adult male present but no workers.

The age of the woman is also a factor in the incidence of poverty. Those black female-headed families with heads under the age of 24 had a poverty rate of 84% in 1983 in contrast to a rate of 51% for those black families headed by women between the ages of 35 and 44. In fact, the incidence of poverty among the families headed by very young women is at least 20 percentage points higher than for black families headed by women over age 24 or for white families headed by women of any age.

THE IMPACT OF GOVERNMENT PROGRAMS

Twenty years ago the federal government launched a "War on Poverty" that was designed to reduce the incidence of poverty in the United States through a combination of income support and human development programs. These programs have, in fact, done little to reduce the incidence of poverty among female-headed families. The current poverty rate among black female-headed families is virtually the same as that in 1970 (54.3) and only marginally lower than it was in 1966, at the beginning of the "war" (59.2). This does not mean that government programs have not

TABLE 1
Income by Family Type and
Employment Status, 1983

Median Income for All Families

Family Type	Race of Head			
	Black	White	Hispanic[a]	All
Married-Couple				
Two Earners	$26,389	$32,569	$24,419	$32,107
One Earner	13,821	22,359	16,099	21,890
Male Head	15,552	23,208	18,032	21,845
Female Head	7,999	13,761	7,797	11,789

Median Income: Household Head Employed Full-Time

Family Type	Race of Head			
	Black	White	Hispanic[a]	All
Married-Couple				
Two Earners	$31,363	$36,457	$28,970	$36,110
One Earner	21,765	29,788	20,599	29,381
Male Head	23,946	29,616	22,531	28,334
Female Head	16,055	19,607	16,305	18,623

Source: U.S. Department of Commerce, Bureau of the Census, Money Income and Poverty Status of Families and Persons in the United States: 1983 Current Population Reports Series P-60, No. 145. (Washington: U.S. Government Printing Office, 1984.

[a]Persons of Spanish origin may be of any race and are included in racial totals.

alleviated the conditions in which these families live. A number of programs such as Food Stamps, subsidized housing, and Medicaid provide noncash benefits that are not included in the income totals that are used to calculate poverty rates. However, while economic expansion reduced poverty incidence among married-couple and male-headed families prior to 1980 and more generous Social Security and Supplemental Security Income benefits brought poverty down among the elderly, neither expanded employment opportunities nor more generous income transfers

TABLE 2
Poverty Rates for Families by Race, Employment Status, and Number of Workers, 1983[a]

Employment Status and Number of Workers	All Families		Female-Headed Families	
	White	Black	White	Black
All Families	9.7	33.4	28.3	53.8
Employment Status of Household Head				
Full-time, year round	3.4	7.0	4.6	11.1
Part-time, year round	3.9	9.3	7.3	16.1
Part year	16.9	42.7	41.7	67.2
No Work	20.1	60.2	46.0	77.6
Number of Workers in Household				
None	24.4	75.4	63.7	89.8
One	13.5	33.5	25.3	41.0
Two	4.4	11.0	7.6	25.2

Source: U.S. Department of Commerce, Bureau of the Census, Money Income and Poverty Status of Families and Persons in the United States: 1983 Current Population Reports Series P-60, No. 145. (Washington: U.S. Government Printing Office, 1984.

[a]Poverty threshold for a family of four was $10,178 in 1983.

have helped black families headed by nonelderly women. In fact, income transfers from Aid to Families with Dependent Children (AFDC)—the source of 9% of all income for black female-headed families—declined in real terms over much of the period. And in the post-1981 period changes in means-tested programs have further eroded the economic well-being of these families.

A study of the economic and policy changes during President Reagan's first term by the Urban Institute found that black families were adversely affected by the policies of the Reagan administration.[5] In addition to higher rates of unemployment (a 60% increase in unemployment rates among black adult women), a number of changes in transfer and other benefit programs were deterimental to these families. Programs of particular importance were AFDC, Food Stamps, and Medicaid. Since black women who head families have lower incomes even when they work, many continue to be dependent on government programs when employed. In the late 1960s and early 1970s several program changes were instituted to reduce the work disincentives of income transfer programs and to provide noncash benefits to the working poor. Many of these features were modified in 1981 when President Reagan put forth the philosophy of helping only the "truly needy."

Deductions from gross income were modified, with recipients only allowed to use the $30 plus one-third of income disregard for 4 months of any 12-month period. A gross income ceiling of 150% of the state need level was instituted and states were allowed to count Food Stamps and housing assistance as income. Children over age 17 who are in school need not be included in benefit payments, a change that might have a disproportionate impact on blacks since black children are more likely to be enrolled in high school beyond age seventeen.

In combination with changes in Food Stamp eligibility, the AFDC rule changes represented a step backward in terms of increasing the well-being of the poor and near poor. This was compounded by the fact that loss of AFDC benefits meant loss of Medicaid, leaving many of these families without access to medical care.

How much worse off were these families? The Urban Institute estimated that black female-headed families lost 3.6% in real disposable income between 1980 and 1984 (see Table 3). This means that after adjusting for changes in taxes, changes in employment, AFDC and Food Stamp cuts, these families were considerably worse off. If alternative policies had been in effect, these families would have had a slight increase in real disposable income and they would have been better off relative to other types of families. The loss in real disposable income for black families headed by women was in contrast to a 3.1% gain for white families and a 0.6% gain for black families with two earners. Losses in real disposable income were comparable for white female-headed families but much larger for black married-couple families with only one earner. Nevertheless, of all family types, black female-headed families continued to have the lowest incomes, having only 75% of the disposable income of white female-headed families and 63% of the disposable income of black married-couple families with only one earner. Black families (mostly female-headed) represented 44% of those on AFDC in 1979 and it is estimated that black families who received AFDC benefits had an average decline in real benefits of about 12%. In addition, it is estimated that 400,000 to 500,000 families were removed from the rolls completely due to the 30 and ⅓ disregard.

Another feature of the Omnibus Budget Reconciliation Act of 1981 (OBRA) was a provision allowing states to institute "workfare." Workfare is a requirement that recipients of public assistance work off their grants

TABLE 3
Real Disposable Income for 1980 and 1984 for Households Headed by a Person Under Age 65, by Race (1982 dollars)

| Household Type | Disposable Income[a] | | Change in Disposable Income | |
	1980	1984	Dollars	Percent
All Families	21,042	21,569	527	2.5
White	21,768	22,432	664	3.1
Black	15,232	14,795	437	-2.9
Black/white ratio	70.0	66.0	--	--
Couples With One Earner	21,704	22,111	407	1.9
White	21,959	22,509	550	2.5
Black	17,243	15,181	-2,062	-12.0
Black/white ratio	78.5	67.4	--	--
Couples With Two Earners	23,999	25,032	1,033	4.3
White	24,219	25,333	1,114	4.6
Black	21,358	21,489	131	0.6
Black/white ratio	88.2	84.8	--	--
Female-Headed	12,215	11,812	-403	-3.3
White	13,202	12,806	-396	-3.0
Black	9,976	9,618	-358	-3.6
Black/white ratio	75.6	75.1	--	--
Unrelated Individuals	10,449	11,385	936	9.0
White	10,852	11,741	889	8.2
Black	7,807	8,820	1.013	13.0
Black/white ratio	71.9	75.1	--	--

Source: Margaret C. Simms, The Economic Well-Being of Minorities During The Reagan Years (Washington, D.C.: The Urban Institute, 1984)

[a] Includes the value of Food Stamp bonus.

in unpaid public service jobs. Prior to 1981, workfare was prohibited except by federal waiver. President Reagan had proposed that workfare be made mandatory, a position that some observers found contradictory to his elimination of the public service employment option under CETA. Congress rejected his proposal, but removed the prohibition against workfare provided that: (1) the number of hours worked not exceed the total grant divided by the minimum wage; (2) welfare recipients not displace regular employees; and (3) the unpaid job is a last resort after other employment or training options have been exhausted.[6] After some initial skepticism, workfare appears to be "catching on" in several states. For women who are subject to workfare requirements there will be the added burden of child-care arrangements with no additional income; inequities when some are subject to workfare and others are not, and the prospect of jobs that may do little to increase their employability. While all of these are issues that legislators and program operators are supposed to address, it is not clear that they will do so. (See the legislative and policy agenda section for further discussion.)

CHILD SUPPORT PAYMENTS

In addition to earnings and government transfer payments, women with children have another potential source of economic support: the fathers of the children. The recently implemented child support enforcement legislation places more responsibility on fathers to support their children. In 1982, only 59% of all women with children and no husband present had voluntary or court-ordered agreements for child support. Fewer than one-half of these women (47%) actually received the full award amount in 1981.[7] For those women below the poverty line, only 40% had awards and 60% of them (or 24% of all female-headed families in poverty) received some amount in 1981. The mean payment received was only $1,440.

Among black women with children and no husband present, only 34% had child-support agreements in 1982, and 67% of them received awards in 1981. The mean amount was $1,640, down 9.1% in real terms from 1978. Even with award payments, mean income for these women was only $8,887. Those without awards were somewhat poorer. Black women below the poverty line were less likely to have award agreements than either white women in poverty or black women not in poverty. Only 27% of these women had agreements and only one-half of those (12.3% of all black mothers in poverty) actually received money from the absent fathers in 1981.

TABLE 4
Total Money Income for Black Males Aged 15-29, 1983

	Median Income	Percent With Incomes Below $10,000[a]
Age		
15–19	$1,559	99.2%
20–24	4,354	82.6
25–29	10,830	50.1

Source: U.S. Department of Commerce, Bureau of the Census, Money Income of Household, Families and Persons in the United States: 1983 (Washington, D.C.: U.S. Government Printing Office, 1985) Table 46.

---

[a] Includes those with no income.

Never-married women are the least likely to have voluntary or court-awarded child-support payments (only 14% for all women), and this is the group that has the lowest incomes and the highest poverty rates. Yet it is not clear how fruitful a policy of child support enforcement would be for this group. Nearly 60% of the never-married black women who head families are under the age of 30. Black males between the ages of 15 and 29 (who are most likely to be the fathers) are not well situated in the labor market. A substantial proportion have no income and a majority make less than $10,000 (see Table 4).

CONCLUSION

Over the past 15 years, the proportion of black families headed by a woman with no husband present has increased to the point that they represent the majority of black families. The economic problems confronting these black women are tremendous. Family income is low and poverty rates are high. Government policy during the decade of the 1980s has been to reduce government support that might create "work disincentives" and to place greater reliance on absent fathers to support their children. While self-help may be a desirable approach, it will not always result in a decent living standard for these women and their children. Poverty rates are still high among black women who work full-time and government support for this group has been cut back since 1981. Economic support from absent fathers may not always be available and when provided may not be sufficient to raise the family above the poverty line. Clearly a more aggressive set of policies that includes child care, job training, and adequate transfer payments is needed, in addition to support from family and community.

NOTES

1. The Census Bureau has changed its terminology in recent years, recognizing that "many households are no longer organized with autocratic principles" (Series P-23, no. 107, p. 1, 1980). As a result, the term that the Census Bureau uses for "female-headed families" is "families maintained by female householders with no husband present." For ease of exposition, that term is used interchangeably with "female-headed" families. Both terms refer to those families with a female householder (no spouse present). "Male-headed" families are those with a male householder (no spouse present). Husband-wife households will be referred to as "married-couple" or "two-parent."

2. These figures refer to a subset of families, those with children under age 18. The vast majority of households (72%) are composed of families. Over 70% of black family households have children under 18. That is true of 51% of white family households. The sources of information for figures on living arrangements are U.S. Department of Commerce, Bureau of the Census, *Household and Family Characteristics: 1984*, Current Population Reports Series P-20, no. 398 (Washington, D.C.: U.S. Government Printing Office, 1985) and U.S. Department of Commerce, Bureau of the Census, *Families Maintained by Female Householders: 1970-79*, Current Population Reports Series P-23, no. 107 (Washington, D.C.: U.S. Government Printing Office, 1980).

3. William P. O'Hare, "Dramatic Increase in Single Black Mothers" *Focus* vol. 13, no. 9, September 1985.

4. The income figures are for all families headed by women (with or without children in the home). Some but not all income information for 1984 was available at the time this article was written so 1983 figures were used throughout for consistency. Comparison with preliminary 1984 figures indicate that the relative patterns among family types have not changed.

5. See Margaret C. Simms, *The Economic Well-Being of Minorities during the Reagan Years*, Changing Domestic Priorities Discussion Paper (Washington, D.C.: The Urban Institute, 1984), and John L. Palmer and Isabel V. Sawhill (eds.), *The Reagan Record* (Cambridge, Mass.: Ballinger, 1984).

6. For further discussion of employment and training programs for welfare recipients, see Demetra Smith Nightingale, *Federal Employment and Training Policy Changes During the Reagan Administration: State and Local Responses* (Washington, D.C.: The Urban Institute, 1985).

7. Statistics on child support come from U.S. Department of Commerce, Bureau of the Census, *Child Support and Alimony: 1981* (Advance Report), Current Population Report Series P-23, no. 124 (Washington, D.C.: U.S. Government Printing Office, 1983).

STRATEGIES USED BY BLACK SINGLE MOTHERS AGAINST STRESS

Harriette Pipes McAdoo

In a recent study, coping strategies used by 318 black single mothers faced with conflicting role demands and stress were assessed. The women experienced intense stress, but stress levels were lower for women who were living with their extended kin. Conflicts existed between the role of mother and employee and between the women's work and childrearing. For conflicts, women selected the least healthy of the three possible coping strategies. They attempted to meet the demands of their work and family, without trying to change the expectations of either. Stress was highest for women who met demands by restricting their own career or personal choices.

The phenomenon of women who are raising their children without a spouse and who are employed in the labor market has been an increasing trend within all American families and especially within Afro-American families. However, this increased labor force participation has not meant that these women and their children have become more economically secure. Today women with children alone are increasingly becoming impoverished, regardless of their labor force participation.[1] These women who are employed have been restricted to low-paying jobs with limited advancement potential.[2] This process has been called "the feminization of poverty," a phrase that is particularly relevant to single women of color. However, while poverty for blacks may be more intense for women and their dependent children, it is all too common for all family members, regardless of gender.

Most women who support themselves and their children do so without depending upon public or private charity. Yet many of these women are poor, even when they receive some form of child support or alimony.

Even if they are employed, their poverty level is high. In previous research this author has found that women who must raise their children alone and who are in the labor market have high levels of stress.[3] Other writers have found that both black and white employed women who work while rearing children experience a fair amount of conflict between their roles at work and their roles at home, regardless of marital status.[4] It is assumed that black, single, working women will experience these same conflicts and be under even higher levels of stress.

There is wide theoretical agreement on the supportive role that the involvement within the extended family has played in stress reduction within black families. There is almost universal agreement that the family units of mothers and children have been strengthened by the support networks of family and friends. However, few empirical examinations have been made of the actual family involvement and its relationship with the stress levels of the mothers. In addition, not all families are involved in the by now almost stereotypical "extended family." Therefore this article will be an examination of some of the theoretical tenets that have been presented about the supportive networks and individual well-being in the families of black single mothers. The importance of black family support networks has been found to transcend Socioeconomic Status (SES) and mobility over different generations.[5]

The black woman has traditionally relied upon her original family for support when raising children alone.[6] The involvement in kin and friend support systems is felt to provide support for both the instrumental and the expressive functions that fall upon a mother. Instrumental roles are those related to basic survival of family members: food, clothing, shelter, and medical care. The expressive functions are those related to the affective domain: the maintenance of emotional support, love, and security. Mothers in these circumstances have been found to have high levels of stress and depression.[7] Even when in more secure economic status, single mothers appeared to be facing more significant stressful life changes than married women.[8]

The purpose of this article is to examine a group of black, single, employed women with full custody of their children, in an attempt to look at their work patterns, the possible conflicts they may have with their families and their work, the stresses they are experiencing, and the strategies that they use in coping with stress conflicts. It was assumed that when women are under a great deal of stress and when they are facing conflicts within certain important areas of their lives they will be unable to do an effective job of parenting their children and meeting all of the responsibilities that they face as single mothers and still maintain their own mental health.

Holmes and Rahe[9] defined stress in terms of the impact of certain significant life events that are experienced by individuals and the family as a whole. Stress has also been defined and measured by three procedures: (1) intensity, (2) frequency, and (3) perceived sources of stress.[10] Clinical assessment procedures have previously assigned stress *intensity* scores to certain significant events in life (SLE), particularly those that are related to transitional points. For example, the death of a spouse is considered highly stressful and is given an intensity score higher than that for assuming a new job. Life events that would be considered both positive and negative are given stress intensity or life event scores. It is assumed that individuals must make adjustments to both good and bad events and that therefore stress is felt. The birth of a baby may be a desired event, but it causes many stresses as adjustments are made to the "blessed event."

Two concerns existed about the original intensity scores: blacks were not included in the sample upon which the scores were standardized; and the original scale did not include several female-related events. Belle developed an extension of the stress scale that included stress events that were specific to females.[11] The original list was used in order to compare this sample with others across the country, and the extended list of events was used in order to obtain measurements that were more sensitive to women.

Stress *frequency* of the significant events over the past two years was developed to offset the limitation on inferences of the intensity scores but also to obtain a measurement of the frequency of stressful events in the lives of these single mothers. It was felt that the frequency of stressful events was important because low-stress events that occur repeatedly may be just as stressful as one major event that occurs only once.

The mothers' perception of stress from various sources was obtained for each of the types or sources of stress that were identified in the original and extended forms of the stress scale. The factors included were: finances, housing, work, male-female relations, parenting, health, personal relations, legal matters, and personal habits. The women were asked to rate each source of stress independently on a scale of 1 to 10 on which 1 represented low stress and 10 indicated high stress. Nine individual stressor scores and one total score were obtained for each woman. With this combination of measurement, more accurate measurements of the actual stresses within their lives could be obtained.

Role Conflicts

The roles that women play have been found to be conflictual and stressful in several studies. Aldous found that parental and marital roles are conflictual for women and compete for temporal and emotional priority.[12] Women who have full responsibility for the parenting role and who also have to play work roles are expected to face even greater stress and conflict.

When women are faced with conflicts between their roles, and when they are providing for both the expressive and the instrumental needs of their children, they will undoubtedly face conflicts in their roles as mother, provider, and employee. They will have conflicting demands upon their time, emotions, and finances and often will be unable to meet successfully all of the expectations they may have set for themselves and their children and employers. Hall outlined three types of coping strategies that are used by working mothers when such conflicts occur:[13]

Type I: Structural role definition. The mother can establish new sets of expectations for herself, for her children, and for her employers. She will negotiate with all of these "role senders" to expect only realistic behavior of her. For example, she may try to meet her obligations on the job, but will tell her boss that she cannot work overtime because she must be at the day care center before 5:45 P.M. to pick up her child. She would decide what is possible for her to do and refuse to feel guilty if she has to forgo some tasks that she has done in the past, such as keeping a spotless house or working late into the night.

Type II: Personal role redefinition. The woman can cope with conflict by redefining her own roles, establishing priorities for the roles, or by eliminating certain role-related tasks. For example, the woman may decide that she has to quit her job and go on welfare so that she can stay home and care for her children. She can continue to work and send the children to live with their grandparents for a short period. Or she may select a dead-end job in order to concentrate on her mothering role, with the hope that she can focus on her career in 20 years, after the children are grown up.

Type III: Reacting role behavior. The woman will continue to meet all of the demands that are placed upon her. She will attempt to be a "super mom," to become more organized, and to work after the children go to sleep, and she will not attempt to meet her own personal needs. She will risk becoming burnt out and emotionally overextended. This choice is considered the least healthy coping strategy.

Harrison and Minor found that married employed women tended to use Type II strategies of making priorities and not redefining anyone's expectations. The role of mother was prioritized over that of worker or wife. The women simply attempted to cope as best they could and responded in traditional ways to conflict and stress. In a later study of single and married women, Harrison and Minor found that the married mothers used Type II, whereas the single mothers used Type III, the least healthy choice. When the conflicts grew too large, women reacted by eliminating one role. White women eliminated the work role, and black women eliminated the marital role, for they could not eliminate the roles of mother or employee.[14]

If the stress impact of the three coping types were compared, the most healthy strategy would be Type I, because the woman could cause modifications in both the internal and external expectations for her. She would be able to change her own internal perceptions of what appropriate behavior for a woman in her position is, and she would be able to modify the expectations of others for her.

Social supportive networks. Descriptive data on the social support networks for single mothers were obtained from structure grids that were developed from an earlier study of extended family patterns among blacks.[15] Data on the types of relationships with the "closest" relatives and friends were obtained. The nature of these relationships was then examined in conjunction with stress-related factors. The variables of the study were: (1) stress intensity, frequencies, and perceived sources; (2) the presence of conflicts between role of mother and worker; (3) the coping strategies selected by the women to deal with the conflicts; and (4) the extended family support networks of these single mothers.

Hypotheses

Based upon a review of literature, certain hypotheses were generated:

1. These single black mothers will have high levels of actual and perceived stress in their lives, especially in the areas related to finances and their work.
2. Women who receive support from their extended families will have lower perceived stress.
3. The majority of the women will experience conflicts in their roles related to work and to mothering and with their job satisfaction.

4. When conflicts do occur, single women will tend to choose emotionally unhealthy coping strategies.
5. Levels of stress will be higher for women who choose Type II and Type III strategies.

METHODS

Sample

This was a secondary analysis of an existing data set of 318 single black women from Baltimore, who are employed and have custody of their children, who were under the age of 19. The sample was drawn from volunteers from an income-stratified list of all approved day care and nursery schools in Baltimore City with an appropriate black enrollment of at least 25%. Additional older volunteers were contacted through the large women's center's employment service.

All of the women were single at the time of the study, but half had been married at one point (see Table 1). Over half of the women had been 19 years or older when they had their first child, but two-thirds had not been married at that time. They were not now replicating earlier family patterns, for 70% of them had grown up in two-parent homes and their parents had been in their mid-twenties (mothers) or late-twenties (fathers) when these women were born.

The women were, on average, 30 years of age when they were interviewed, and their median income was $12,000. Some level of financial support was provided, on an irregular basis, by the fathers for 37% of the families. Almost half of them received help on a regular basis from family members, with the most help being received from their own mothers (28%) and their male friends (10%).

RESULTS

Stress

The women were found to be experiencing intense and continuing levels of stress in many aspects of their lives. They received stress intensity scores that would put them at the level Holmes and Rahe found in clinical studies to be predictive of impending emotional or physical illness within a rather short period of time. The significant life events occurred frequently in their families in both the standard SLE stress scale and in the

TABLE 1
Background Characteristics of Black Single Mothers

Variable	Total %	Socio-Economic Status	Total %
Previous Marital Status		**Education** (highest level completed	
Ever married	56	Junior H.S.	3
Never married	44	High School/Trade School	37
	100%	1-2 yrs. college	29
		3-4 yrs. college	19
Marital Status		Graduate/Professional	12
			100%
Separated	26		
Divorced	29	**Occupation**	
Widowed	2		
Never married	44	Executive/Professional	25
	101%	Administrative Per.	12
		Clerical	47
Married, 1st Pregnancy		Skilled/Semiskilled	14
		Unskilled	3
Yes	27		101%
No	73		
	100%	**Income**	
		Less than $5,999	9
Age, 1st Pregnancy		$6,000-8,999	16
		9,000-11,999	24
18 and under	46	12,000-14,999	19
19 and over	54	15,000-17,999	12
	100%	18,000-23,999	13
		24,000+	7
			100%
Present Age		**Religion**	
Under 30	54	Baptist	49
Over 30	46	Methodist	18
	100%	Catholic	14
		Other Protestant	15
		No Religion	4
Present Family Structure			100%
Attenuated nuclear (mother-child)	66	**Social Economic Status**	
Attenuated extended (mother, child relatives)	25	Class	
		II Middle	31
		III Working	53
Augmented attenuated nuclear (mother, child, non-relatives)	7	IV Lower	15
		V Underclass	1
			100%
Augmented attenuated extended (mother, child, relative, nonrelative)	2		
	100%		

subscale related to female concerns (rape, unwanted pregnancy or birth, unfaithful lover, etc.). Mothers felt that stress most frequently came from economic areas of their lives: finances, housing, and work (see Table 2).

TABLE 2
Rank Order of Mean Scores of Women's
Perceptions of Sources of Stress (N = 301)

RANK	STRESSORS	MEANS
1	Money	7.54
2	Housing	5.55
3	Work	5.08
4	Male-Female Relations	4.83
5	Parenting	4.37
6	Health	3.86
7	Personal Relations	3.84
8	Legal	3.19
9	Personal Habits	3.05
	Total	41.26

The women who perceived that they were under high levels of work-related stress: (1) had actually experienced frequent significant life changes in their lives in general, (2) had significant life events that were intense, and (3) had frequently experienced gender-related stress. All of these stresses were significantly correlated ($p < .001$). Women who had experienced great stress at work also perceived that they were under significantly higher levels of changes in their personal habits, had health problems, and had problems in their personal relations.

Demographic differences in perceived stress. No significant differences in the levels of perceived stress were found to be based on the demographic variables of marital status, age or marital status at first pregnancy, religion, or income (see Table 3). However, there was a definite tendency for stress to be higher for those women who had lower incomes. Linkages were found between family structural and household structural variables. Women who lived with their children and other family members had significantly lower levels of perceived stress (median = 35.74) than those who lived alone with their children (median = 42.47) or in any other type of arrangement; (median = 44.07; F [3,297] = 3.32; $p < .01$). Likewise, women who lived with their extended family in general (median = 35.74) had perceived stress that was lower than those in nuclear (median = 42.41) or augmented (median = 44.02) families.

Those with the highest levels of stress were the women living with their children and with nonrelatives; often these nonrelatives were other single mothers and their children. Sometimes there also were dependent older

TABLE 3
Means and Analysis of Variance of Perceived Stress by Demographic Variables

Demographic Variable	Group	Perceived Stress		
		N	M	SD
Household Structure	Mother and Child	199	42.47	14.21[1]
	Mother, child, kin	74	35.74	15.30
	Mother, child, nonkin	22	45.23	14.93
	Mother, child, kin, nonkin	6	37.67	16.54
		301		
Family Structure	Nuclear	200	42.41	14.20[2]
	Extended	74	35.74	15.30
	Augmented	27	44.07	15.83
		301		
Marital Status	Never married	130	39.21	13.90
	Separated	76	43.07	14.67
	Divorced	89	41.85	16.07
	Widowed	6	49.17	12.04
		301		
Age at 1st Pregnancy	18 and younger	140	40.82	14.56
	19 and older	158	41.74	15.04
		298		
Married 1st Pregnancy	Yes	77	42.39	15.05
	No	222	40.86	14.73
		299		
Religion	Baptist	146	40.69	15.83
	Methodist	56	40.89	13.68
	Catholic	42	39.62	12.83
	Other Protestant	46	43.87	14.74
	None	11	43.36	14.29
		301		
Income	$ 5,000 or less	74	42.62	13.03
	6,000-8,900	129	42.33	15.21
	9,000-11,900	67	39.51	15.61
	12,000-14,000	14	38.64	15.97
	15,000 or more	11	32.18	14.13
		295		

[1] $F_{(3, 297)} = 3.32$, p .01)

[2] $F_{(2, 298)} = 4.64$, p .01)

relatives, especially in the case of women who had higher incomes. Middle-class women often were supporting relatives who had supported them when they were young, single mothers. Seldom were these nonrelatives reported to be men with whom they were romantically involved (6%). The women's housemates tended to be persons who were also under stress and who might be making demands upon them for financial or emotional support.

Role Conflicts

The women were asked if they felt conflicts between their roles. Conflicts between their work and family roles were found on two areas of conflict, but not on the third. Just over half of the women reported that they experienced conflicts between their roles of mother and worker (54%) and between their children and their work roles (52%). However, only a third (33%) felt conflicts between their role of mother and their own job satisfaction (see Table 4). These responses indicated a significant association between the presence of conflict and the particular type of possible conflict (X^2 [2] = 34.02, $p < .001$). Their mother roles did not influence job satisfaction, but they did feel conflictual pressures between being mothers and caring for their children.

When conflicts were reported by the women, each was asked about how she handled each of these conflicts. The responses were coded according to Hall's three typologies. Each response was evaluated independently by two coders, with a reliability of .88. In cases of differences between the coders, discussions were then held between the two until they could reach agreement upon a consensual final code.

When conflicts were present, the women used the least healthy coping strategy. The majority of them selected Type III strategies for each of the three possible points of conflict. When conflicts occurred between work and mother roles, 64% selected Type III and, 3% Type I. Type III strategies meant that the women did not try to change the expectations of others but tried to meet everyone's demands. When conflicts arose with work demands and their children, 73% selected Type III and 21% chose Type I. The same pattern was found in the coping strategy selected for mother role and job satisfaction, for 65% selected Type III and only 6% selected Type I, the healthiest choice. The association was significant between the type of strategy used and the type of conflict, when the women overwhelmingly selected Type III (X^2 [4] = 33.76, $p < .001$) strategies, the most mentally unhealthy.

TABLE 4
**Chi-Square of Types of Role Conflicts by Presence of Conflicts and
Coping Strategies Used**

	Mother & Worker Roles		Children & Worker		Mother Role & Job Satisfaction				
	$\underline{f}$	%	$\underline{f}$	%	$\underline{f}$	%	x^2	df	P
Conflict Present									
Never	145	(46)	151	(48)	211	(67)	34.02	2	.001
Sometimes	170	(54)	164	(52)	104	(33)			
Total	315	100%	315	(100)%	315	(100)%			
Coping Strategies Used if Conflict was Present									
Type 1[1]/ Structural Role Defin.	21	13	35	(21)	7	(6)	33.76	4	.001
Type 11 Personal Role Defin.	35	22	10	(6)	32	(29)			
Type 111 Reacting Role Behav.	101	64	122	(73)	72	(65)			
Total	157	99	167	(100)	100	(100)			

Conflicts Between Roles As:

1/ Considered the most health strategy to use.

Stress and Coping Strategies

The last step was to examine the differential levels of stress for the women who made each of the three coping strategy choices on the summary scores. It was predicted that women who selected Type II and Type III strategies would have higher levels of stress. On Stress Intensity, mothers who used Type II had significantly higher stress (median = 228.80), than mothers who selected Type III (m = 217.20) or Type I (M = 156.64) coping strategies (F [2,162] = 3.13, $p < .05$). The same results were found when Stress Frequency was examined; Type II mothers (M = 11.60) and Type III mothers (M = 10.35) had significantly higher stress frequency than mothers who chose Type I (M = 7.85) coping strategies (F [2,162] = 3.18, $p < .05$)(see Table 5). Mothers who selected the choices that Hall had considered the healthiest had the lowest stress intensity and frequency. Type I choices of structural role definition that required their bosses and children, the senders of "role expectations," to modify their expectations had the lowest levels of stress.

TABLE 5
Analyses of Variance of Stress Levels by Chosen Coping Strategy

Coping Strategy	Stress Intensity			Stress Frequency		
	M	df	F	M	df	F
Type I Structural Role Defin.	156.64	2,162	3.13*	7.85	2,162	3.18*
Type II Personal Role Defin.	228.80			11.60		
Type III Reacting Role Behavior	217.20			10.35		

*($p < .05$)

Family Support

The support and help provided by the intergenerational family units were the key ingredients that enabled these black women to maintain positive mental health and to cope with the stresses and role overload that they experienced as employed single mothers. They experienced stresses more strongly in the areas of finances, housing, and work-related areas. They were maintaining themselves above the poverty level while under severe levels of perceived and actual stress. They were experiencing a growing impoverization in spite of their employment. Child care issues were of particular concern.

Family ties were reinforced by dense family interactions. As a group, the women felt very close to their kin and comfortable about their amount of contact with them. They tended to feel closest to their female relatives, usually their mothers or sisters. There was almost daily, or at least weekly, telephone contact with kin, and they frequently visited these relatives. The most frequent types of help that they gave back and forth were advice and emotional support, money, and child care. They received help from, and gave help to, an average of three relatives. They felt that the reciprocity was balanced.

The levels of interaction were higher when the income of the mother was lower and when she had more children, especially if they were younger. Kin interactions could be predicted to be greater when the mothers felt emotionally close to their kin, when more expressive help was given, and when both sides were actively involved in the exchanges of support and goods. Interactions intensified when the mothers tended to be unhappy and were under greater stress. Help was exchanged more when it was easy to visit and when the mother was younger and had younger children.

Women who perceived themselves to be under less stress were significantly more satisfied with their family situations, felt it was easy to visit their kin, had more kin upon whom they could count to provide help, and were not called upon excessively to help other family members. Satisfaction with kin and ease in visiting kin predicted the greatest variance in stress. However, single mothers with higher self-esteem appeared to be those who were able to maintain themselves in independent households but who felt close to their family and were able to get to the different generations of their families easily in times of crisis.

It would appear that the ties between these single mothers and their extended kin were crucial in maintaining the family's integrity, especially during traumatic periods of transition: birth outside marriage, divorce, and great financial stress. These were found to have the greatest impact on the mental health of the single women and their children.

SUMMARY

This group of single black mothers was found to have very high levels of actual and perceived stress and to be under very high stress in financial and work related areas. The women experienced stress and conflicts in the multiple roles they were attempting to maintain. The strategies they were using with these conflicts were for the most part putting greater stress upon them. However, those employing the most assertive coping strategies were those able to maintain themselves in these roles with the lowest levels of stress.

These women were making choices similar to those in Harrison's and Minor's study, with the one exception that they were not able to eliminate any of the roles that may have become too overwhelming for them. Their financial and marital status precluded them from some earlier choices, for these women were permanently in the state of single parenthood. One positive aspect of their dilemma was that the supportive networks and links between the women and their families appeared to be providing much-needed support. Mothers who were to maintain frequent and warm relationships with their own families of origination were under lower levels of stress. Women who were not involved with their extended families became very isolated, unless they were able to recreate familylike support networks with their friends, who often were other single mothers. Women who were involved with warm, supportive persons tended to have lower stress and to cope better with their roles within the workplace and within their families.

The importance of the linkages between family and work cannot be overlooked. This trend will intensify as more women have full financial custody of their children and must be able to blend and maintain these two roles of mother and worker.

NOTES

1. Pearce, D., and McAdoo, H., *Women and Children: Alone and in Poverty*. National Advisory Council on Economic Opportunity, (Washington, D.C.: 1981).
2. U.S. Commission on Civil Rights, *Unemployment and Underemployment Among Blacks, Hispanics, and Women, 1982*.
3. McAdoo, H., "Factors Related to Stability in Upwardly Mobile Black Families," *Journal of Marriage and the Family* 40(4), (1978): 761-776.
4. Harrison, A., and Minor, J., "Interrole Conflict, Coping Strategies, and Satisfaction Among Black Working Wives," *Journal of Marriage and the Family* 40(4) (1978).
5. McAdoo, H., "Societal Stress: The Black Family" in *Stress and the Family*, vol. I, *Coping with Normative Transitions*, H.I. McCubbin and C.R. Figley, eds. (Larchmont, N.Y.: Brunner/Mazel, 1983).
6. Aschenbrenner, J. *Lifelines: Black Families in Chicago* (New York: Holt, Rinehart and Winston, 1975). Hill, R., *The Strengths of Black Families* (New York: Emerson Hall Publishers, 1971); Stack, C., *All Our Kin* (New York: Harper & Row, 1974).
7. Holmes, T.H., and Rahe, R.H., "The Social Readjustment Rating Scale," *Journal of Psychosomatic Research* 11, (1967).
8. McAdoo, H., "Role of Black Women in Maintaining Stability and Mobility in Black Families," in *The Black Woman: Current Research and Theory*, L. Rose, ed. (Beverly Hills, Calif.: Sage Publications, 1980). Also See Aschenbrenner, op. cit.
9. Holmes and Rahe, op cit.
10. Aschenbrenner, op cit. and McAdoo, "Role of Black Women."
11. Belle, D., "Lives in Stress: A Context for Depression," Stress & Family Project, Harvard School of Education, Grant no. MH28830, Mental Health Services Branch, NIMH, January 1980.
12. Aldous, J., *Family Careers: Development Change in Families* (New York: John Wiley, 1978.)
13. Hall, D.T., "A Model of Coping with Role Conflict: The Role Behavior of College Educated Women," *Administrative Science Quarterly* 4 (December 1972).
14. Harrison and Minor, op. cit.
15. McAdoo, H., *The Impact of Extended Family Variables Upon the Upward Mobility of Black Families*, Final Report, OCD, DNEW grant no. 90-C-631, December 1977.

Book Review

Losing Ground: American Social Policy, 1950-1980

(By Charles Murray. New York: Basic Books, 1984)

Reviewed by William A. Darity, Jr. and Samuel L. Myers, Jr.

Charles Murray, in a remarkable examination of American social policy since 1950, arrives at some unconventional conclusions about the potential of social transfer programs to reduce poverty. The conclusions of *Losing Ground: American Social Policy, 1950-1980* (New York: Basic Books, 1984) are unconventional from the perspective of the vast array of academic scholars and social science researchers who have sought solutions over the past decades for poverty and inequality. Of course, the conclusions are not so startling to policymakers and politicians of the New Right. Indeed, much of what Murray urges in his extensively documented account of the failures of government intervention already is part of the policy posture taken by the Reagan camp; all of his reasoning long has been gospel among advocates of capitalism since the English poor laws. It certainly is the gospel among those around the White House since 1980. But Murray's provocative book is stirring up a storm among liberal intellectuals and the architects of the New Society and the War on Poverty.

Murray's story is quite simple. The post-1960s era saw an explosion of federal social transfer programs. Expenditures on welfare, crime, housing, and education reached unimaginable heights by the 1970s. Although aimed at the poor, the programs and expenditures resulted in unconscionable costs for the very people they were intended to help. Affirmative action programs hurt blacks; welfare programs encouraged increased dependency and reduced work incentives; Food Stamps and Medicaid eroded the work ethic and produced the stigma of being the recipient of charity; more humane criminal justice policies resulted in increased numbers of poor blacks being victimized by violent criminals in their neighborhoods. The upshot of the social transfer ideology was that the

deserving poor were hurt at the expense ostensibly of helping the un-
deserving poor.

This story unfolds in *Losing Ground* in an inventive way. First, Murray
traces an ideological transformation among the elites of policymaking in
America. The traditional consensus had it that the poor should be given
no more than enough to prevent starvation.

> The very existence of a welfare system was assumed to have the inher-
> ent, intrinsic, and unavoidable effect of undermining the moral
> character of the people. Not working is easier than working; not saving
> is easier than saving; shirking responsibility for parents and spouses
> and children is easier than taking responsibility. It was seen as a truism
> that a welfare system was perpetually in danger of tilting the balance in
> favor of the easy way out. (Murray, p. 16)

This consensus survived for more than 100 years. At least, it survived
until the liberal years of the social reform after the Kennedy administration. The shift from the traditional consensus to a radically different
posture came abruptly:

> In only three years, from 1965 to the end of 1967—what I shall refer to
> as the "reform period"—social policy went from the dream of ending
> the dole to the institution of permanent income transfers that em-
> braced not only the recipients of the dole but large new segments of the
> American population. It went from the ideal of a color-blind society to
> the reinstallation of legalized discrimination.(Murray, pp. 24-25)

The reform period, according to Murray, gave birth to an ideology of
"blaming the system":

> What emerged in the mid-1960s was an almost unbroken intellectual
> consensus that the individualist explanation of poverty was altogether
> outmoded and reactionary. Poverty was not a consequence of indo-
> lence or vice. It was not the just deserts of people who didn't try hard
> enough. It was produced by conditions that had nothing to do with
> individual virtue or effort. *Poverty was not the fault of the individual
> but of the system.* (Murray, p. 29, emphasis in original)

This was a radical shift away from an important morality that located the
burden of eliminating poverty squarely at the feet of the poor. According

to Murray, the result was a legitimization of a view that would have devastating consequences for the lives of poor people:

> But the intellectual analysis of the nature of structural poverty had given a respectable rationale for accepting that it was not the fault of the poor that they were poor. It was a very small step from that premise to the conclusion that it is not the fault of the poor that they fail to pull themselves up when we offer them a helping hand. . . . It was the system's fault. It was history's fault. (Murray, p. 39)

To demonstrate that the social welfare policies of the 1960s *caused* the deterioration in the well-being of the poor, Murray shifts to an intriguing empirical argument. In the years since the onslaught of the "reformers," expenditures on social welfare quadrupled; yet poverty remained unchanged. Moreover, black unemployment increased, labor force participation declined, crime soared, and illegitimate birth rates jumped to an all-time high. The social welfare programs of the sixties, and their accompanying ideology, Murray concludes, directly contributed to the increased entrenchment of the poor in a permanent underclass.

What to do? For Murray, the answer is to get rid of welfare, eliminate Food Stamps, Medicaid, and the like. In his own words:

> The proposed program . . . consists of scrapping the entire federal welfare and income-support structure for working-aged persons, including AFDC, Medicaid, Food Stamps, Unemployment Insurance, Worker's Compensation, subsidized housing, disability insurance, and the rest. It would leave the working-aged person with no recourse whatsoever except the job market, family members, friends, and public or private locally funded services. (p. 227-228)

These conclusions have the liberal intellectuals fuming. Murray resorts to the very tools and numbers that social science researchers have amassed in their entreprenuerial efforts to study poverty; but he uses them to try to put his rivals out of business. Murray cites and summarizes an enormous volume of mainstream, orthodox academic research, but he arrives at interpretations often at odds with what their seemingly apolitical authors had intended. No wonder so many authors allege he has given their work twisted treatment. Indeed, given the stake that some in the social research community have in salvaging what is left of the credibility of poverty research, it is no surprise that there is an uproar.

The most audible indications of distaste for Murray's analysis come from the University of Wisconsin's Institute for Research on Poverty. Leaner now than during the heyday of massive social experiments and innovative research on transfer programs, the institute's senior members have responded to Murray's arguments with a vengeance. Beginning with Institute Director Sheldon Danzinger's recent *Challenge* review article, co-authored with Peter Gottschalk, and followed by a series of chapter by chapter critiques in the form of an institute report, the Wisconsin group has sounded the loudest battle cry.[1] Not only do they contend that Murray has misinterpreted their and other social researchers' data; they also contend that Murray is patently wrong in numerous instances in the conclusions he reaches, even when he gets the numbers right.

For example, Glen Cain, one of the principals of the income-maintenance experiments in New Jersey and Seattle, reports:

> I confess that I took part in the research on these experiments, and I further confess that I do not recognize the motivations for or the results and interpretations of these experiments as Murray describes them. (p. 23, McLanahan, et. al.)

About the work-reduction effect of social transfers, Murray claims:

> The key question was whether a negative income tax reduced work effort. The answer was yes. The reduction was not the trivial one that NIT sponsors had been prepared to accept, but substantial . . . the NIT [in the SIME/DIME sites] was found to reduce "desired hours of work" by 9 percent for husbands and by 20 percent for wives. (p. 151)

About the motivations underlying the experiments, Murray contends:

> The NIT experiment made a shambles of the expectations of its sponsors. . . . [it] directly answers the question we posed about causation, at least for the outcomes relating to welfare, work and marriage: The only time we have been able to put the question to a controlled test, the causal effect was unambiguous and strong. (p. 153)

Here, Murray claims to find support for his conclusion that social transfer programs reduce the incentives to work and create other nasty outcomes like broken families and chronically dependent welfare recipients. Cain's response is that none of this surprises the designers of the transfer programs. These are *expected* outcomes. Economic theory predicts these effects. The purpose of the experiments was to determine how big the disincentives would be and how large the resulting work reductions and the like would be. Cain argues that the largest disincentives occurred at those levels of transfers that never have been and probably never will be contemplated by any political party. Why test the impacts of an unfeasible plan? Cain replies, because the experiment was one-sided: benefits only could be increased. They could not be reduced. To assure sufficient variance in the treatment, the upper bounds on the experimental transfer had to be extraordinarily high. Thus, argues Cain, within the range of politically feasible transfers, the deleterious effects seem much less damning.

Cain concludes his critique by questioning the theory that underlies Murray's attack on social welfare programs:

> [F]or Murray the rationality of the poor extends only to the fleeting short run. In the relevant long run, the poor, especially the black poor, behave irrationally when they choose to avail themselves of program benefits. In Murray's words, they strike a "Faustian Bargain." They hurt themselves.
>
> Murray's model of self-destructive behavior has no basis in economics, which is not to say the model is incorrect. But his model should be recognized for what it is: his own set of assumptions about what is good or bad for the poor. . . . I conclude that Murray's theory of behavior . . . like his empirical evidence, does not support a verdict of failure of Great Society programs. (p. 30, McLanahan, et al.)

At Wisconsin, at least, faith in social transfers as a means of reducing inequalty survives.

Other examples of disputes with Murray's data and his interpretations abound. For example, the authors of this review found in a recent article that the statistical correlation between the growth in welfare and the growth in female-headed families does not support the causal interpretation that Murray advances.[2] Welfare attractiveness or welfare dependency are not found to explain the rise in the fraction of *black* families headed by females.

Murray cites cross-sectional evidence—ironically much of it published by the same group of Wisconsin researchers—to support his claim about the effects of welfare on family structure. In addition, using trends on the ratio of illegitimate births to all live births, Murray concludes that the formation of single black female-headed families was caused by the expansion of welfare.

The individualistic, economizing behavior that supposedly leads women to have babies out of wedlock and to form households without a male head as a result of the incentives and inducements of public assistance is not revealed in our research using time-series evidence from 1955 to 1980. Indeed, since *real* AFDC benefits were falling in the period of the 1970s when female-headed families experienced their most explosive growth, a Gary Becker inspired theory would point to just the opposite pattern of family change.

Welfare payments are not a fundamental cause of female headship among white families either. In the most complete and exhausting econometric analysis of structural changes among white families to date, Sheila Ards similarly fails to find a statistical effect of welfare attractiveness or recipiency on female-headedness.[3] What distinguishes the Ards analysis is her attempt to include Food Stamps, Medicaid payments, rent subsidies, and other measures of "welfare" in her proxy for welfare attractiveness. The accumulated time-series evidence simply contradicts the simple trends to which Murray appeals.

But this tangle of conflicting statistical findings obscures the basic insight to be drawn from the debate between Murray and the Wisconsin group. What we see in the controversy between Murray, on one hand, and liberal intellectuals, especially conventional social science researchers, on the other, is an intra-class dispute of the type we have discussed in detail elsewhere.[4] Social programs have been conceived, implemented, administered, and evaluated in the decades since the New Deal by a cadre of professionals and intellectuals whose class interests do not lie unambiguously with the poor. This is a class distinct from the traditional capitalist class. This managerial class has acquired an increasing stake in the decision-making and resource allocation in the public sector. As the public sector has grown, so too has the professional-technical managerial class.

The ideological shift in poverty policy described by Murray can be better understood by differentiating among the elites involved in the formation of public policies in the past decades. On the one hand, there is the business elite. For the past half a century, this elite group has sought to restore the economic and social world of free enterprise that existed in the 1920s. The corporate interests have maintained a continuing hostility toward income redistribution schemes, generally, and toward welfare programs that reduce work incentives, specifically. On the other hand, there is the managerial elite, of which both Murray and his critics are a part. This second elite has been in conflict with the business interests in part because of the former's insistence on regulatory and market intervention strategies for solutions to problems of poverty, pollution, work-place safety, and similar examples of market failure. The managerial class, comprised of the intellectuals and intelligentsia, is precisely the class to which Murray attributes the shift in ideology towards the poor. Murray says: "the salient feature of the intelligentsia is not that it holds power—though many of its members occupy powerful positions—but that at any given moment it is the custodian of the received wisdom" (Murray, p. 42). We would contend that the thirst for power is no small motive for the policy shifts, nonetheless. Within the sphere of public policy towards the poor, the managerial class has completely wrested authority and control away from the capitalists. Whereas the pre-New Deal mentality was to let the unfettered labor markets regulate the poor, the post-New Deal era saw the rise of a government-centered mode of regulation. The role of the courts and of the federal government, and particularly of the administrative agencies delegated the authority to promulgate rules and to enforce legislation, *continued* to expand along the charted path created during the New Deal. The managerial class' power rested squarely with its ability to shape the direction and scope of the newly powerful courts and administrative agencies.

Murray focuses on an apparent power shift of the 1960s to discover the transformation in poverty policy. Here, Murray's historical account is embarrassingly oversimplified: the apparatus for the expansion that Murray sees in the late 1960s was placed in operation long before the welfare explosion of more recent years. Understanding growth of welfare in the 1970s requires a history that begins at least in the 1930s, when the competition between the business and managerial elites originated.[5] Nevertheless, the expansion of the managerial class's role in public policymaking and its thirst for power contributed to the development of its brand of regulating the poor.

Frances Fox Piven and Richard A. Cloward suggest that those who regulate the poor may not have interests that coincide with the interests of the poor. As the poverty population expands, the interests of political stability are served by reducing the misery of the masses.[6] We agree with Piven and Cloward that the changing demographics of the poverty population had an important influence on the *politics* of poverty policy. Thus, the coincidental rise in single-parent families with the expansion of welfare was really the reflection of policy responding to demographics rather than demographics instantaneously responding to policy. If there are to be found long-term demographic shifts as a result of our social transfer policies, they will be found in the slower, more permanent changes embedded in several generations of efforts to regulate and control the superfluous and redundant segments of the population, of which poor blacks are a conspicuous component.

While the new managerial class has assumed the commanding position of regulating and controlling the poverty population, a schism has occurred within its ranks. There has been a gravitation by many, like Murray, towards the right. The move has accompanied a vocal and persistent effort by the capitalist-leaning elements to eliminate welfare for the poor and to return to a modified version of the pre-New Deal days when the sweat shops, chain gangs, and labor queues did the job of keeping wages low. The liberal-leaning element of the managerial class has been infused with a massive growth of employment from black professionals. In some respects, there is a short-sighted attempt among these members of the class to solidify the employment gains made as the welfare bureaucracy grew. But in the long haul, even the black managers are likely to be drawn rightward by shifting winds.

The important struggle within the managerial class as it affects poverty policy is not over whether the Great Society failed or succeeded. Both factions acknowledge many program failures and both factions support the curtailment and reduction of the provision of social transfers to the poor, particularly to the black poor. The struggle is over the control of the policy and decision-making apparatus for regulation of the poor. By forging an alliance with the political right, some members of the managerial class can now claim a position of authority and power that rested in the hands of "liberals" a generation ago.

Much of the battle within the managerial class with respect to poverty policy can be perused in Murray's extensive footnotes. Virtually all of the work cited is from the "authority" of the conventional, orthodox social science research community—an esteemed component of the managerial class. Murray relies heavily on the "consensus" opinions of the managerial class to support his view that blacks and the poor have gotten worse off.

Two separate footnotes illustrate this. On the racial disparities in intelligence, Murray cites Jensen and Jencks, among others, to conclude:

> Among specialists in educational testing . . . [cultural bias in test
> scores] has fallen to the status of a minor issue for which a great many
> of the interesting questions have been answered. . . . [L]iberal scholars

were not seriously questioning the reality of racial differences in tests of cognitive skills. (p. 279, fn. 14)

On the racial disparities in crime as measured by arrest rates, he says:

Researchers have conducted numerous studies of the extent to which such deformations [distortions in arrests statistics] affect arrest data at any given time, and a consensus has been forming that the racial differences in real rates of crime are just about as large as the official data would have us believe. (p. 282, fn. 11)

Here is the managerial class at its best: damning the poor generally and indicting the black poor specifically. Murray is correct that there are the bleeding hearts among intellectuals who, when they damn and indict, still uncover a role for further government spending—that is regulatory control. But they are just another faction within the managerial class, a faction to which Murray's footnotes frequently are addressed.

Murray makes a major point of his effort to discredit social welfare by accusing the "humanitarian" wing of his class of embracing "white liberal guilt." That guilt is the source of the "Blaming the System" logic behind most of the Great Society programs. A more important point would have been that whenever black community-based organizations began self-help projects and enterprises in the sixties, both segments of the managerial class rushed to dismantle the efforts. So strong, for example, was the opposition to the Nation of Islam's entreprenuerial moves toward self-sufficiency and self-reliance that the managerial class sought to have its black members take a more explicit and visible stance in denouncing the Muslims.

We do not agree with Murray's conclusion that the welfare safety net must be ripped away in order to save the family, reduce crime, and eliminate poverty. But we find much of his conservative analysis and entertaining style on the mark for quite another reason. In the battle between the conservatives and the liberals of the managerial class, one issue at stake has been: Has black-white inequalilty diminished? During the heyday of the liberal-wing of the managerial class, the resounding response was, "Yes!" With the lone exceptions of Lazear and Heckman, both Chicago economists, the economics profession reached conclusions contrary to those that the authors of this review published five years ago in *The Review of Black Political Economy*.[7] Murray vindicates our efforts—without citing our work explicitly—by acknowledging two aspects of the marginalization of black males that we believe are at the root of the declining economic status of a significant core of blacks at the bottom. Murray convincingly describes the declining labor force participation rates for teenage black males, and the striking gap in the unemployment rates between blacks and whites. He calls prominent attention to the increasing size of that gap between black and white teenage males. For Murray, however, there is no explanation. The same young black males that Murray describes as being out of work and out of the labor market are the ones that he identifies as the criminals, who were not being rehabilitated by the failed policies of the 1960s. Yet they are also often the fathers of the babies born out of wedlock; they are the males that are absent from the families, which without welfare, would be better off because there would be "no recourse except the job market." Where all the jobs would come from to employ these young black males, or how marriages will suddenly materialize out of a new "responsibility" urgently pressed upon youths who are now in prison, or about to be imprisoned, is never made clear. What is clear is that this pool of marginalized black males poses so serious a puzzle for Murray, that, in his few encounters with them in the course of the discussion of black poverty, he must acknowledge his utter ignorance. Not surprisingly, the declining labor force participation rates, increasing black youth unemployment rates, increased imprisonment rates, and the resulting reduced pool of marriageable black men are unsolved dilemmas for the managerial class.

In sum, what is valuable about Murray's book is that it helps to expose the ongoing tensions within the managerial class while at the same time it reveals some truths about some of the devastating conditions faced by the black poor. Murray sees the self-destructive *behavior* of the recipients of social transfers as being at the root of poverty. His ideological commitment to the managerial class, regardless of the internal conflicts within that class, prevents him from recognizing that indeed there are long-term deleterious effects of welfare policies on blacks, but that these are the *intended* consequences, given the not-so-benign motives of the policies' makers. Since he is unable to connect the marginalization of black males to the welfare crisis, Murray remarkably exposes his work to a new line of thought that could help stimulate a break from the stifling, conventional modes of social science research.

NOTES

1. Sheldon Danzinger and Peter Gottschalk, "The Poverty of *Losing Ground,*" *Challenge*, May-June 1985, pp.32-38; Sara McLanahan, Glen Cain, Michael Olneck, Irving

Piliavin, Sheldon Danzinger, and Peter Gottschalk, "Losing Ground: A Critique," Institute for Research on Poverty, Special Report Series, SR #38, August 1985.

2. See William A. Darity Jr. and Samuel L. Myers Jr., "Does Welfare Dependency Cause Female Headship?: The Case of the Black Family" *Journal of Marriage and the Family* 46, no. 4, November 1984.

3. Sheila D. Ards, "White Female-headed Families: What Causes Their Increase?" Carnegie-Mellon University, School of Urban and Public Affairs (unpub. paper), May 1985.

4. See William A. Darity Jr. and Samuel L. Myers Jr. "Public Policy and the Black Family," *The Review of Black Political Economy* 13, nos. 1-2, Summer-Fall 1985, pp. 165-187.

5. Understanding welfare policy towards black, moreover, requires a history that begins at least with Reconstruction. See our paper "Down on the Killing Floor: The Courts and The Economic Dependency of the Black Family." University of Wisconsin Law School, Legal History Program, Summer 1985.

6. *Regulating the Poor: The Functions of Public Welfare*, New York: Pantheon, 1971.

7. William A. Darity Jr. and Samuel L. Myers Jr, "Changes in Black-White Income Inequality, 1968-1978: A Decade of Progress?" *The Review of Black Political Economy* 10, no. 4, Summer 1980. The battle over whether blacks have gotten worse off brings together two uncommon allies: conservative economists and progressive black scholars. The liberal wing of the managerial class contended that affirmative action and equal employment opportunity legislation had reduced the earnings gap between blacks and whites. In contrast, conservatives like James Heckman and Edward Lazear contended that the reductions in earnings disparities were more apparent than real. See Edward Lazear, "The Narrowing of Black-White Wage Differentials is Illusory," *American Economic Review* 69, no. 4, September 1979; Richard Butler and James Heckman, "The Impact of the Government on the Labor Status of Black Americans: A Critical Review of the Literature and Some New Evidence," in Leonard S. Hausman, et al. (eds.), *Equal Rights and Industrial Relations* (Madison, Wisconsin: Industrial Labor Relations Research Association, 1977); and Butler and Heckman, "A New Look at the Empirical Evidence That Government Policy Has Shifted the Aggregate Relative Demand Function in Favor of Blacks," University of Chicago, unpub. paper, 1978. Our research, consistent with this latter view, has drawn on the notion that a statistical illusion is created by the analysis of individuals with positive earnings, especially in a world where upward of one-quarter of young blacks are without labor market earnings.

SECTION INTRODUCTION

Julianne Malveaux

Federal involvement in the national health-care system has had a positive effect on the access black women have had to health services. In 1964, just 57% of the black population (compared to 67% of the white population) saw a doctor at least once a year. By 1977, three-quarters of both blacks and whites saw physicians almost five times a year.[1] These statistics show improvement in the health status of the black population, and of black women (who visit physicians more than men do) in particular.

There are other indicators of progress: between 1964 and 1977, black treatment in voluntary and private facilities (as opposed to public, tax-supported facilities) rose significantly.[2] Further, more black workers are employed in the health-care system, as physicians, nurses, and support staff.

But it is a mistake to describe the present state of health delivery in the United States as a "health-care system." There is a diverse set of deliverers, some public and some private. There are various levels of health access, some only implied by the Medicare/Medicaid subsidy, others guaranteed by health insurance and health maintenance plans. Too many blacks still use emergency rooms as their primary provider of health care. And too few blacks provide health care for their communities—fewer than 3% of all physicians are black.[3]

The crazy quilt we call a "health-care system" leaves too many people out. Perhaps 10% of the population is not covered by employer-provided or public plans. One of the costs of the 1981-83 recession was an increase in the number of persons excluded from comprehensive health-care coverage. Clearly, with black unemployment twice the rate of white unemployment, a disproportionate number of those not covered are black.

Despite the improvement in black access to health care, there remain gaps in the health-care status of black and white Americans. Alvin and Sandra Headen discuss differences in status, especially as they refer to women, noting differences in mortality and morbidity in the black community. Their research echoes the concern of other researchers. Howze describes the black infant mortality rate as "an unequal chance for life."[4] Hall describes the black cancer rate as alarming.[5] Beryl Jackson, in her comments in this section, emphasizes issues raised by the Headens about health-care quality.

Much research has focused on the physical health of black Americans, but mental health status has been less frequently reviewed. The articles in this section on health care also provide only minimal focus on black mental health problems. Yet the resources to treat these problems have become more sparse in recent years.[6] And issues of preventive mental health become critical, especially as the levels of drug and alcohol abuse rise, and as it becomes clear that blacks experience somewhat more stress than do their white counterparts.

Attention to mental health and stress is especially important when the physical outcomes of poor mental health are considered. A survey of working women noted, for example, that women who reported themselves under stress experienced more health symptoms (like muscle aches, eyestrain, depression), and actual health effects (high blood pressure, gastritis) than did women who experienced less stress.[7] Similarly, there is correlation between stress, race/ethnicity, substance abuse, and long-term physical side effects.

Who should deliver health care? Fred McKinney addresses this question by discussing the impact on black women workers of changing systems of health-care delivery. Bernadette Chachere suggests that McKinney might broaden his perspective. Indeed, while McKinney focuses on the status of the black physician, he gives less attention to the changing character of medical support staff. As concern with cost containment becomes more important, and competition among medical support staff is sharper, it is possible that black women will experience employment losses as health support workers.[8]

Ron Law, who administrates the Paul Robeson Health Organization, raises a set of complementary questions in his article on public policy and health-care delivery. Law describes a successful alternate model for health-care delivery: privately owned, for-profit, fee-for-service ambulatory care facilities. His discussion of the need present in Harlem, and the service that developed to meet that need, translates the data presented by the Headens and McKinney into a "hands on" perspective on health service. Law raises important policy questions when he questions the way Medicare patients are treated by the medical establishment. He further raises questions of access when he notes the need for more physicians in inner cities. His discussion of the availability of prenatal care has far-reaching implications.

Ultimately, this section on the health status of black women raises more questions than it answers. While the health-care status of black women is documented, as are black women's employment prospects in health care, a policy quandry is posed by these descriptions. Is cost containment incompatible with a goal of improving the health status of black women? What policies can combat rising medical malpractice rates and reductions in health access that result from such high rates? Are resources available to combat the problems of mental health and substance abuse among black women? Clearly the health status of black women poses a challenge to those legislators determined to close the "health gap." Whether reference is made to the physical health or the mental health of black women, it is clear that this health status is important to maintaining the health status of the black community.

NOTES

1. George Hariston and W. Michael Byrd, "Medical Care in America: A Tragic Turn for the Worst," *Crisis*, 92, no. 8, October 1985.

2. Ibid.

3. Ibid.

4. Dorothy Howze, "The Black Infant Mortality Rate: An Unequal Chance for Life," *Urban League Review*, 9, no. 2, Winter 1985.

5. Howard Hall, "Cancer and Blacks: The Second-Leading Cause of Death," *Urban League Review*, 9, no. 2, Winter 1985.

6. Woodrow Jones Jr., "Preventing Mental Disorders in the Black Community: Approaches and Problems," *Urban League Review*, 9, no. 2, Winter 1985.

7. Julianne Malveaux, "Black Women and Stress," *Essence*, April 1984.

8. Julianne Malveaux and Susan Englander, "Race and Class in Nursing Occupations," presented at the Mid-Atlantic Women's Studies Association Meetings, George Washington University, October 1985.

GENERAL HEALTH CONDITIONS AND MEDICAL INSURANCE ISSUES CONCERNING BLACK WOMEN

Alvin E. Headen, Jr. and Sandra W. Headen

In the last 30 years the health status of black women has improved. However, the likelihood of health problems from complications of pregnancy and childbirth or prolonged illness from combined effects of diabetes, hypertension, and obesity remains. The need for continuity of care for these conditions and the low economic status of black women suggest that current policy shifts away from emphasis on increased access to medical care will adversely affect the health status of black women. Policies to contain health-care costs should therefore be designed to assure appropriate access to needed care for black women and other low-income groups.

Black women represent a sizable portion of the population and make significant economic contributions. Based on recent estimates from the U.S. Bureau of the Census, in 1984 black females accounted for 12.4% of the total female population and 52.5% of the black population.[1] Approximately 41% of all black families are headed by women with no husband present, and in 1981 the median income of these families was $7,506. The median income was $13,380 for the subset of these families in which the woman household head was able to work "year-round, full-time"—a 78.3% difference. Black families headed by males with the wife in the paid labor force earned a median income of $25,040; those in which the wife was not in the paid labor force had a median income of $12,341.[2] Although many factors affect the decision to participate in the labor force, whether black women are healthy enough to engage in productive work is vital to the social and economic well-being of the black family.

The need for concern over the health status of black women is heightened by current public policy shifts away from increasing access, a major health issue during the 1960s and much of the 1970s, toward the goal of containing costs. This shift will ultimately reduce access to care and utilization of medical services. The intellectual basis for this policy change is provided by the argument that in the United States there is substantial overutilization of medical services.[3] Therefore, by implementing changes in medical insurance that reduce utilization, health care costs can be reduced without adverse effects on health status. A basic issue facing black people today is whether the health status of black women will in fact not be adversely affected by this shift in policy.

Our analyses lead to the conclusion that policies that focus on cost containment at the expense of access to care are not in the best interest of black women. The rationale for this conclusion is related to three issues— the particular health needs of black women, the pattern of health care utilization exhibited by black people, and the low economic status of black women. Low income makes black women reliant on public insurance programs such as Medicare and Medicaid, where policy changes are being aggressively implemented.

The objective of this article is to assess the impact of public health insurance and changes in health insurance policy on the health status of black women. To accomplish this objective, the article will first discuss the health needs of black women as exemplified by their specific health problems. Subsequent discussion will focus on the relationship between health status and utilization of medical services, and the relationship between utilization of medical services and health insurance.

OVERVIEW OF GENERAL HEALTH STATUS

According to 1983 estimates published in *Health United States 1984*, black women had a life expectancy at birth of 73.8 years. This was 0.9 years shorter than life expectancy for the total U.S. population and 5.0 years shorter than that for white women. However, it was 8.6 years longer than the life expectancy for black men and 2.2 years longer than that for white men. Thus, if one uses mortality rates (deaths per unit of population) as health indicators, black women appear to be relatively healthy and have made substantial gains in health status. A downward trend in overall mortality and mortality from specific diseases reflects a substantial improvement in the health of black women over the last 30 years. From 1950 to 1981, death rates for black women from a variety of causes decreased (Table 1): heart disease by 45%, cerebrovascular disease by 63%, complications of pregnancy by 76%, and malignant neoplasms by 4.0%. The relative health status of black women compared with black men and with whites also improved. For six of nine leading causes of death in the U.S. in 1981 (Table 2), black women had lower mortality rates than men of either race. With the exception of suicide, rates for white women were consistently lower.[4]

The health of black women has improved in an absolute sense, but many health problems remain. For example, death rates from cerebrovascular disease, homicide, and diabetes were considerably higher for black men and women compared with whites. For black women, mortality from diabetes exceeded that of any other group. Like black men, young black women under the age of 35 were frequent victims of accidents and homicide. With age, black women were more likely to succumb to cancer, heart disease, stroke, and diabetes.[5]

Although mortality rates are the most widely used indicators of or proxies for the health status of populations, from a policy perspective they are incomplete and, for many purposes, inadequate indicators of health status. For example, if a black woman is not able to work full time because of illness or poor health, her own and her family's well-being will be impaired. If she is a single mother, her family faces a 44% cut in income; if she is married, family income may be reduced by 50% or more. These societal implications of morbidity (illness) are not reflected in death rates.

TABLE 1
Changes in Mortality from Selected Causes, 1980-81: Black Women

	Mortality Rate	
	(deaths per 100,000 U.S. population)	
Cause of Death	1950	1981
Heart Disease	349.5	191.2
Cerebrovascular Disease	155.6	58.1
Pregnancy Complications	92.1 (1960)	22.1
Malignant Neoplasms	131.9	127.1

Source: U. S. Department of Health and Human Services, National Center for Health Statistics, Health United States, 1984, Hyattsville, Maryland, December, 1984, Table 16, pp.59-60.

TABLE 2
Morality from Nine Leading Causes of Death

Mortality Rate

(deaths per 100,000 population)

Cause of Death	White females	Black females	White males	Black males
Heart Disease	129.8	191.2	268.8	316.7
Malignant Neoplasms	107.2	127.1	158.3	232.0
Cerebrovascular Disease	33.1	58.1	38.9	72.7
Pneumonia/Influenza	9.0	11.3	15.6	26.4
Cirrhosis of the Liver	6.7	12.7	14.8	27.3
Diabetes Mellitus	8.4	21.3	9.3	16.8
Accidents/Adverse Effects	20.2	21.6	59.1	74.7
Suicide	6.0	2.5	18.9	11.0
Homicide	3.1	12.9	10.3	69.2

Source: U.S. Department of Health and Human Services, National Center for Health Statistics, Health United States 1984, Hyattsville, Maryland, December, 1984, Table 16, pp. 59-60.

Furthermore, the disruption caused by disability from chronic diseases may have a greater impact on the family than the disruption caused by death. A family may receive financial compensation upon the death of a member, but disability due to chronic illness is often not adequately compensated. However, death certificates make mortality rates more readily available than morbidity data, and they have become the empirical basis for many policy discussions. The importance of morbidity data should not then be diminished. When life is prolonged, its quality is gauged by the extent to which illness and disability are minimized. This article examines mortality data for black women, but it attempts to focus more heavily on the limited morbidity data. In particular it examines the impact of reproductive activities and chronic diseases on the health needs and health outcomes of black women.

REPRODUCTIVE HEALTH

Today black women and their children more often survive the rigors of pregnancy and childbirth than they did 30 years ago. Maternal deaths from reproductive complications have decreased by 76% (from 92.1 deaths per 100,000 live births in 1960 to 22.1 in 1981) and infant mortality by 54% (from 43.9 deaths per 1,000 live births in 1950 to 20.0 in 1981). However, a sizable gap in health outcomes for black and white women remains. During the same time period, maternal mortality for white women decreased from 22.4 per 100,000 to 6.5 and infant mortality from 26.8 per 1,000 to 10.5. Thus, while improvement was noted for both groups, mortality rates were much higher for black women.[6]

The relatively poorer reproductive health of black women compared with that of white women can be attributed in part to their higher overall birthrate and the frequency of high-risk pregnancies. By having more children in a lifetime, a woman increases the likelihood that one or more pregnancies will be complicated. Maternal death from complications of pregnancy and childbirth is three times higher among black than among white women. In 1981, there were 22.1 deaths per 100,000 live births for black women, but only 6.5 per 100,000 deaths for white women. Although this ratio becomes more favorable in the optimal childbearing years— between 20 and 29,—mortality increases with maternal age and rates are extremely high for black women over 30.[7] In addition, the infant mortality rate among blacks is almost twice that of whites, 21 versus 11 deaths per 1,000 live births.

For black women, risks of pregnancy are also increased by factors associated with maternal age. Compared with white women, black women under age 20 have higher birthrates and bear a greater proportion of total births for their group. For example, although birthrates for women 10 to 14 years old are low, the birthrate for black women in this group is seven times that of white women of comparable age. Birthrates for black women 15 to 19 years old are also higher than those of whites of similar age. Also, in 1981 24.3% of total births to black women were to women under 20, whereas only 12.9% of total births to white women were to women under 20. The risks of childbearing are also high when the mother is over 35 years old. Black women in this age group bear a smaller proportion of total births for their group than white women over 35 (15% in 1981 compared with 21.4%), but their birth rate is slightly higher than that of white women of similar age (Table 3).[8]

In addition to higher maternal and fetal mortality rates for black women compared with white women, low birth weight is another adverse outcome of pregnancy that particularly affects black women. This problem is also associated with maternal age in that women under age 20 and over 35 have more low-weight births than women in other age groups.

TABLE 3
Birthrate by Age and Race of Mother

Age

(births per 1,000 women)

Race	10-14	15-17	18-19	20-24	25-29	30-34	35-39	40-44	45-49
White	.5	25.1	71.9	106.3	111.3	60.2	18.7	3.4	.2
Black	4.1	70.6	135.9	141.2	108.3	60.4	24.2	5.6	.3

Source: U. S. Department of Health and Human Services, National Center for Health Statistics, Health United States, 1984, Hyattsville, Maryland, December, 1984, Table 2, p.43.

Low birth weight has been associated with birth defects and mental retardation and is an underlying condition in at least half of infant deaths. Counter to expectations, it is not a result of prematurity; birth weights of preterm babies born to black and white women differ only slightly. Instead, it is the full-term baby born to a black woman that is more likely to be underweight.[9] This statistic suggests that the health of the mother in the last two months of pregnancy is important to birth outcome.

For whites, a substantial reduction in low-weight births is found among older, married, better-educated women, especially if prenatal care is obtained early. By comparison, black women have low-weight births regardless of their circumstances. For example, black women with more education have fewer low-weight babies than black women with less education. However, black women with 16 or more years of schooling still have more than twice as many low-weight babies as white women of comparable education. This trend holds for all educational levels. In addition, white women in the major childbearing ages, 20 to 34, have few underweight babies; black women in these age groups have twice as many low-weight births. Thus, with improved education and optimal reproductive age, black women experience less dramatic decreases in low-weight births than white women.[10]

Low birth weight has also been associated with delayed prenatal care, especially among young, unmarried women. An important finding is that early onset of prenatal care has considerably greater effect on birth outcomes for white women than for black women. For example, black women who seek prenatal care in the first three months of pregnancy have almost twice as many low-weight babies as white women who seek care this early. In addition, the number of low-weight births to black women who wait until the last trimester of pregnancy to seek care is only slightly higher than that of black women who seek care early. This finding suggests that early prenatal care has a less dramatic effect on birth outcomes for black women than would be expected.[11]

In summary, because they have a higher number of lifetime births and more high-risk pregnancies, black women experience more adverse outcomes from pregnancy and childbirth than white women. Higher birthrates in the extremes of the age distribution, under 20 and over 35, elevate these risks even more. Adverse health effects are realized in the form of higher maternal and infant mortality and more low-weight births. Improvements in personal and social circumstances of the mother, which result in substantial decreases in low-weight births for white women, have less dramatic effects on low birth weights for black women.

MORBIDITY FROM CHRONIC ILLNESS

Although black women live longer now, the chances that they will spend a sizable portion of their lives being sick or disabled are high. They will need continuous medical care for a variety of chronic conditions that will individually and collectively contribute to deterioration in health. For example, the importance of diabetes mellitus in the health of black women goes beyond its prominence in mortality statistics for older women. With obesity and hypertension, it forms a triumverate of associated risks for numerous secondary conditions that increase morbidity as well as mortality. Because they are more likely to be overweight than whites or black men, black women will be the primary recipients of adverse health outcomes resulting from independent and combined effects of these conditions.

Diabetes is a condition that represents a primary health threat from chronic hyperglycemia (elevated blood sugar) and is believed to be the underlying cause of a number of secondary conditions, including cardiovascular and cerebrovascular diseases, blindness, cataracts and glaucoma, diseases of the nervous and vascular systems, kidney disease, skin problems, and complications of pregnancy.[12] Thus, although mortality from diabetes is low (9.8 deaths per 100,000 U.S. population in 1981), morbidity is considerable.

The incidence of diabetes is only 2.4% in the U.S. population, but mortality rates for individuals with diabetes are twice that of similar-aged individuals without diabetes. Morbidity from secondary complications of diabetes is also high. Diabetics are twice as likely as nondiabetics to suffer from stroke, coronary heart disease, and hypertension. Eye disease is six times higher in diabetics and amputation of the lower extremities is 16 times more likely. Diabetes is the leading cause of new cases of legal blindness in people 20 to 74 years old, and 50% of amputations of the lower extremities are performed on diabetics. In addition, diabetes is the second leading cause of renal disease in the United States, accounting for 25% of cases. For some conditions, blacks with diabetes are at higher risk than whites with diabetes. They are twice as likely to need amputations, 1.2 times more likely to have hypertension, and three times more likely to have renal disease; and their children's perinatal mortality is three times higher.[13] While the incidence of these complications varies among diabetics, the likelihood that an individual will suffer from one or more conditions increases with age and duration of illness.

Black women most often develop noninsulin-dependent diabetes mellitus, a condition that is strongly associated with obesity. Four-fifths of individuals with noninsulin-dependent diabetes are classified as obese (those 20% or more over ideal body weight), and 75% experience a return to normal levels of blood sugar after losing weight. Diabetes is the sixth leading cause of death for black women. This statistic is no doubt related to the fact that, at all ages past 25, black women are more likely to be overweight than whites or black men. Sixty percent of black females over the age of 45 are overweight whereas 30% of white women in this age group are.[14]

The high association between diabetes and obesity can have profound effects on health. Each condition has been separately linked to increased morbidity and mortality from secondary complications. Obesity is independently related to increased mortality from diabetes mellitus, heart and circulatory diseases, coronary artery disease, hypertensive heart disease, and diseases of the digestive system. Obesity and overweight are also associated with increased morbidity from hypertension, cardiovascular disease, hyperlipidemia (a risk factor for heart disease and coronary artery disease), and pulmonary and renal problems. Although there is some controversy over the impact of being overweight by less than 30%, obesity in excess of this amount has been linked to increased mortality and morbidity.[15]

Hypertension is a third factor that increases the health risk of obesity-related diabetes. As noted earlier, blacks with diabetes are 1.2 times more likely to have hypertension than whites with diabetes. Also, it has been well established that hypertension increases the risk of mortality and morbidity from some of the same conditions associated with obesity and diabetes.[16]

In summary, over the last 30 years, the health of black women improved substantially with respect to mortality. However, a closer look at morbidity data reveals that black women are at increased risk (compared with other groups) for illness and disability from a variety of chronic illnesses that require a lifetime of medical care to control both acute and long-term effects.

MEDICAL INSURANCE ISSUES: A QUESTION OF ACCESS

As a result of the enactment of the Medicare and Medicaid programs in 1965 and the growth in employment and income, the majority (about 87%) of people in the United States are covered to some extent by some type of medical insurance plan. Most are covered through employer-sponsored private plans. Those over age 65 and many of the handicapped are covered by Medicare, and selected low-income groups—primarily single parents with dependent children, the blind, aged, and disabled—are covered by the Medicaid program. These plans are supplemented by locally financed public hospitals and clinics that provide services to low-income people on an ability-to-pay basis. All who have studied the issue agree that expanded health insurance has resulted in increased utilization of medical services.[17] Thus, the improved health status of black women over the past 30 years can be attributed in part to increased utilization of medical services, facilitated by the expansion of health insurance.

In the 1980s a change took place in public policy toward cost containment policies designed to reduce utilization of medical services.[18] It was based on the belief that decreased utilization would not adversely affect the health status of the population. A basic policy issue concerning health insurance for black women is whether their health status will remain unaffected by these changes.

In order to address this issue, two areas must be examined. The first concerns the relationship between health status and utilization of medical services, and the second concerns the relationship between utilization and health insurance. The discussion will support the following contentions: (1) utilization of medical services improves health status, (2) the setting in which primary care is provided affects the quality of care and health status by implication, and (3) the health needs of black women require a shift toward more appropriate settings for primary care.

Compelling empirical evidence that increased utilization of medical care is associated with better health has been developed by Hadley. After a multivariate statistical analysis of 1970 data which controlled for factors such as race, sex, age, income, education, marital status, work experience, cigarette smoking, and disability, he concluded that "medical care use has a negative and statistically significant impact on mortality rates. This implies that health status is better when medical care is higher." His results for black females aged 45 to 65 showed that a 10% increase in medical care use is associated with a -1.5% decline in mortality. For older black women, aged 65 and over, a 10% increase in use is associated with a -1.7% decline in mortality. The magnitude of these relationships is slightly larger than those for white women, -1.3% and -1.4%, respectively.[19] If Hadley's results for the 15-year-old data still hold, and there is little reason to believe that they do not, the health status of black women increases with utilization of medical care and decreases symmetrically with reductions in utilization of medical care.

Regarding the question of the setting in which primary care is received and its relation to quality, two facts are relevant: (1) blacks are more likely than whites to use hospital outpatient departments, as opposed to physicians' offices, as their primary source of care and (2) black people appear to be sicker than whites in that they are hospitalized more frequently and have longer average stays once hospitalized.

In 1981 there was almost no difference between blacks and whites in the number of physician visits per person, 4.7 and 4.6, respectively.[20] However, proportionately fewer blacks than whites used doctors' offices, clinics, or telephone consultation, while proportionately more blacks used hospital outpatient departments.[21] This difference in utilization patterns suggests possible differences in the type and quality of care received. For example, personal physicians and Health Maintenance Organizations (HMOs) are better able to treat problems for which continuity of care is important; hospital outpatient departments and free-standing acute care centers are designed primarily for acute problems. Many of the health needs of black women, such as chronic illness, family planning, and prenatal and postnatal care, require continuity of care over an extended period. When acute care settings are used for these problems, quality of care may be compromised, resulting in lower general health status and higher use of hospital inpatient services.

In fact, hospital inpatient statistics for 1982 show that blacks had more discharges for every 1,000 people than whites—147.3 and 125.2, respectively—and the length of stay for blacks was considerably longer than for whites—9.3 and 6.5 days, respectively.[22] Higher discharge rates and longer average stays indicate higher levels of illness. It seems reasonable to propose that this adverse outcome may be attributed in part to inadequate quality of care resulting from the utilization of acute care services for chronic medical problems. In such settings the continuity of care needed for chronic illness would not be provided.

In summary, this analysis indicates that the health status of black women is positively related to the level of medical service utilization as well as to the quality of those services. As indicated in previous discussions, black women have a particularly high incidence of chronic conditions such as diabetes, hypertension, and obesity. It follows that both the health status of black women and the quality of health care services received would be improved if care were obtained in settings that provide continuity of care. The data suggest that this desirable utilization pattern has not been achieved. The adverse effect of this situation is reflected in longer hospital stays for blacks than for whites. Thus, health status is affected by both the level of medical service utilization and the quality of care received.

Turning to the relationship between medical insurance and utilization it is important to remember that medical insurance plans, public or private, reduce financial barriers to utilization of medical services. In 1982 data, hospital discharges for every 1,000 people increased from 106.2 to 178.6 as family income declined from $25,000 or more to $7,000 or less. Average length of stay increased from 6.2 days in the highest income group to a peak of 8.9 days in the next-to-lowest income group. It declined by one day to 7.9 in the lowest income group.[23] These data show that low-income groups are more likely to use hospital inpatient services than high-income groups. Because hospital services are extremely costly, this pattern of utilization could not have occurred in the absence of health insurance plans, especially public plans such as Medicare and Medicaid.

Variations in benefits, health insurance coverage, and economic status often combine to affect the setting in which medical care is received and ultimately its quality. Data for 1981 clearly show that as family income increases a patient is more likely to have a visit in a physician's office and conversely as income declines a patient is more likely to have a visit in a hospital's outpatient department.[24] This pattern of utilization can be attributed to financial incentives built into the various insurance plans—in particular, more complete coverage for hospital services than for those provided in physicians' offices. The potential adverse effects of such utilization practices on the quality of health care for black women was discussed above.

While there is little comprehensive data on the clinical effects of reduced insurance coverage, it is clear that reduced coverage will reduce utilization.[25] If services are not being overutilized, health status will deteriorate. Empirical evidence to support this proposition has been found in data on low-income, chronically ill patients in the state of California after the state eliminated its Medicaid program for 270,000 medically indigent adults in 1982. The study, which included patients with hypertension and diabetes, reported that "six months after termination of the Medi-Cal benefits, there was a clinically meaningful deterioration in the health status of the medically indigent adults as measured by the General Health Perception scale."[26]

Black women, while clearly benefiting from medical insurance, are unlikely to be overutilizers of health care services. Indeed, it appears that they would benefit from changes in the coverage and design of most plans to provide more incentives for greater utilization in settings other than hospital outpatient departments or acute care centers—for example, movement toward use of personal physicians or *HMOs* for primary and maintenance care. More importantly, any decrease in benefits is likely to reduce the utilization of health services by black women and exacerbate problems they now face in obtaining the continuity of care required by the chronic conditions from which they suffer.

RESULTS AND POLICY RECOMMENDATIONS

In summary, from examination of mortality data it is evident that there has been a substantial improvement in the health of black women over the past 30 years. This improvement can be attributed in part to increased access to medical services resulting from expanded insurance coverage. However, when morbidity is used as the health indicator, the following health problems emerge:

- For younger women, under age 34, violence, pregnancy complications, and accidents are the major health problems.
- For older women, chronic illnesses (e.g., diabetes, cardiovascular and cerebrovascular diseases, and hypertension) are the major health problems.
- For black women of all ages, obesity is a major health risk.

Although not exhaustive, this list of problems represents considerable risks to the health and well-being of black women. We also concluded from our analysis that current public policies concerning health insurance that focus more on containing costs than on increasing access will increase health risks for black women and their families.

The health problems of black women identified here suggest several policy recommendations for action by the black community and its representatives. First, in order to address the risks faced by younger women, additional efforts should be made to initiate effective programs to reduce violence in the black community. Continued support should also be provided for programs that focus on family planning and prenatal and postnatal care. Two proposals that will help older black women are suggested. Policies and programs that emphasize continuity of medical care should be promoted over those that allow fragmented care—for example, those that force black women to turn to hospital outpatient clinics for primary care. Also, support should be provided for medical insurance plans that minimize the out-of-pocket expenses for health care for low-income people. This latter recommendation is counter to the current trend regarding public and private medical insurance plans that increase costs to individual patients.

Because obesity is the primary cause of noninsulin-dependent diabetes and a major risk factor for other illnesses, reduction of obesity for black women should be a primary health objective. In this regard, the black community should support the expansion of public health insurance benefits to the coverage of preventive services.

In conclusion, it appears that a shift in the focus of current health policy toward cost containment and away from its historical goals of increasing access is not in the best interest of black women or the black community in general. More favorable policies would emphasize increased access to physicians' offices and Health Maintenance Organizations where black women can obtain the continuity of medical services required for adequate care of health problems associated with reproduction and chronic illness.

NOTES

The views and opinions expressed herein are those of the authors and do not necessarily reflect the official policy or position of the American Medical Association.

1. U.S. Department of Commerce, Bureau of the Census, *Estimates of the Population of the United States by Age, Sex, and Race: 1980 to 1984* (Current Population Reports, Population Estimates and Projections), Series P-25, no. 965 (Washington, D.C.: Bureau of Census, March 1985), Table 1, p. 9.

2. U.S. Department of Commerce, Bureau of the Census, *Money Income of House-*

holds, Families, and Persons in the United States: 1981 (Current Population Reports, Consumer Income), Series P-60, no. 137 (Washington, D.C.: Bureau of the Census, March 1983), Table 13, pp. 32-34.

3. Center for National Policy, American Medical Association, *The Environment of Medicine*, Report of the Council on Long Range Planning and Development (Chicago: American Medical Association, 1983 and 1985).

4. U.S. Department of Health and Human Services, Public Health Service, *Health, United States, 1984* (Hyattsville, Md.: National Center for Health Statistics, December 1984), Table 11, p. 53.

5. *Health, United States, 1984*, Table 16, pp. 59-60, and American Cancer Society, *Cancer Facts and Figures for Minority Americans, 1983* (New York: American Cancer Society, 1983).

6. *Health, United States, 1984*, Table 12, p. 54; Table 25, p. 76.

7. *Health, United States, 1984*, Table 25, p. 76.

8. U.S. Department of Health and Human Services, National Center for Health Statistics, *Trends in Teenage Childbearing, United States 1970-81*, Series 21, no. 41, Table 4, p. 17.

9. U.S. Department of Health, Education, and Welflare, National Center for Health Statistics, *Vital and Health Statistics: Factors Associated with Low Birth Weight, United States, 1976*, Series 21, no. 37, p. 2.

10. *Factors Associated with Low Birth Weight, United States, 1976*, Table 4, p. 27; *Trends in Teenage Childbearing, United States, 1970-81*, Table 9, p. 20.

11. *Factors Associated with Low Brith Weight*, Table 4.

12. *Diabetes Mellitus* (Indiana: Eli Lilly and Company, 1980), p. 179.

13. The Carter Center of Emory University, "Closing the Gap: The Problem of Diabetes Mellitus in the United States," *Diabetes Care*, 8, no. 4 (July-August 1985): 391-406.

14. *Health, United States, 1984*, Table 39, p. 94; Carter Center, "Closing the Gap: The Problem of Diabetes Mellitus in the United States," p. 391.

15. Terence Wilson, "Weight Control Treatments," In *Behavioral Health*, Joseph Matarazzo et al., eds. (New York: John Wiley & Sons, 1984), pp. 657-670; George Bray, "The Role of Weight Control in Health Promotion and Disease Prevention," in *Behavioral Health*, pp. 632-656.

16. Wilson, "Weight Control Treatments," p. 634; James Alexander, "Blood Pressure and Obesity," In *Behavioral Health*, pp. 877-888.

17. Karen Davis and Dianne Rowland, "Uninsured and Underserved: Inequalities in Health Care in the United States," *Milbank Memorial Fund Quarterly: Health and Society* 61, no. 2 (Spring 1983): 149-176.

18. Center for National Policy, *Health Care: How to Improve It and Pay for It* (Washington, D.C.: Center for National Policy, April 1985), p. 1. This book contains articles by Lynn Etheredge, Uwe Reinhardt, Theodore R. Marmor and Andrew Dunham, Karen Davis, and David Blumenthal, and an introduction by Ben W. Heineman, Jr. A conclusion of this panel of prominent researchers convened by the Center for National Policy is that "current health finance policy in the United States will not stop the rise in medical care costs, and more people will be left out of the system as pressures of competition increase" (p. 1). Also see Karen Davis, "Access to Health Care: A Matter of Fairness," in *Health Care: How to Improve It and Pay for It* Series Alternatives for the 1980's, no. 17, (Washington, D.C.: Center for National Policy, 1985), pp. 45-57.

19. Jack Hadley, *More Medical Care, Better Health?: An Economic Analysis of Mortality Rates* (Washington, D.C.: The Urban Institute Press, 1982), Table 11, p. 62.

20. Because specific data on black women's health care utilization patterns by setting are not readily available from published sources, the following discussion is based on

data for all blacks. Since black women constitute the majority of the black population and head a substantial plurality of black households, these data should provide a reasonable basis for analysis. Note, however, that women of all races use more health care services than men.

21. *Health, United States, 1984*, Table 41, p. 97.

22. *Health, United States, 1984*, Table 51, p. 109.

23. *Health, United States, 1984*, Table 51, p. 109.

24. *Health, United States, 1984*, Table 42, p. 971.

25. Joseph P. Newhouse, et al., *Some Interim Results from a Controlled Trial of Cost Sharing in Health Insurance* (Santa Monica, California: Rand Corporation, 1982).

26. Nicole Lurie, Nancy Ward, Martin Shapiro, and Robert Brook, "Termination From Medi-Cal: Does it Affect Health?" *New England Journal of Medicine* 311, no. 7 (August 16, 1984): 480-484.

EMPLOYMENT IMPLICATIONS OF A CHANGING HEALTH-CARE SYSTEM

Fred McKinney

The American health-care system has undergone rapid growth and structural change over the past 20 years. Because of the increase in expenditures flowing into the system, total employment in the industry has increased significantly. Along with total employment, the employment of black women has also grown. Unfortunately, however, black women continue to be concentrated in the lowest paying of the health occupations. Efforts to improve the occupational distribution of blacks in general and black women in particular are going to be more difficult in the future because of the dominance of cost containment as the nation's primary health policy goal.

There are few industries in the American economy that have changed as rapidly and dramatically as the health care industry. There has been growth, as well as attempts at structural change. Both of these factors have had an impact on the employment of minority workers in the industry. The growth in health expenditures is the engine for the expansion in total health employment. The attempts at structural change have had mixed results, but the current success of the prospective payment system and the growth of for-profit firms have the potential for changing the number of blacks working in the industry, their growth in particular occupations, and their work conditions.

This article will examine both the past growth and the ongoing structural change and their impact on the employment of black women in the industry. Although the changes discussed affect all workers, particular emphasis will be placed on the employment status of black women in the health occupations.

Black women are disproportionately represented in many of the health occupations. Changes in the industry will therefore affect the status and the progress for black women in the industry. In particular, many observers think that the health industry will not grow at the same rate as it has in the past 20 years. If this is the case, black women may find it increasingly difficult to secure jobs in the higher-paying health occupations as the system contracts or holds steady.

THE GROWTH IN THE HEALTH INDUSTRY

By far the most important change in the nation's health care system in the past 20 years has been the introduction of Medicare and Medicaid in July of 1965. Prior to 1965, older Americans were selected out of commercial insurance plans because their expected health expenditures would have exceeded the community-rated premiums that were offered at that time. Low-income Americans also has limited access because health services were too expensive and because they had little health insurance since many low-wage jobs did not offer insurance as a benefit. As a result low-income persons had significantly fewer physician visits and had substantially poorer health than the general population. The elderly poor suffered even more than the nonelderly poor when it came to being locked out of the system because of the inability to pay. The emotional stories of the elderly being forced to sell all their possessions in order to pay hospital bills was enough to move even the most intransigent congressman and senator into supporting a system of public insurance for those who were old or poor and for those who had been made poor by their ill health.

The government's role as a third-party payer grew substantially as a direct result of the Medicare and Medicaid programs. In 1963 the federal government provided only 18% of hospital revenues.[1] By 1980 this figure had grown to 54%.[2] Like the half-empty, half-full glass of water, the Medicare and Medicaid programs were seen by some as having gone too far and by others as not having gone far enough.

Before the introduction of Medicare and Medicaid in 1965, health expenditures made up 6% of the gross national product. In 1985 health expenditures will account for almost 11% of the GNP. It is estimated that by the year 2000 health expenditures could make up 15% of the GNP. In a recent issue of *Medical Care* Ginzberg and Ostow estimate that real per capita health resource use increased from $51 a year in 1935 to $524 in 1983. In absolute dollar terms total health expenditures increased from $41.9 billion in 1965 to $355 billion in 1983.[3]

Not only has there been an absolute increase in health expenditures; there has been a major shift in dollar expenditures from the private sector to the public sector. Table 1 shows that federal, state, and local expenditures as a proportion of total health expenditures have grown from 26.2% in 1965 to 41.9% in 1983. The major change has been due to the growth in Medicare and Medicaid expenditures. In 1967 total Medicaid expenditures amounted to $2.5 billion; by 1982 the total (federal) Medicaid budget topped $30 billion, with another $20 billion being spent by the states.[4]

TOTAL HEALTH EMPLOYMENT

Employment in the health industry grew as a direct result of the growth in health expenditures. The number of physicians grew from 326,200 in 1970 to 466,600 in 1982. The number of registered nurses has increased from 750,000 to 1,357,000 in the same period.[5] Over the period the active supply of workers in the heterogeneous allied health occupations has increased from 658,000 to 1,166,000. Similar changes were also present in the other health professions and for workers in non-health-specific occupations that work as support personnel in the industry. In 1982, for instance, there were 1.18 million clerical workers in the health industry.

TABLE 1
National Health Expenditures by Source of Funds, Selected Years*

Year	Private Expenditures	% of Total	Public Expenditures	% of Total	Total Expenditures
1965	$ 30.9B	73.8%	$ 11.0B	26.2%	$ 41.9B
1970	$ 47.2B	63.0%	$ 27.8B	37.0%	$ 75.0B
1975	$ 76.3B	57.5%	$ 56.4B	42.5%	$132.0B
1980	$142.2B	57.3%	$105.8B	42.7%	$248.0B
1983	$206.6B	58.1%	$148.8B	41.9%	$355.4B

*Source: Health United States, 1984

Total employment in the health industry in 1982 amounted to just under 7 million in 1982. Table 2 uses census data to show the rapid growth in the supply of health personnel between 1960 and 1980. Unquestionably the driving force for this rapid employment growth was the increase in financial resources flowing into the system.[6]

BLACK EMPLOYMENT IN THE HEALTH INDUSTRY

Although less than 4% of all physicians are black, black representation in some of the other health occupations is substantial. Table 3 shows the proportions of blacks in selected health occupations. One clear pattern that emerges is that black workers are concentrated in the lower-wage health occupations of aides, practical nurses, and technicians. This occupational distribution is very similar to the distribution of minority workers in other industries. Without question the occupational distribution of black workers is due to past discrimination practiced by the nation's medical schools, hospitals, and other institutions in the industry, as well as the nation's consumers.

Discrimination in medicine has been well documented.[7] As recently as 1972, 85% of all active black physicians were graduates of Howard and Meharry medical schools, which were the nation's only two "black" medical schools until the opening of Morehouse Medical School in 1981.[8] In the late 1960s predominately white medical schools increased the numbers of black medical students. First-year enrollments of blacks increased from 882 in 1971 to a high of 1,085 in 1977 but dropped to 984 in 1981.[9] In percentage terms, there was a drop in blacks' first-year enrollment from 7.6% to 6.7% between 1971 and 1981, despite the absolute increase.

Black women in medicine were even more underrepresented than black men or white women in the profession. Whereas 11.6% of all physicians were women in 1980, only 2.7 were black and only .8% of all physicians were black women. In contrast, black women make up more than 5% of the total labor force.

Not long after the nation's white medical schools recognized and acted on the shortage of black physicians, health policy analysts began to talk about the looming physician surplus. The cynic might interpret the shift in policy, demanded by the physician surplus, another example of past discrimination having the permanent effect of reducing the representation of blacks in the profession, with all of the subsequent consequences. The Graduate Medical Education National Advisory Commission (GMENAC) was well aware of the political dilemma of advocating a re-

TABLE 2
Employment Growth in Health Occupations, 1960, 1970, and 1980*

	1960	1970	1980
Physicians	229,671	279,658	431,418
Dentists	86,887	92,563	124,772
Registered Nurses	581,289	835,797	1,266,801
Pharmacists	92,233	110,331	143,490
Dietitians	26,470	40,225	65,221
Inhalation Therapists	N.A.	15,000[A]	47,600
Occupational Therapists	N.A.	5,000[A]	17,518
Physical Therapists	N.A.	11,000[A]	42,462
Physician's Assistants	N.A.	N.A.	29,690
Clinical Laboratory Technicians	N.A.	118,264	238,362
Dental Hygienists	N.A.	17,458	45,446
Health, Records Techician & Technologists	N.A.	10,946	14,803
Radiologic Technicians	N.A	52,566	84,345
Licensed Practical Nurses	219,085	235,546	424,960
Dental Assistants	N.A.	90,497	151,755
Nursing Aides, Orderlies & Attendants	391,136	733,576	1,295,957
Therapists Medical	36,568	75,690	N.A.
Technicians Medical	138,813	N.A.	N.A.
Midwives	896	941	N.A.

*Source: U.S. Census, 1960, 1970, 1980

[A]From Status of Health Personnel in the United States, May 1984

TABLE 3
Black Employment as Percentage of Total Employment in
Selected Health Occupations, 1983*

Occupations	Percentage of Black Workers
Physicians	2.7%
Dentists	3.2%
Registered Nurses	6.7%
Physicians Assistants	7.7%
Licensed Practical Nurses	17.7%
Health Technologists and Technicians	12.7%
Nursing Aides, Orderlies and Attendants	27.3%
Therapists	7.6%

*Source: January 1984 Employment and Earnings

duction in the total supply of physicians at a time when black doctors continued to be underrepresented and the gap showed little sign of closing. Sensitivity to this issue led the commission to recommend that the committment made by the nation's medical schools to blacks and to women continue in the now-changed environment. According to the interim GMENAC report:[10]

Greater diversity among the medical students should be accomplished by promoting more flexibility in the requirements for admission; by broadening the characteristics of the applicant pool with respect to socio-economic status, age, sex, and *race* [emphasis added]; by providing loans and scholarships to help achieve the goals; and by emphasizing, as role models, women and under-represented minority faculty members.

Other occupations in the health industry effectively absorbed labor that was becoming redundant in the manufacturing sector. Many urban areas began to lose their manufacturing base at about the same time the health industry experienced its expansion. The urban hospitals not only served as places for the sick to receive treatment but played a significant role in the employment of low-skilled and minority workers. It must be noted that 40% of all hospital employees work in hospitals in the nation's 100 largest cities.[11] New York led the nation's cities with 74 hospitals and 140,000 health workers.

The income and purchasing power of these workers has bestowed upon them political power that forces urban politicians to support their continued employment in the face of falling hospital demand. Whenever and wherever urban hospitals are threatened with closure, workers are able, in most cases, to mobilize grass-roots support to fight the closing because of the loss of "needed" services, but also to protect the jobs of workers, many of whom live close to the hospital and are well connected in the community. Because many of the nation's 6,300 hospitals are located in areas with significant minority populations, minority workers have been a major source of the low-wage, low-skill workers needed in the hospital. Local 1199 in New York City reports that of their 90,000 active members, 65% are black and 65% are women.[12]

Minority workers and women in some of the other health professions fared only marginally better than black physicians. Table 3 shows that in dentistry, among registered nurses, among physicians' assistants, and in the therapy professions, blacks were underrepresented in comparison to the percentage of blacks in the labor force. As with the medical profession, these other professions recognized the lack of minority representation. Some of them have aggressively attempted to improve the distribution of minority health professionals with the help of the federal government. But the president vetoed the Public Health Act (1984), which would have authorized money for aid to educational institutions training all health workers and would have provided some monies for increasing the number of minority health professionals. From all indications, the current administration does not see increasing the proportion of minority health professionals as a priority.

From a systems point of view it might be the appropriate policy to begin to slow down the growth in training grants to the health professional schools, since there are indications that the growth in total expenditures may be slowing. Again medicine provides an example of pursuing goals of slowing down total supplies while increasing minority supplies. Although medicine has not been successful in accomplishing either of these goals, it and other professions should be encouraged to continue along these lines.

Black women in the health care industry are concentrated in the lowest-paying health occupations; these same occupations are also female dominated. Over 90% of dieticians, registered nurses, dental assistants, practical nurses, nursing aides, and dental hygienists are women. The earnings of women in these occupations are generally low; given changes taking place in the industry, earnings are not likely to grow as rapidly as they did in the 1970s.

For years health workers were considered to be underpaid, but they were not covered by collective bargaining until 1974. Since then they have increasingly become unionized and have "caught up" with other workers with similar skills. But because of the emphasis on cost containment, the ability of health workers to bargain successfully for higher wages is now constrained. Strikes at hospitals across the country have been acrimonious and protracted. The wage pass-throughs of the late 1960s and 1970s are no longer the rule.

The earnings of black health workers, and particularly of black women workers, are significantly below the earnings of white male health workers. These differences partly reflect the effects of discrimination, but some of the earnings differential is probably due to differences in experience, differences in the incomes of the consumers served by black professionals, and in medical specialty. Black health professionals are younger, more likely to serve predominately black clients and, more likely to work in the public sector. Black workers are also concentrated in the lower-paying occupations, and more likely to be in the lower-paying primary care settings and specialties. Table 4 shows that these factors have had a profound effect on the earnings of black women relative to the earnings of black men and white men and women. Black women physicians, for example, made less than 35% of the income earned by white male physicians in 1979.[13] Since the earnings are for physicians employed full-time and year-round only, this difference cannot be attributed to differences in hours of work. Black women physicians also earned significantly less than black male physicians but fared better in comparison to white women. There was a similar pattern in dentistry. Interestingly, black women did relatively better than white women in a number of occupations in terms of income. Black women dentists, registered nurses, LPNs, and nursing aides and orderlies reported higher incomes than white women in the same occupations. But even in these predominantly female occupations (with the exception of dentistry) black women earned lower incomes than males of both races.

One development likely to have a negative impact on the earnings of black women in nursing is the proposed changes that would increase the educational requirements of professional nurses. Currently there are three ways to become a registered nurse. The first is to earn a diploma at a hospital with a clinical nursing program. The second is to enroll in an associate degree program in nursing. And the third is the baccalaureate degree program. The diploma degree program graduates dominated the newly trained RNs until the early 1970s. By 1982 there were more RNs coming out of associate degree programs than from the other two sources combined.[14]

National organizations of RNs such as the National League of Nurses and the American Nurses Association have for a number of years attempted to control the supply of newly trained RNs as a way of increasing the earnings of RNs. One proposal that has been pushed to achieve this goal is to limit the title of professional nurses to those who have a baccalaureate degree or higher.

TABLE 4
Black Female Earnings as a Percentage of Black Male, White Male, and White Female Earnings for Selected Health Occupations, 1980*

Occupation	Black Female Earnings as a Percentage of		
	Black Males	White Males	White Females
Physicians	46.4%	34.6%	88.2%
Dentists	57.2%	47.5%	169.0%
Registered Nurses	98.0%	91.7%	102.0%
Pharmacists	81.3%	77.3%	100.0%
Therapists	87.1%	72.9%	89.1%
Health Technologists	84.9%	73.7%	99.8%
Licensed Practical Nurses	92.4%	94.5%	108.0%
Nursing Aides, Orderlies and Attendants	84.6%	77.1%	106.0%

*Source: 1980 U.S. Census

The effect of a proposal of this nature would be to exclude a potentially large supply of workers from the occupation by legislative fiat. Furthermore, and particularly germane to the focus of this article, the greatest percentage of black nurses are coming out of the associate degree programs. If the degree requirement is changed, black women would be forced to increase their preparation. Should black women and other associate and diploma degree nurses be compelled to bear increased costs to enter the profession?

The impact of proposals to change entry requirements is neither trivial nor inconsequential. In the near future, direct reimbursement may be available to registered nurses. If a large proportion of the nursing population is excluded from this direct reimbursement, and an even larger percentage of black nurses are excluded, the gains made by a few will not be transferred to others. Similar attempts to restrict entry into allied health professssions also threaten to reduce the supply of black women in these occupations.

STRUCTURAL CHANGE IN THE HEALTH INDUSTRY

Development economists distinguish between growth and development.[15] A similar analogy can be made in the analysis of the health industry. The growth in the size of the industry has been matched by some successes and some failures at structural change. Current demands for structural change are partly the result of the improvements in access to health services to all population groups. The improved access for the poor and the elderly took place without altering the fee-for-service payment system and the reimbursement of hospitals on a basis of costs, and without any change in the system's emphasis toward overmedicalization. The increase in demand brought about by Medicare and Medicaid led to inflation in the health sector. In the mid-1970s the health care component of the Consumer Price Index increased at almost twice the overall rate.[16] As health care prices rose, the political support for national health insurance faded. Even supporters of national health insurance acknowledged the need to get health care costs under control.

Economists pointed to a number of factors that would have to be addressed in order to control health care prices. The experience of the Economic Stabilization Plan (ESP) price controls in the early 1970s was one model of an unsuccessful attempt at controlling not only health prices, but all prices; not long after the price controls were lifted, prices for health services and other goods ratcheted up to what they would have been in the absence of the ESP controls. Between 1965 and 1970, health care prices increased at an annual rate of 6.1%, and all prices increased by 4.2%. During the period of controls, 1971 through 1975, medical care prices increased by 6.9%. But it was soon after the period of price controls that health care inflation attracted the attention of most economists. From 1975 through 1980 health care prices increased at an annual rate of over 9.5%. Only energy prices exceeded the inflation experienced in the health sector.[17]

The experience of the early 1970s brought to light a peculiar aspect of the market for health services. While prices were moderating during the ESP, total expenditures were growing faster than they ever had. Puzzled by this experience, economists argued that because physicians acted as patients' brokers they had the potential to create demand in a period of falling or moderating prices.[18] If they could increase the demand for their services, total health expenditures could rise. When one combines this aspect of the market with the dominance of nonprofit institutions and a system of reimbursement whereby consumers paid only a fraction of the cost of the service, there was little doubt that the structure of the market was largely responsible for the rapid increases in prices and expenditures. After the ESP program was ended in 1974, health care prices resumed their upward spiral.

During the Carter administration the focus shifted from access to cost containment. President Carter and his planners at the Department of Health, Education, and Welfare felt they could enact national health insurance. Karen Davis, then assistant secretary for planning and evaluation, had written extensively on the need to improve access to the poor by federalizing the Medicaid program in order to eliminate major cross-state inequities.[19] But inflation had changed the priorities and the consciousness of Congress and forced the Carter administration to submit a hospital cost containment bill to Congress as the first step to a national health plan. The hospital cost containment bill never received serious attention. By 1979 political problems had all but taken the initiative from the health reform efforts. Just as Watergate killed the Nixon administration's Family Assistance Plan, Iran and a slowing economy derailed national health insurance and other radical changes in the structure of the industry.

The growth in for-profit hospitals was a change that most policymakers would have opposed in the radical days of the 1960s. Health care was perceived as different from other goods, and the overwhelming majority of hospitals are still considered nonprofit institutions. The American

Medical Association and the American Hospital Association have been opposed to the "corporate" practice of medicine because it was viewed as conflicting with both the interest of the patient and the professionalism of the provider. In spite of these objections from the professional associations and some consumer groups, the for-profit movement has taken hold and threatens to change the practice of medicine significantly. This development of the entreprenurial spirit in health care took place for the same reasons that profit-making firms and entrepreneurs enter any industry: the prospect of earning higher profits than can be earned with any other use of a given set of resources. Corporations like the Hospital Corporation of America, Cigna, Humana, and American Medical International, to name a few, have captured a significant part of the market. The Hospital Corporation of America, for example, grew from 2 hospitals in 1968 to 425 hospitals in 1985.[20] This growth cannot be translated into net gains in employment, since most of these HCA hospitals are the results of takeovers and mergers. The for-profits have infused a competitive spirit into the hospital market, where nonprofit hospitals previously had considered themselves above the plebian pursuit of profits. The entreprenurial spirit brought with it the marketing of hospital services as never before. Republic Hospital Corporation in Texas recently advertised to perform cataract surgery on weekends for discount prices. Republic reported the marketing was successful, and nonprofits have invited Republic to assist them in improving their own marketing schemes.

The for-profits are not without their critics. Foremost among them is Dr. Arnold Relman, editor of the *New England Journal of Medicine*, who argues that the for-profits sacrifice quality medical care for profits, refuse to treat low-income uninsured patients, and engage in practices inconsistent with the profession of medicine.[21] The issue of "dumping" poor and uninsured patients on public hospitals is potentially the most important access problem for black health care consumers. A study of the current practice of dumping is one well worth black policymakers' attention. Another issue that has important ramifications for minorities is the employment practices of the for-profit hospitals. In many cases, for-profit chains take over failing nonprofit institutions. Some of these institutions have labor contracts that are either abrogated or substantially modified as a condition of the takeover. Unions are aggressively fought off and long-established work rules are changed by the for-profits. Given the focus on profit maximization, these developments are not surprising, but the impact on hospital workers, is an issue that needs further study.

A conscious effort on the part of the federal government to change the distribution, production, and financing of health services resulted in some changes. The focus of structural change has been a shift from concern for increased access to a concern for controlling health care prices and expenditures. The evolution of health policy directed at controlling prices and costs is analogous to the unsuccessful efforts of a big-league manager in a pennant race to get runners in scoring position. A fair assessment of past health policy in this area would have to conclude that we have not moved beyond first base.

The Tax Equity and Fiscal Responsibility Act of 1982, provided for the experimental prospective payment system of diagnostic related groups (DRGs). Hospital services previously had been reimbursed on a retrospective basis, a system similar in design and outcome to the system of procurement of military equipment. Medicare, Medicaid, private insurance companies paid hospitals for services rendered plus an operating profit. The prospective payment system of DRGs reimburses hospitals on the basis of diagnosis. If the hospital can produce the service for less than the set price, it can keep the difference. If the hospital cannot produce the service for an amount equal to or less than the DRG price, it absorbs the loss. The effect of the new payment system is to put pressure on hospitals to get their costs under control and operate as efficiently as possible.

Expectations that DRGs would reduce patients' lengths of stay and workers' employment in hospitals have been realized. Since June of 1983 lengths of stay are down, and hospital employment is down by 70,000.[22] This quick response to the new payment system has led the Health Care Financing Administration to extend the system to states that were previously exempt because they had another cost containment system in place.

The DRG system combined with the industry's response, primarily in the form of the growth in for-profits and new types of delivery systems, has permanently changed employment opportunities in the industry. The first change, the reduction in hospital employment, is likely to continue for the rest of the decade. Pressure by insurance companies and corporations on hospitals to produce services for less has been effective. Estimates recently completed as part of a three-year study for the Commonwealth Fund of New York concluded that hospital employment will fall by another 300,000 by 1990.[23] Much of the employment reduction will take place in low-wage service jobs that have substantial minority representation. Licensed practical nurses, nursing aides, custodial workers, dietitians, and kitchen workers, as well as other support workers, will likely experience significant reductions in demand for their services by the nation's hospitals.

On the positive side, there will be increases in employment in non-hospital settings. Since hospital reimbursements are being reduced, hospitals and other entrepreneurs, physicians as well as nonphysicians, are quickly moving into the market for outpatient services. Ambulatory surgery centers, ambulatory care centers, and other organizations are expanding rapidly. The National Association of Ambulatory Care Centers estimates that the number of these centers has grown from 1,100 in 1983 to 2,500 in 1985.[24] They also estimate that by 1990 ambulatory care centers will capture 40% of the ambulatory care market.

If these institutions are close to reaching their expectations, and there is good reason for their optimism, it means that employment in these institutions will grow commensurately, offsetting the expected reductions in hospital employment. It is difficult to estimate whether the displaced hospital workers will be the ones hired by the expanding ambulatory care centers. One concern policymakers should be aware of is the mismatch between where the new jobs in the industry will be and where the workers likely to have the most problems in finding jobs are. The new jobs in the industry are going to be in upper-middle-class and middle-class neighborhoods. One characteristic of the for-profits, whether they be hospitals or ambulatory care facilities, is their desire to receive cash for services. This desire forces them to locate in higher-income neighborhoods. This situation is not necessarily an employment barrier; however, employment shifts are usually neither smooth nor painless, particularly for minority workers.

CONCLUSIONS AND POLICY RECOMMENDATIONS

The growth and structural change in the health industry over the past 20 years has been rapid and dramatic. Total dollars flowing into the industry and changes in the way health services are produced and financed have contributed to an expansion in total industry employment. The structural changes, particularly recent growth in the multi-institution, for-profit hospital sector and the establishment of the DRG system, have affected the geographic distribution of employment. The health care system is moving toward an organization that resembles other industries. Competition, cost control, marketing, and a decreased reliance on regulation to achieve social goals are trends that most observers predict will continue in the foreseeable future.

There are two major concerns blacks should consider when thinking about the consequences of these industrywide changes. First, a subject that this article did not address in detail, is the effect these changes have had on access to health services. The second concern is the employment effects of the changes. The predominance of cost containment as the No. 1 health policy goal is unfortunately being pursued without adequate consideration either for people who still do not receive enough quality medical services or for workers whose livelihoods depend on the jobs created by the system.

The worst fear is that black health workers will find employment prospects increasingly limited in most of the health professions in urban areas. In the 1970s there was the exodus of jobs in the basic industries. In the 1990s there may be an exodus from one of the sectors that was supposed to absorb the labor displaced from manufacturing. Whereas cost containment is an appropriate goal and the increase in for-profits may not necessarily be detrimental to minority employment, we must consider the distributional impacts of this policy on all citizens—workers as well as patients and providers.

In urban areas across the country minority workers are at risk of losing a large number of jobs, and at present there is no federal or state policy in place that addresses the shift in employment growth. To make matters potentially worse, educational institutions in general have not scaled down the production of health professionals so that future supplies will match future demands. There are currently thousands of black youth training in the nation's high schools, trade schools, and community colleges for jobs that simply may not exist in 10 years. Currently no one is disseminating that information to guidance counselors, parents, and students.

The primary way to improve the status of black health care workers should be to increase the number and proportion of black professionals in the higher-paying health occupations. This goal will require federal, state, and private initiatives to increase the numbers and proportions of blacks enrolled in the nation's health professional schools. In light of attempts to slow down the growth in the system, the case for increasing the numbers and proportions of black health professionals is likely to meet with resistance from white workers competing for those same limited slots. It has become a zero-sum game. But the case for increasing the proportion of black women and men in the higher-paying health professions is solid and worthy of policmakers' undivided attention. Without federal help it is unlikely that this goal can be accomplished. A recent study by Ruth Hanft shows that medical school students are acquiring significant amounts of debt.[25] She reports that medical students in private schools owe, on average, $31,000 by the end of their fourth year. The cost of education in the health professions is a barrier to increasing the proportion of black health care professionals. This constraint cannot be eliminated, but it can be reduced with targeted loans to qualified black health care students.

A second major policy recommendation that follows from the discussion addresses the problems black health care professionals currently in practice are facing. Currently over 80% of the clients of black physicians are black, but over 80% of black patients report having a white physician as their primary provider. For black physicians and other health care professionals this distribution of clients translates into lower incomes and greater economic instability. One change that could significantly improve the survival rate of black health care professionals would be to increase Medicaid fees up to the level other insurers pay for similar services. The second-class treatment of Medicaid patients often means second-class treatment for black health care professionals. Increasing fees would go a long way toward improving the viability of black health care providers. In an era of cost containment, recommending an increase in Medicaid fees is not likely to generate much congressional support. However, these increases can be financed by an increase in the taxes on cigarettes and alcohol. The revenue from these taxes could completely pay for increasing the viability of black health care professionals, improving the health of Medicaid recipients, and improving the health status of all Americans.

A final recommendation would be for policymakers to push for vigorous enforcement of antidiscrimination laws and affirmative action, particularly in the new for-profit firms in the industry. We currently do not know much about workers in the newer parts of the industry. A study of how minority workers are faring in the for-profits is overdue.

In conclusion, the changes taking place in the health industry provide black workers with challenges and opportunities. How well we do in manipulating the system to our advantage will depend on both external and internal factors. A government that realizes the continued underrepresentation of black health care professionals, particularly black women in the traditionally male-dominated professions, can be an indispensable ally, or a formidable foe. But our success ultimately will depend on the motivation and support each one of us can muster to accomplish small but significant victories in our struggle for economic and political equality.

NOTES

Research on this article was supported by the Commonwealth Fund of New York.

1. U.S. Department of Health and Human Services, *Health, United States, 1984* (Washington, D.C.: U.S. Government Printing Office, 1984).

2. *Health, United States, 1984.*

3. Eli Ginzberg and Miriam Ostow, "Organization and Financing of Medical Care," *Medical Care* 23, no. 5 (May 1985): 421-431.

4. *Health, United States, 1984.*

5. Ginzberg and Ostow and *Health, United States, 1984.*

6. Unpublished data from the Department of Labor.

7. James Curtis, *Blacks, Medical Schools and Society* (Ann Arbor: University of Michigan Press, 1971).

8. Manning Marable, "Black Education, Economics, and Social Policy: An Historical Perspective" (Working paper presented to Brandeis University Heller School, September 1985).

9. "Datagram," *Journal of Medical Education* 57. (June 1982).

10. U.S. Department of Health and Human Services, *Report of the Graduate Medical Education National Advisory Commission, Interim Report* (Washington, D.C.: Public Health Service, 1980).

11. Fred McKinney, "The Demand for Allied Health and Nursing Personnel by Employment Setting: Where Will the Jobs be in 1990 and 2000?" (Paper submitted to the Commonweallth Fund, September 1985).

12. Telephone conversation with representative of Local 1199 of New York City, August 20, 1985.

13. U.S. Department of Commerce, Bureau of the Census, *Detailed Population Characteristics, United States Summary, 1980 Census of the Population* (Washington, D.C.: GPO, 1982).

14. U.S. Department of Health and Human Services, *Report to the President and Congress on the Status of Health Personnel in the United States* (Washington, D.C.: Public Health Service, 1984).

15. R.B. Sutcliffe, *Industry and Underdevelopment* (London: Addison-Wesley Publishing, 1971).

16. *Health, United States, 1984.*

17. *Health, United States, 1984.*

18. Frederick W. McKinney, *Market Determinants of the Distribution and Quality of Physicians' Services* (Ph.D. dissertation, Yale University 1983).

19. Karen Davis and Cathy Schoen, *Health and the War on Poverty* (Washington, D.C.: The Brookings Institution, 1978).

20. Hospital Corporation of America, *Annual Report, 1984.*

21. Arnold Relman, "The New Medical-Industrial Complex," *The New England Journal of Medicine* 303, no. 17 (October 23, 1980) 963-970.

22. American Hospital Association, *Hospital Statistics, 1984* (Chicago: American Hospital Association, 1984).

23. Frederick W. McKinney, "The Demand for Allied Health."

24. Frederick W. McKinney, "The Demand for Allied Health."

25. Ruth Hanft, "Minorities and the Health Professions in the 1980s," *Health Affairs* 3, no. 4 (Winter 1984): 71-84.

PUBLIC POLICY AND HEALTH-CARE DELIVERY:
A PRACTITIONER'S PERSPECTIVE

Ron Law

Primary health care for inner-city residents is generally provided in institutional settings. This article describes a successful alternate model for health-care delivery: privately owned, for-profit, fee-for-service ambulatory care facilities. The Paul Robeson Health Organization in Harlem is described as an example of such a facility. Most of PRHO's patients are black; 55% are adult females. Some of the special health needs of inner-city women and the range of services available to them at PRHO are described. A conclusion of this article is that the economic and social benefits derived from a health delivery center like PRHO make this model one worth consideration for replication in other communities.

Health care is a multi-billion dollar industry. It has shown consistent yearly and record profits. Within the health-care industry, primary care has been the largest growth component. Despite industry-wide numerical and economic growth, inner-city areas are lacking in the number of available primary care facilities where health consumers can receive routine examinations, early detection and diagnosis of diseases, follow-up treatment, maternal and child care and immunization for preschool and school-age children.

Primary care for inner-city residents, in significant proportions, is generally provided in institutional settings. In New York City, for example, over half of what would qualify as ambulatory care services is provided at either a hospital outpatient department, an emergency room, or a neighborhood community health center.[1] This heavy reliance on institutional services places a tremendous burden on an already overtaxed health-care delivery system, which is simultaneously coping wth escalating cost and a growing ambulatory care population. The 1984 U.S. Public Health Statistics show that the two largest groups of health-care consumers were black women single heads of household and dependent children.[2]

According to federal criteria, communities similar to Central Harlem in demographic, socioeconomic, and health-status needs often qualify as "medically underserved areas." The certification of an area as "medically underserved" is given after an assessment is made of the factors that affect the need for and the uses of health resources and it is shown that there is less than one doctor for every 2,200 people. (The average for the nation is one doctor for 1,500 people.)

For the immediate population of Central Harlem there is one doctor for 4,500 people. This statistic alone points to a deficiency in health-care delivery. The implications are supported, in measure, by the type and incidence of reported illness and the number of facilities available to service this population.

It has been studied and documented that black women at the lower end of the economic scale usually use hospital emergency rooms and outpatient departments for ambulatory care, while their counterparts at the other end of the economic scale use a private physician's office.[3]

Regardless of the reported progress in health-care delivery, the rates of mortality, morbidity, and life expectancy reflect the differences in health statistics and health standards for black women. The National Center for Health Statistics reported that in 1981 the rate of heart diseases for black females was more than twice as high as the rate for white females. It was also reported that in 1981, 79% of white mothers received prenatal care in the first trimester of pregnancy compared with 62% of black mothers. And for the first time since 1970, the percentage of black mothers with early prenatal care remained stable.[4] The health-care reality for black women is the same whether they live on "Sugar Hill" or Lenox Avenue, whether employed with "good" health insurance coverage or a Medicaid recipient.

Harlem Hospital, the only municipal hospital servicing Central Harlem, reported in 1983 that it had 1.3 million patient visits and estimated there were at least 500,000 potential patient visits not seen by any service provider or hospital in the area. From a public policy prospective the impact is obvious. Harlem Hospital has become the doctor's office for the residents of Central Harlem. Harlem is located in a city of extreme wealth, with a multitude of renowned medical centers, seven medical teaching schools, and an abundance of skilled medical practitioners.

However the economically depressed areas of New York and its indigent population groups lack ready accessibility to ample primary-care services.

For low-income black women, Medicaid apparently alleviates the financial barriers to health care; but this is a myth. A perception has been created that these women, or even the aged and the poor, are receiving "acceptable" medical care when in fact the care available is limited. This perception is an illusion that must be shattered. Neither Medicaid nor Medicare has truly opened up the opportunities for medical care for the most needy because doctors in private practice are absent from inner cities.

Health-care delivery should be judged in terms of accessibility, availability, cost, and quality of care. For a Medicaid recipient the program pays for all medical and dental services in full, provided a medical practitioner can be found who will accept the Medicaid payment as full payment. (In New York State, 95% of dentists refuse to accept Medicaid payments because of the low fee schedule.) A financial outlay for a deductible or co-insurance payment is not required, as it would be for a private insurance. Medicaid addresses the cost of health care and allows access, but neglects a portion of the equation: availability.

Medicaid's purpose is to assure access to health care. It is limited in its ability to assure the availability of doctors in private practice. In urban areas like Harlem, where there is a high demand for health care among black women and dependent children, there are too few private practitioners to offer an alternative for any segment of the population. Likewise it is inequitable to force low-income black women living in inner cities to continue receiving primary care at institutional settings.

Proprietary (for profit) ambulatory care facilities are springing up across the country, specifically in suburban areas. The phenomenon of private practitioners abandoning the inner city is caused by the unprofitability of a practice based on current government program reimbursement levels. Likewise, propriety facilities shun the inner cities because their targeted patient population is self-payers or individuals with private insurance coverage, not Medicaid recipients. Truthfully, a private practitioner would find it difficult to operate profitably solely on Medicaid, even though there is a high health consumer demand population in inner cities.

Conversely, a large, privately-owned, multiservice center can operate profitably. In the heart of Harlem such a facility exists: the Paul Robeson Health Organization (PRHO). Its unique experience as a two-year old privately owned, fee-for-service, comprehensive, freestanding ambulatory care center offers a viable alternative in the health-care delivery system and it is worthy of consideration, study, and replication.

PRHO was designed as a diagnostic and treatment center to meet the specific demographic, socioeconomic, and health-status needs of the Harlem community. Most forms of health insurance are accepted by the center, particularly Medicaid. Because it does accept Medicaid, 70% of PRHO's patient population are Medicaid recipients, another 20% are third-party insured (insurance, union plan, or other private medical coverage), and 10% are identified as self-payers. To date, the patient population at PRHO is 55% women, 30% children, and 15% men. More importantly, PRHO offers a multiplicity of services within its 17,000 square feet, 32 exam rooms, and 15 doctors in a wide range of medical specialties: internal medicine, family practice, gynecology, pediatrics, podiatry, dermatology, clinical psychology, radiology, and laboratory facilities. It also contains a full service pharmacy and maintains a livery/ambulette service. In December 1985 the center began offering dental services. An additional feature of the center is its fully integrated online computer that permits efficient data collection and retrieval, medical diagnosis systems, appointment scheduling, and direct billing to Medicaid. Because of the center's large size, its patient visit capacity—based on concerns of quality care—is approximately 90,000 annual visits. The center is profitable at the rate of 30,000 visits. Now, over 14,000 patients use PRHO as their family physician.

The success of PRHO should be attributed to two primary factors: its staff and its investors. The staff of PRHO is a dedicated and committed group of doctors, physician assistants, ancillary medical staff, and support personnel who believe in the center's concept and feel a sense of accomplishment because of the quality of care offered. During a difficult period, the entire staff demonstrated their concern by offering to forgo receiving their salaries, enabling the center to keep its doors open.

The center's administration exemplified a sensitivity by establishing a community hiring program in an effort to hire black medical professionals who would not have otherwise benefited from proprietary medicine.

Equally, the investors, during the same difficult period, were willing to provide additional infusions of capital until the center was financially stable. The investors not only had a vested interest in the success of the center, but they also recognized the social benefit the center provided for a community where health-care facilities are limited. The combined efforts of the staff and the investors made PRHO a conceptual and financial success.

From its inception PRHO sought to be sensitive to the kind of services its patients would require. As a comprehensive diagnostic, treatment, and preventive health-care facility, there is an insistence on quality care and continuity of care and service. Admittedly the term "quality of care" is subjective. The health-care system is too big, too diffuse, too complex to lend itself to any one set of goals or standards. There is no common agreement as to the purpose and role of health care. It is a system rooted in the personal relationship that exists between the health-care consumer and the practitioner who supplies it.

The motivation for the consumer is derived from a perceived set of goals and needs. At PRHO the emphasis on "quality care" is intended to change the patient's behavior and attitudes toward health care and the need for it. For a black female receiving care at PRHO, who may be on Medicaid, a single head of household, and living in a hotel for homeless families, this behavioral and attitudinal change could lead to better health habits in the form of preventive care, good dietary habits, routine check-ups, and screening for undetected diseases.

The reference to single women living in a hotel for homeless families is based on empirical experience. PRHO built a solid base of medical care consumers through an aggressive outreach program. Because of the success of the outreach program, the center is the authorized medical provider for the following: the New York City Agency for Child Development, which supervises 61 day care centers in the Harlem area; the City University of New York, City College campus, where PRHO operates a satellite clinic as the official health center for students, faculty, and staff; The New York State Department of Substance Abuse Services, which funds all substance rehabilitation programs; and the New York City Human Resources Administration Crisis Intervention Center, which supervises homeless families temporarily sheltered in hotels. From the HRA Crisis Intervention Center alone, over 2,200 women received care between June and October 1985. This figure represents approximately 20% of the homeless families and is exclusive of the children. Within this population the types of illnesses detected were: anemia, breast cancer, tuberculosis of epidemic proportions, pregnancy, communicable diseases, and psychological problems related to stress. Among the children there was a high incidence of malnourishment, physical and sexual abuse, communicable diseases, teenage pregnancy, and one case of rickets. These are

the diseases that have been identified in a small percentage of the homeless who have come in for treatment. It is not known what poverty-related
illnesses have not been detected or treated in the remaining 80%.

Even a freestanding primary care ambulatory center is limited in the
services it can provide. The delivery of prenatal care in Harlem is a good
example. Within the general confines of Harlem there are at least four
facilities where prenatal care can be obtained. One is the OB maternity
clinic at Harlem Hospital, which has an approximately 60-bed capacity;
the other three facilities are community based, publicly-funded clinics
that offer limited services. A black woman living in Harlem and seeking
prenatal care has limited choices: either she receives her care in an institutional setting, which may be overcrowded and understaffed, or she can
receive limited care at one of the neighborhood clinics.

Early prenatal care is important because of its influence on the successful completion of the pregnancy, and because it is a determinant of
the overall health of the child. Studies have shown that adequate prenatal
care is generally accepted as an efficient way to improve the outcome of
pregnancy.[5] Additional studies prove that there is a close relationship
between the socioeconimic status of the mother and the probabilty that
she will seek and/or obtain needed prenatal care.[6] The availability of
private physicians offering prenatal care in Harlem is limited.

Private physicians hesitate to accept Medicaid recipients as patients
because of the low reimbursement allowed for complete global care. Another more important reason why private physicians are not available is
because of the 50% increase in the cost of medical malpractice insurance
within the State of New York. The rate increase has created a discentive
for private practitioners to continue their practices, even a practice located in the suburbs. From a public policy perspective it is quite apparent
that there is a need for greater availability and accessibility to prenatal
care in Harlem. Unfortunately, the alternatives are limited. The institutional setting is adequate to handle the heavy demand and the community
clinics offer abbreviated services.

At one time, PRHO offered prenatal and obstetrical care for its patient
population. But the malpractice insurance rate increase altered the delivery of these services. It becomes problematic to continue to offer
obstetrical care when physicians are closing their practices and refusing to
treat patients, regardless of race, economic status, or location. Of the two
physicians who provided the OB/GYN care, one quit and the other moved
to California to join a group practice. For a black women living in
Harlem, obtaining prenatal and obstetrical care becomes an onerous task.

To further demonstrate the impact on this community, when PRHO offered prenatal and obstetrical care it serviced approximately 800 women in a 10-month period. If the studies are correct and the socioeconomic characteristics of a population are also important determinants of both the need for and use of health services, will the infant mortality rate continue to rise for black women?

Health can be defined as a state of optimal physical, mental, and social well-being and not merely as the absence of disease and infirmity. In an ever-changing world of new scientific discoveries, new technology, changing population trends, and the disclosure of new illnesses, is it really possible to find the most appropriate use and distribution of health resources? Are the real issues confronting the health-care delivery system a question of painful choices between the trade-offs in the allocation of resources, the uncovering of gaps in the existing system, or the pinpointing of areas that have received too little attention? When private practitioners refuse to participate in the Medicaid program, this indirectly forces black women to seek care elsewhere or to forgo care altogether. There is a negative consequence in leaving the determination of health care to market forces, especially when the market forces have not been responsive to the needs of a significant portion of the population who already lack ready access to health services. Very few persons would argue against the need to control cost and make it more predictable, but at the expense of what segment of the population?

The health-care system currently operates under the influence of conflicting priorities: the need to contain escalating costs and the need to provide additional support to consumers of health services. The capability of existing facilities to expand to meet proven needs are limited by fiscal realties.

A strategy to encourage the establishment and construction of new freestanding primary-care centers is a temporary solution. The demonstrated economic and social benefits derived from a freestanding center like PRHO make it worth exploring for other communities. Our experience indicates that if there were more facilities where black women living in Harlem could receive primary and preventive care, there would very likely be a reduction in the high incidence of infant morality, the rate of deaths related to stroke or breast cancer, and an extension of the life expectancy for black women.

Providing additional facilities addresses only one part of the issue. The lack of private practitioners remains an unanswered question. To ignore the paucity of physicians in the inner-city areas only begs the issue. The

Reagan administration decision to shift the placement of National Health Service Corps doctors from urban to rural areas further reduces the available pool of trained medical personnel to serve the inner-city areas, while the urgency still exists.

The administration's shift to rural areas is based on the method used to determine if an area has a health manpower shortage. The current ratio for determining an area as being a "health manpower shortage area" is an inaccurate reflection of the medical personnel shortage for an area. It includes both office and institutionally based physicians in its computation. The impact on a community like Harlem, where a substantial majority of the physicians are institutionally based, is to have a medically underserved area deemed ineligible as a "health manpower shortage area" and thus denied even minimal assistance from federal agencies. This seemingly small differentiation of whether a doctor is office or hospital-based is significant because counting medical licenses in an institution does not speak to the doctor's availability to meet patients or adequately serve their medical needs. The count is taken of teaching personnel, specialists, interns, and residents as if they were equally competent, or available for primary care needs.

Also, the federal designation affects the way states evaluate medical needs which can have negative impacts even on institutions; e.g., limiting in-hospital beds, certificate of need concerns for high tech equipment, increasing or even maintaining certain teaching services at community hospitals, etc. The formula must be re-evaluated to provide equitable distribution of services.

The question of financial access to health care for low-income black women has been removed by the Medicaid program. But Medicaid cannot eradicate medical indigency because there are some medical services the program will not subsidize. It is too simplistic to assume that the problem of cost and access are merely those of economics and can be resolved merely by economic methods. This type of approach to health-care delivery ignores the complexity of our societal view of health care as well as having an adverse impact on the "quality of care."

NOTES

1. *Health Systems Plan 1980-85*. Health System Agency of New York City, p. 155, March 1980.
2. *Health, United States, 1984* (Washington, D.C.: U.S. Department of Health and Human Services National Center for Health Statistics, December 1984), Tables 45, 91.
3. *Health Statistics*, U.S. Depatment of Health, Education and Welfare, Public

Health Services, Health Resources Administration, Office of Health Resource Opportunity, Melvin H. Rudov, Ph. D. and Nancy Santangelo, MPH, p. 7, January 1978.

4. *Health, United States, 1984*, p. 10.
5. *Health Systems Plan 1980-1985*, p. 225.
6. *Health Systems Plan 1980-1985*, p. 226.

Discussion I

Beryl B. Jackson

Alvin and Sandra Headen and Fred McKinney's excellent essays "General Health Conditions and Medical Insurance Concerning Black Women" and "Employment Implications of a Changing Health-Care System," respectively, have stimulated my thinking in several directions. The main theses of these two essays were similar: concerns were expressed for the well-being of black women in areas of health, access to health care and employment, and existing and impending difficulties facing black women in terms of the inflationary condition of the health industry. This latter situation will increase in seriousness as the continued reliance on cost-containment to control the inflationary expenditures of the health industry goes forth.

McKinney provided in-depth analysis of the rapid growth and heavy expenditure of the health-care industry including a description of structural changes, organizational functioning, and black representation in the health field across socioeconomic and occupational statuses. He found a heavy concentration of black women in the lowest-paying jobs of the health care industry. In this respect, he addressed the tenuous positions of black women employed in the health industry and their vulnerability to changes in employment as a result of the cost-containment programs of the federal administration. Alvin and Sandra Headen focused primarily upon the alarming morbidity and mortality rates of black women across the lifecycle with their increasing vulnerability to the major chronic diseases and the reproductive health pattern of black women. Within the constraints of space the authors of both articles adequately addressed the topics they were assigned, raised related issues, and made a number of pertinent recommendations worthy of action.

A consideration of the central themes of these essays leads to the conclusion that the primary issues are: (1) poverty, which is inextricably linked to poor health and renders black women very vulnerable and places them at high risk to a number of health problems and chronic diseases, (2) failure of the Reagan administration to be sensitive to and propose programs of viable economic considerations that would be targeted to these high risk groups, and (3) underrepresentation of black health-care professionals across disciplines, a fact exacerbated by the reduction of federal programs that were designed to increase the number and proportion of black professionals in higher paying health occupations. There is no doubt that the present condition will only get worse because, as cutbacks are made in the name of cost-containment and accountability, the population that is going to be most profoundly affected are black women because of their increased representation in low-paying jobs and in unemployment. Regrettably, the present state of affairs highlights the perpetuation of the federal government's attitude of benign neglect towards blacks in general in the United States.

My comments address the following issues: (1) the interrelatedness of the biological, psychological, and social factors, and the linkage and relationship of these to the socioeconomic factor in the domain of health and illness; (2) the health implications that result from limited access to the health delivery system; and (3) the need for an alternative health-care delivery model that would facilitate more equitable access to health services and would be less disease-oriented and more health-focused.

My clinical experiences in different inpatient settings—community mental health center, neighborhood family health center, and home visitation have helped me to bring into focus not only the physical dimensions of health-care problems and needs of black women but also the psychological, social, emotional, and economic components. Koldjeski has stated that "health in its broadest context takes into account physical, mental, and social functioning of a person and the environments in which the person copes in order to try to achieve a measure of satisfaction in life.[1] This suggests that it is the interrelatedness and integration of these different dimensions of one's life that help to identify patterns in health and illness. Health has value because it makes the individual a happier and more productive person. Consequently, it is essential that both human and economic resources are made available and utilized to provide opportunities so essential for health if a person is to personally develop and socially contribute as well as to lower the incidence of physical and emotional disorders.

RELATIONSHIP BETWEEN PHYSICAL, EMOTIONAL HEALTH AND SOCIOECONOMIC RESOURCES

Since the turn of this century, the highest rate of mental disorders has been found among persons falling within the lowest socioeconomic levels.[2] Interestingly, these differences vanished or were reversed when socioeconomic status was controlled. These results support the conclusion that socioeconomic status rather than race per se is a more important factor in accounting for variations in mental health among black Americans. Within this group, "Black women still comprise the most destitute . . . educationally, economically, and politically,"[3] and presumptively are the most vulnerable. For all combinations of race and sex, black women are clinging to the lowest rung of the socioeconomic ladder and falling. There is a predictive pattern that suggests this downward trend will continue. It would be noted that despite the enormous implications of these findings for social, economic, and health policy reform, the lamentable fact is that today, as in 1970, the median income of blacks is just above half of the median income for white families.[4]

The effects of economic deprivation usually go beyond physical illness. In 1978 the United States Commission on Civil Rights Report indicated that black women, historically because of racism, social class, restrictive participation in the labor force, and unemployment, have been psychologically affected in terms of their self-esteem. Also, black women have had to take jobs that are less valued by society and with less upward mobility than majority men and women, and they are often placed in traditional stereotyped jobs. This has been noted to have had deleterious effects on their mental health.[5]

In addition, it has been empirically documented that not only are black women exposed to greater psychological stress due to the lack of economic resources and low self-esteem but are more likely to be subject to stressful life events. Unemployment, marital instability, loss of job, long-term joblessness, low or irratic income, poverty, and frequent changes and relocations have been identified as powerful stressors that tend to produce stress, and have been heavily implicated in a number of physical and mental problems.[6]

It has been estimated that life events account for 4% to 15% of the variance in physical and mental symptoms. Such changes, however measured, have been associated with a wide range of impairing or disabling consequences such as physical illness, sudden cardiac arrest, myocardial infarction, anxiety, depression, social maladjustment, neuroticism, somatic preoccupation, aggression, paranoia, suicidal tendencies, and psychiatric symptomology.[7] Since the cadence and density of stress events is influenced by the availability of socioeconomic resources, it is not surprising that black Americans are exposed to higher levels of stress than their white counterparts and to the greater incidence of mental and physical problems associated with stress.

LIMITED ACCESS TO HEALTH CARE: IMPLICATIONS FOR HEALTH

Although federal health expenditures have increased over 350% since 1970 and now absorb almost 11% of the gross national product, a change in national health policy shows that real federal expenditure for health in the 1980s has been reduced to less than one-third of that of the 1970s.[8] Consequently, health and social institutions have responded by formulating priorities and allocating resources accordingly. Unfortunately, the "downsizing" of these programs affects populations already at the lowest rung of the ladder—black women.

Under the Reagan administration, economic considerations have been the driving force for public policy formulation of health care and this factor determines not only access to health delivery systems but also the quality and quantity of care provided. At the beginning of the budget cuts, some 12% of Americans, or 24 million people, were without adequate access to medical care. Of this number, 2% were not able to obtain regular health care of any kind. According to Richardson, "If you . . . happen to be poor your health problems are likely to be greater and your access to proper health care services are more difficult than that of the rest of the population."[9]

Interestingly, the national policy to cut health cost, which results in the difficulty poor people experience in accessing health-care systems, "is not based on economic necessity but rather on political choice. The Reagan administration and Congress have not reduced government spending but shifted it from domestic to military purposes and interest payments on accumulating national debt."[10] Aiken, in a related statement appraising access to health care in America, said: "It is not clear that in a time of constricting resources the country will be willing to place a high priority on the expenditures necessary to bring about marginal improvements in quality in a health care system believed to be one of the best in the world."[11] In the same vein, the National Council of State Human Service Administrators reported that:

Inflation took its toll on social and health-care services for low-income families and children, as federal funding of these services failed to keep pace with rising cost of providing them. . . . Programs for low-income families and children, while constituting less than 10% of the federal expenditures, sustained 30% of all the budget cuts in the last four years. . . . The effects of cuts have been statistically verified by the U.S. General Accounting Office. Up to 60% of the families losing AFDC had no health-care coverage, more than half reported running out of food, and more than a fourth had utilities shut off in their homes. These families were pushed deeper in poverty and their children lost health, nutrition and day-care services.[12]

In response to McKinney's perception that the possibility exists that many of the retrenched workers from the health industry may find employment in other health-related areas such as the ambulatory care settings, it should be noted that such a shift may be accompanied by many hardships because of the increased use of technology in the health-delivery system that neccessitates special education and training, which black women as a group do not have and may experience difficulty in obtaining. Such changes will likely create additional stress for these employees following the loss of employment. Many women will either be asked to acquire the necessary skills before employment can be offered them or younger women prepared in health technology may be hired over them.

Given the structural inequities characterizing the employment of black Americans in general and black women in particular, the disemployment effects of the shift in health-care delivery systems is serious, especially for older black women. This concern for black women at midlife and older looms in magnitude as the population gets older and more female.

AN ALTLERNATIVE HEALTH-CARE MODEL

There is no question that an alternative set of health-care and management intervention strategies, one that is more sensitive and responsive to the needs of black women, is much overdue. It is very unfortunate that the hospital cost-containment bill signed by President Jimmy Carter, which he had intended only to be a precursor of a national health insurance plan, has been allowed to remain a permanent regulatory mechanism in the health-care industry. What is more, this cost-containment plan is in part responsible for the mushrooming of a competing "for profit corporate practice of medicine" that directly contributes to the inflationary cost of health care and indirectly to the increasing difficulty poor black women experience in accessing the health-care services.

Obviously, what is needed is a national insurance plan that is embedded in an alternative health-oriented system of care rather than a disease-oriented one. The concept of a health insurance plan is not new. It has been the goal of many concerned politicians for decades but continues to be a goal that has not yet been realized. The idea of changing to a philosophy of care that is more health-oriented has already been utilized by many health-care providers, but needs to be generalized across the nation. "The newly perceived importance of ambulatory care, primary care, and family care centers, home health services, and other patterns of care, the increasing utilization of such types of care, and the provision of public and private payment of it clearly show the impact of the evolving health orientation."[13]

There is no doubt that the health-oriented model of care, though limited in scope at the present time, has demonstrated that it can help to prevent or modify disease and illness and can be used successfully to collaborate and augment the hospital's care of the sick. Marieskind, concerned about the quality of health care available to women in general and to minority women in particular, has also advocated an alternative policy consideration and new goals for health status. She stated that "one of [the] pressing health status goals concerning women in the United States is to improve the morbidity and mortality rates of minority women." She further expressed this belief for one area of care: "Women's health needs might be more appropriately served (and at lower cost to the nation) through a health care model that utilizes family practitioners, working in conjunction with midwives for the obstetrical and contraceptive needs of women."[14]

The integration of a national insurance plan and a health-oriented philosophy of care would more appropriately serve the health-care needs of women in general and black women in particular by providing continuity of care across the lifespan. Regrettably, the present trend towards specialization in obstetrics and gynecology has provided poor black women with health care that is disproportionately centered around the reproductive years and at best is limited and unsatisfactory.

With an alternative national health policy there would be greater collaboration among care providers in different disciplines. It would be possible and more economical using this model of care to assemble, coordinate, and utilize the necessary expertise of various professionals and technicians such as: the general practitioners, professional nurses, technical nurses, nurse midwives, clinical nurse specialists from the different clinical areas, primary care nurses, family nurse practitioners, social workers, psychologists, as well as the internists, the specialists from all areas of surgery, obstetrics, and gynecology to meet the total range of women's health needs.

To summarize: (1) poverty is the primary contributing influence affecting the physical and psychological health status of black women, and (2) public policy has done little to curb the inflationary health-care industry and reduce the difficulty poor black women experience in adequately accessing health-care services. These are crucial issues that should appeal to the sensitivity of the federal, state, and local governments as well as the public and private sectors of the American society. Bold new actions should be taken to intervene appropriately to change the alarming rates of morbidity and mortality from chronic diseases and the psychological problems among black women. A national health insurance plan is one approach that would address the health problems of black women.

NOTES

1. D. Koldjeski, *Community Mental Health Nursing: New Directions in Theory and Practice* (New York: John Wiley and Sons, 1984).

2. G. Antunes, C. Gordon, C. Gaitz, et al. "Ethnicity, Socioeconomic Status and Etiology of Psychological Distress," in *Sociology and Social Research 53* (1974), pp. 361-368; G. Comstock, & K. Helping, "Symptoms of Depression in Two Communities." *Psychological Medicine* 6, (1976), pp. 551-565; B.P. Dohrenwend, and B.S. Dohrenwend, "Social Class and Stressful Events," in E.H. Hare and J.K. Wing (Eds.), *Psychiatric Epidemiology: Proceedings of the International Symposium* (Oxford University Press, 1969, pp. 321-328); B.S. Dohrenwend & B.P. Dohrenwend, "Overview and Prospects for Research on Stressful Life Events," in B.S. Dohrenwend and B.P. Dohrenwend (Eds.), *Stressful Life Events: Their Nature and Effects* (New York: John Wiley and Sons, 1974); W. Eaton & G. Kessler, "Rates of Symptoms of Depression in a National Sample," *American Journal of Epidemiology* 114 (1981), pp. 528-538; R.R. Frerichs, C.S. Aneshensel, and V.A. Clark, "Prevalence of Depression in Los Angeles County," *American Journal of Epidemiology,* 113 (1981), pp. 691-699; C. Gaitz and J. Scott, "Age and the Measurement of Mental Health," *Journal of Health and Social Behavior* 13 (1972), pp. 55-67; F. Ilfeld, "Psychological Status of Community Residents Along Major Demographic Dimensions," *Archives of General Psychiatry* 35 (1978) 716-724; J. Mirowsky and C. Ross, "Minority Status, Ethnic Culture, and Distress: A Comparison of Blacks, Whites, Mexicans and Mexican Americans," *American Journal of Sociology* 86 (1980) 479-495; G. Warheit, C. Holzer, and S. Arey, "Race and Mental Illness: An Epidemiological Update," *Journal of Health and Social Behavior* 16 (1975), pp. 243-256; W. Yancy, L. Rubsby, and J. McCarthy, "Social Position and Self Evaluation: The Relative Importance of Race," *American Journal of Sociology* 78 (1972), pp. 338-359.

3. L. Rodgers-Rose, "Some Demographic Characteristics of the Black Woman," in L. Rodgers-Rose (Ed.), *The Black Woman* (Beverly Hills: Sage, 1980), p. 40.

4. B.E. Anderson, "Economic Patterns in Black America," in J.D. Williams (ed.), *The State of Black America* (New York: National Urban League, 1982).

5. U.S. Commission on Civil Rights, *Social Indicators of Equality for Minorities and Women* (Washington, D.C., 1984, pp. 39-46.

6. S. Cobb, "Social Support as a Moderator of Life Stress," *Psychosomatic Medicine* 38 (1976), pp. 300-314; S. Gore, "The Effects of Social Support in Moderating the Health Consequences of Unemployment," *Journal of Health and Social Behavior* 19 (1978), pp. 157-165; R.F. Kelly, "The Family and the Urban Underclass," *Journal of Family Issues 6*(2, June 1985), pp. 158-184; L.I. Pearlin, M.A. Liberman, E.G. Managhan, and J.T. Mullan, "The Stress Process," *Journal of Health and Social Behavior 22* (1981), pp. 336-356; L.S. Syme and L. Berkman, "Social Class, Susceptibility and Sickness," *Journal of Epidemiology 104* (1976), pp. 1-8.

7. D.T. Dekker and J.T. Webb, "Relationships of Social Readjustment Rating Scale to Psychiatric Patients Status, Anxiety and Social Desirability," *Journal of Psychosomatic Research 18* (1974), pp. 125-130; J.H. Johnson and I.G. Sarason, "Moderator Variables in Life Stress Research," *Stress and Anxiety 6* (1978), pp. 151-168; E.S. Paykel, "Recent Life Events of Clinical Depression," in E.K. Gunderson and R.H. Rahe (Eds.), *Life Stress and Illness* (Springfield, Ill.: Thomas, 1974).

8. L.H. Aiken, *Health Policy and Nursing Practice* (New York: McGraw-Hill, 1981).

9. W. Richardson, "Poverty, Illness and the Use of Health Services in the United States," *Hospitals 43* (1969), pp. 34-40.

10. The National Council of State Administrators. *Public Welfare*, Summer 1985.

11. Aiken, p. 12.

12. National Council of State Administrators, p. 6.

13. American Nurses' Association, Congress for Nursing Practice. *Nursing: A Social Policy Statement* (Kansas City, Mo., 1980).

14. H.I. Marieskind, "Toward a National Health Policy for Women's Health," in *Women in the Health System: Patients, Providers and Programs* (St. Louis: C.V. Mosby, 1980), pp. 312, 314.

DISCUSSION II

Bernadette Chachere

It was stated in a committee report submitted to the secretary of the Department of Health, Education, and Welfare that "the key fact about the health service system as it exists today is the disorganization . . . fragmentation and disjunction that promote extravagance and permit tragedy." Perhaps it is appropriate and consistent that the same might be said of Fred McKinney's analysis and policy recommendations in the "Employment Implications of a Changing Health-Care System."

From his analysis of the structural changes taking place in the health-care industry, McKinney concludes that the two major issues facing blacks are access to quality health care and employment. Three policies are proposed to address these concerns: (1) increase the number and proportion of black professionals in the higher paying health occupations via targeted loans to black health-care students; (2) increase the economic viability of current black health-care providers via higher Medicaid payments to black physicians; and (3) push for vigorous enforcement of antidiscrimination and affirmative action in the new for-profit firms in the industry. McKinney proposes that a tax be levied on cigarettes and alcohol to raise the necessary revenue to implement these policy recommendations. While one could take issue with the fairness of such a tax, which will undoubtedly exhibit a high degree of regresssivity as well as further subsidize physicians who on average earn $68,000 per year, this critique will instead focus on the extent to which the policies proposed can address the problems posed.

The "access to health-care problem" stems primarily from two interrelated sources: the geographical and functional distribution of providers, in particular physicians. Alternatively stated, there is a mismatch between where health care is most critically needed and where providers are geographically located. Additionally, there is a mismatch between the *kind* of care needed and the *kind* of care provided. That physicians, both black and white, tend to locate in high-income areas has been well documented and researched and is partially explained by the functional distribution of providers, i.e., the extensive phenomenon of medical specialization. In general, health-care services in the United States are oriented toward curative rather than preventive care. This orientation produces the need for specialists (for each illness) rather than generalists; episodic care (for each illness) rather than continuous care; crisis-induced demand inelasticities (for each illness) rather than normal downward sloping demand curves. This curative orientation increases the costs of health care and further exacerbates the access problem for low-income minorities.

In short, the access problem is not likely to be alleviated with policies that focus only on increasing the total number of providers, again physicians in particular, with no regard for geographical and functional distribution of the providers and their orientation toward curative health care. This is supported by the conclusions of the analysis by Headen and Headen on the health conditions of black women. Their findings are that for black women of all ages, obesity is a major health risk; for black women under the age of 34, pregnancy complications, violence, and accidents are the major health problems; and for older black women, diabetes, cardiovascular and cerbrovascular diseases, hypertension, and obesity are the major health problems. It is not clear that "access" problems of black women will be corrected by increasing the number and/or fees of black surgeons, radiologists, dermatologists, anesthesiologists, etc., nor is it clear that nontargeted general subsidies to medical school students would change the existing functional distribution of health providers. Admittedly black women are but a part of the total black community, but the findings of the Headen analysis certainly suggest the necessity of considering specific health problems prior to making policy recommendations to increase the total number of providers. Supply-side policies must be formulated to meet demand-side problems. In fact, the health problems of black women may be substantially reduced with education programs aimed at dieting, weight-gain prevention, pre- and postnatal self-care, nutrition etc., none of which require extensive medical training of eight years, the current minimum required in U.S. medical schools. There have been studies which suggest that a greater use of paramedical personnel would reduce costs without losses in quality of care. Moreover the use of paramedical personnel also has positive employment implications for blacks in the health-care sector, the second major concern addressed by McKinney.

McKinney predicts declines in the employment of black health-care workers as a consequence of current cost containment policies. The cost-containment policies discussed are the use of the prospective payment system of diagnostic-related groups (DRGs) to determine Medicare and Medicaid reimbursements and the promotion of for-profit hospitals. Because DRGs are expected to reduce "lengths of stay" in hospitals, employment of hospital personnel is predicted to decline as a consequence. Given the newness of the DRG policy, data to test the hypothesis are scant. However, McKinney finds the decrease in lengths of stay and employment reported in the June edition of *Hospital Statistics* supportive of his hypothesis. While simultaneous decreases in lengths of stay and employment may establish a correlation between the two, it does not establish causation. If the total number of patients admitted remains the same, the fact that any one patient stays a shorter period would not affect the number of hospital personnel needed to provide services to all patients. Why should higher patient turnover reduce the required number of nurses, assistants, orderlies, dieticians, etc.? Hospital personnel employment is a function of hospital admissions. If hospital personnel are viewed as variable inputs and hospital services measured on the basis of number of patients served, then high turnover (reduced length of stay) may have a positive effect on employment. Unless the DRG policy reduces total hospital admissions, the explanation for declining hospital personnel lies elsewhere.

The growth of for-profits, McKinney predicts, will have little impact on employment "since most of these . . . are the result of takeovers and mergers" of failing non-profits. But as a condition of the takeover, for-profits either abrogate or substantially modify labor contracts. Additionally, "unions are aggressively fought off and long established work rules are changed." What is surprising is that McKinney concludes this discussion of the for-profits with the statement that it ""is not surprising or necessarily bad for hospital workers but it is an issue that needs further study." Certainly further discussion, if not study, is necessary to show how such union relations are *not bad* for hospital workers. This conclusion perhaps explains why no policy recommendations are made on this issue even though the majority of black health-care workers are in hospitals and in occupations affected by union contracts. See Table 3 and note McKinney's reference to New York City hospital workers Local 1199—"of their 90,000 active members, 65% are black."

A general weakness of the McKinney analysis and subsequent policy recommendations is that he approaches the topic as if there were a health-care system or health-care industry. When in fact what creates the access problem and, to some degree, the employment problem for minorities is that health-care services are *not* delivered within a system, as we commonly use the term. Nor can we view hospital services and physicians services as they are currently delivered as being in the same industry; products between the two are not substitutable. Additionally, physicians operate as entrepreneurs in a fee-for-service compensation arrangement that permits supply to create its own demand, while the majority of blacks are employees of hospitals. Hospitals have long been characterized by intense stratification of personnel by occupation. Internal dual labor market theory provides a more appropriate paradigm for analysis of economic conditions of hospital workers. Health-care analysis that fails to recognize the heterogeneity of the services provided and the inputs used fall prey to the economic fallacy of composition. What is appropriate resource utilization for one good or service, such as primary care, may not be for another, such as emergency care. What serves the economic interest of one provider, such as physicians, may not serve the interest of another provider, such as orderlies.

SECTION INTRODUCTION

Stephanie Y. Wilson

This section contains three articles. The first is "Women and Self Employment in Urban Tanzania" by Willene A. Johnson; the second, "Jamaican Working Class Women: Producers and Reproducers," is authored by Beverly J. Mason. Johnson and Mason state boldly that black women have always worked; this is not to be disputed. The question for researchers and policy analysts remains as to how to evaluate and recognize their efforts given the deficiency of an appropriate database. For this reason both articles are based on independent surveys. The third article, "You Have Struck a Rock: A Note on the Status of Black Women in South Africa" by Julianne Malveaux, lends personal insights into the role black women are forced to assume in a developed country divided by apartheid. The author establishes the link of denied opportunities between black women in the developing world and black women subjugated to a low-income status in a developed one. This introduction places these essays in the context of the role of women in the world and regional economies and in the individual country situation.

THE WORLD

The postwar period has been one of unprecedented economic growth. From 1955 to 1980 the world's output tripled in real terms, and despite the sharp increase in population, income per capita on average doubled. A rapid expansion of trade, production, and capital flows made way for an expansion in the paid labor force of an estimated 700 million people, 40% of them women. The economic growth, however, was not uniform. In the developing countries, population growth outpaced the expansion of the modern industrial sector. There were increasing numbers of unemployed and underemployed. Overall, the disparity in income between developing and developed countries continued to widen and there was little change in the distribution of income between the richest and poorest countries of the world.

Another feature of this period was the decline of agriculture in the world economy. The agricultural sector, which in 1950 had employed about two-thirds of the world's paid labor force, accounted for less than half of the total by 1980. Employment in both industry and services by International Labor Organization (ILO) estimates grew twice as fast as agriculture. The expansion of the service sector became important for the growing number of women seeking jobs. During the 1980 to 1983 period, the world recession, marked by a high rate of inflation coupled with large-scale unemployment, bore most heavily on the developing countries and poorer populations. Women continued to enter the labor force in large numbers, but their unemployment rate rose faster than men's. The implications of stronger women's participation in the labor force and its social, political, and economic effects on the world and country economies are important topics demanding careful attention.

THE REGIONS

From 1950 to 1980, six regions of the world showed a rise in the representation of women in the paid labor force (ages 15-64)—South Asia, Oceania, Western Europe, the Far East, Latin America, and North America; two regions showed a decline—the Middle East and Africa; and one region showed no change—Eastern Europe. The largest influx of women into the labor market occurred in North America. Despite these variations, the dominant trend in most of the world is toward greater visibility of women in the labor force.

THE CARIBBEAN

In the Caribbean there is a rapid urbanization due to high rural-to-urban migration and high birth rates in the cities. In Jamaica, the country examined in Mason's study, 46.6% of migrants to the capital city of Kingston are female. This movement of women into urban areas has led to two patterns of development. The first is an accelerated movement of women into paid employment in the formal sector. The second is a continuing high rate of female participation outside of the formal structures in primarily urban areas. In Jamaica, the labor force participation rate of women is 70%. The ILO has found that in practically all of the Caribbean countries more than one half of the female urban work force works in the service sector.

Between 50% and 70% of women work in domestic service, which constitutes between 30% and 45% of the total urban female economically active population. In Jamaica many women engage in what the locals refer to as "scuffling," which comprises activities ranging from trading and bartering to performing various odd jobs. It is not unusual to have women working in both the formal and informal sectors either simultaneously or cyclically as dictated by economic conditions or seasonal fluctuations. Studies have found that while men were preferred by employers, women often guided the varied employment strategies of the family, including male decisions to work in the modern sector.

This high participation by women calls for a well-defined response and a well-thought-out strategy by governments in this region to channel attention and resources to vocational and educational programs that target women. Failure to do so may result in a gross underutilization of the labor and brainpower of this segment of the population.

AFRICA

In Africa, unlike the Caribbean, the urban areas are growing rapidly but the population of Sub-Saharan Africa is still primarily rural. A mere 17% of the estimated 1980 population was living in urban areas of any size according to World Bank figures. The percentage of women living in urban areas in the most recent two censuses for Tanzania, the country studied by Johnson, was about 5% in 1967 and 12% in 1978. The female/male ratio in the urban population of Tanzania was .90 in 1978. Women constitute at least 40% of all within-country migrants in Africa, and in some cases there are a greater number of female than male migrants. Age distribution also plays an important part in the labor force participation of women. The female age distribution in the African cities is younger than that in the rural areas, although it is older than that of urban males. The female/male ratio of the economically active population is .85.

A large informal sector exists throughout Africa that is similar to that in the Caribbean. Small-scale traders and street-vendor ranks are comprised of women, including those who do odd jobs for households and work as midwives, seamstresses, caterers, launderers and factory piece workers. In this context, where there is a high correspondence between gender and occupation, there is a great opportunity for structuring the delivery of government support services to focus on women.

THE COUNTRY ECONOMIES

Tanzania and Jamaica, two of the countries studied in these articles, share the Pan-African exprience. There, however, the macroeconomic similarities end. Tanzania is a low-income country ranked 12th in the world, based on ascending order of its gross national product (GNP) by the World Bank. Jamaica is a middle-income country ranked 63rd. The population of Tanzania in 1983 was 20.8 million; Jamaica has a mere 2.3 million. The total area of Tanzania is 240,000 square kilometers; for Jamaica it is only 11,000. Life expectancy in Tanzania is 55 years, and for Jamaica it is 70 years. The growth of production across sectors of the economy was positive in Tanzania during the period 1965-83; in Jamaica growth was also positive in 1965-73 but negative in 1973-83.

More specifically, the industrial and service sectors in Tanzania grew by 0.2% and 5.4%, respectively, between 1973 and 1983. The declines in these two sectors in Jamaica were 4.3 and 0.3, respectively. Also, population in Tanzania between 1973 and 1983 grew 3.3%, while Jamaica's population grew a mere 1.3%.

Out of these two divergent countries similarities emerge about women; particularly women who work. The dearth of information about such women has been recognized. The need for more information has been argued. The fact that women head households and have a significant impact on the development process has been documented.

In contrast, South Africa is listed as an upper-middle-income country by the World Bank and, according to United Nation statistics, one out of every three black South African workers is a woman. However, most women are limited to domestic farm and factory work. The average earnings of black South African women are less than one-half of South African male workers and about 8% of the income of white males. A large reason for this disparity is the limited access to education. Boys are given preference in education, and steep educational fees limit a family's ability to educate their children.

Agriculture in South Africa is second only to gold as an earner of foreign exchange. Black South African labor greatly contributes to both industries with little to show for the effort. Capital intensive mechanization has resulted in a decline in permanent workers and has led to the use of seasonal workers—mostly women who receive compensation solely "in kind," which increases their dependence on money sent from husbands and sons in urban areas.

In the industrial sector, black S.A. women tend to be concentrated in low-paying jobs such as the clothing, textile, food processing, and canning industries. These women provide a "cheap labor" source to the bantustan industries, which were planned to curb the flow of black South Africans into the urban areas.

The Malveaux article discusses the constraints faced by black women when subjected to the system of apartheid. Her study contributes to a sparse literature on the plight of such black women in South Africa.

As Gloria Scott notes in her comments, the literature on women in developing countries is extremely limited. The articles in this volume add to that small body of literature which attempts to give further explanation to the vital economic role women play within their societies. The essays by Mason and Johnson attempt to analyze what heretofore has remained elusive—the role of women not only in the formal but also the informal sector. The research should be seen as an important contribution to a further refinement of our thinking on women in international development.

WOMEN AND SELF-EMPLOYMENT IN URBAN TANZANIA

Willene A. Johnson

This study examines the employment and earnings of self-employed women in urban Tanzania. Most of the empirical evidence comes from a household survey that interviewed 5,543 adults in seven mainland towns during 1971. Although women represent almost 28% of all urban self-employed, they are clustered into a few low-income activities. Women's involvement in household and subsistence production leads them to work fewer hours in market activities, but their lower earnings are mostly due to their restricted access to education and capital.

This article focuses on one aspect of Tanzanian women's economic activity: their involvement in urban self-employment. Our analysis of women's earnings from self-employment is a part of a larger study of women's economic activity in urban Tanzania. The responses to the NUMEIST household survey conducted in seven towns in mainland Tanzania during 1971 provided the empirical evidence for this analysis of women's employment and earnings.[1] Most of the larger study deals with women's earnings in wage employment. This part of the study examines women's role within the self-employment sector, looks at the determinants of women's earnings in that sector, and considers the effects of traditional law and colonial and independent government policy on women's earnings from self-employment. We begin with a brief description of women's involvement in the Tanzanian urban economy and then move on to issues of women and self-employment.

WOMEN IN URBAN TANZANIA

The women of the urban areas of Tanzania are women in transition. In 1971, two-thirds of Tanzanian urban women were rural-urban migrants.

Some were primarily involved in household production or schooling before migrating to town. A few were involved in wage activities or non-agricultural self-employment. But most were economically active in subsistence or cash-crop agriculture in the rural areas. For many urban women, then, their transition was from an active involvement in rural production to a still active but less clearly defined involvement in the urban economy.

African women in general and Tanzanian women in particular remain economically active in the urban areas. Women's economic activity is often overlooked, however, because of survey techniques, definitions of economic activity, and the nature of women's work. Thus, although the 1967 *Population Census* of Tanzania shows a labor force participation rate of 16.9% for urban women, alternative measures based on NUMEIST data yield participation rates ranging up to 41%.[2] Women's economic activity has been overlooked, in part because their activity is not as easily measured as that of their male counterparts. Women are more likely to be involved in multiple roles, supplementing low earnings from wage employment with earnings from self-employment. These market activities are often performed while women are involved in subsistence or household production. Since the market activities may be sporadic or in joint production with nonmarket work, they are often overlooked by census and labor surveys.

Although both men and women are involved in wage-employment, self-employment, and subsistence production, the extent of involvement in each type of activity differs by gender. Uneven technological and structural changes have had differential impacts on the various subgroups of the urban population. The predominance of males in wage employment has fostered the misconception that African women withdraw from the labor force upon entering the urban areas. On the other hand, subsistence production has persisted in the urban areas of Tanzania largely because of the subsistence activities of married women. Single women appear more likely to be engaged in wage employment, while divorced and widowed women are overrepresented among the self-employed. Thus, even though a significant proportion of women are economically active, the social and economic responsibilities which define their role as wife and mother also define their nondomestic economic activities.

Much of the recent work on women and development has revealed that economic modernization and changing patterns in the gender division of labor have created situations where both modern and traditional individuals are juxtaposed within the same family. Thirty years ago, Lewis understood that his metaphor of islands of capitalist employment surrounded by a "vast sea of subsistence workers" could apply to people as well as industrial enclaves. He emphasized that a small number of individuals might be trained in modern techniques and educated in Western culture while the great majority of their compatriots "live in quite other worlds."[3] In terms of wage employment, women and men are for the most part on the same "islands." Both male and female wage earners are exposed to similar economic factors that shape the characteristics of employment in the various sectors of the economy. Although there are some influences on women's earnings that are gender specific, these are overshadowed by factors which affect both men and women in a similar fashion.

If we were to extend Lewis' metaphor to self-employment activities, we might be forced to conclude that women are, for the most part, still in the sea of less productive employment whereas some men have found refuge on islands of high productivity and high earnings. Self-employment in urban Tanzania comprises a wide range of activities, including some using traditional techniques and yielding low incomes, and others more obviously integrated into the modern urban economy.[4] Although self-employment in urban Tanzania is not limited to the marginal, low-productivity economic enterprises so often associated with nonwage employment in developing countries, such enterprises and activities coexist with activities characterized by large capital investments and high earnings. In effect, self-employment, like wage employment, has been shaped by the uneven nature of the development process. Sabot's finding that the distribution of income is clearly bimodal in six out of eight types of self-employment is consistent with the hypothesis that some of the self-employed within each type of activity can be classified as part of the "marginal sector."[5] Our study indicates that gender plays an impotant role in shaping the uneven nature of this distribution and that women are usually at the lower end of the bimodal distribution of self-employment income.

SELF-EMPLOYED WOMEN WORKERS

Self-employed women have lower earnings because they are clustered into low-income activities and because in most of these activities women earn less than their male counterparts. Women represent 27.8% of the self-employed whereas they are only 14% of urban wage employees. Despite this sizable representation, women are involved in fewer types of self-employment activities than men. Table 1 lists the proportion of women involved in each type of activity and their average earnings in each occupation. There are no women in the sample working in portage or other transport services, no women in building construction, none engaged in fishing, and no self-employed women professionals. Except for the work of porters, all of the unrepresented categories have an average income well above the statutory minimum wage of 180 shillings per month (approx. 7 shillings = $1).[6] As a result of their concentration in activities that yield low incomes, the average earnings of self-employed women are 148 shillings per month, well below the male average of 543 shillings. The earnings of women are higher in only one activity: bar and restaurant keeping. These hotels and restaurants provide urban workers with hot meals, while the bars serve beer and roasted meat in the evenings. Bar and restaurant keeping was also the only non-wage activity where the average female earnings exceeded the minimum wage.

Women's self-employment appears to be almost a sector within a sector. Whereas the self-employment sector in urban Tanzania includes a wide range of economic activities, including modern activities that do not correspond to the informal or urban traditional sector model, the non-wage activities of women certainly fit the informal sector pattern. If, like Sabot, we use income as a major criterion in differentiating between the "marginal" and "viable" sub-sectors of self-employment, we find that women are more often in the marginal subsector. Whereas 51% of women have self-employment earnings of 100 shillings a month or less, only 34.8% of men have such low earnings. At the other end of the scale, nearly 15% of men have earnings above the highest reported female income of

TABLE 1
Primary Nonwage Activities of Self-Employed Women

Type of Activity	% of Female Self-Employed	Average Earnings
Crafts/manufacture	11.5	151 shs.
Street trading	23.3	108
Shopkeeping	6.7	79
Bar, hotel, restaurant	4.9	280
House rental	9.3	166
Agriculture	41.8	132
Other	2.5	150

Source: NUMEIST, 1971.

900 shillings per month. Almost two-thirds of self-employed women are employed in either farming or street-trading, activities that yield among the lowest self-employment incomes.

Although the women in the sample are residents of towns, agriculture remains their most important single source of self-employment income. Cash-crop agriculture is done either within the urban areas or on the outskirts of town. Women born in the urban centers or nearby rural areas maintain access to traditional agricultural areas surrounding the towns, while migrant women sharecrop or rent the land of the local population. Agricultural activity has persisted in the urban areas for several reasons: women's need or desire to continue fulfilling the traditional responsibility of feeding themselves and their children, their experience and skill in agriculture compared with their limited skills in other areas, patterns of urbanization that make suitable land accessible to the urban population, and the low levels of capital investment required to farm using traditional techniques.

Street trading might also seem a logical choice of economic activity for women who might have had experience marketing agricultural produce in the rural areas. Trading and cash-crop agriculture were sometimes joint activities for self-employed women. Of the female street traders, 25.6% also grew cash crops. Only 12.7% of male street traders were also engaged in cash-crop agriculture. Bohannan and Dalton stress the difference between marketing (selling one's own produce to buy one's needs) and trading (a separate economic activity involving buying for resale).[7] For many women, urban street trading is closer to "marketing," an activity providing little opportunity to gain additional skills and amass capital. Unlike workers in other self-employment activities, women in farming and trading were rarely integrated with modern economic activities and methods of production. Their transition is therefore incomplete—though their work has been urbanized, it has not yet been modernized.

WOMEN AND CAPITAL INVESTMENTS

In our analysis of the determinants of variation in earnings from self-employment, we found that the level of initial capital investment had a significant, positive effect on earnings in the nonwage sector.[8] Women's earnings are uniformly low because they are restricted to activities that require little capital investment and yield little return on that investment. The vast majority of women street traders, 88.2%, stated that they started trading with an investment of less than 50 shillings. Table 2 compares the capital investment needed to initiate the primary self-employment activity for men and women in self-employment.

Not only is women's average level of investment in physical capital much lower, they have not been able to compensate for this deficit by higher levels of human capital investments. Most women in the self-employment sector have had neither formal schooling nor technical training. Of the 26.4% who did attend school, few went beyond primary school. Despite the importance of nonformal or technical training for work in this sector, only 3.1% of self-employed women have had this type of training. In her study of the limited access of Tanzanian girls to schooling, Mbilinyi concludes that female enrollment is limited because of the interaction of several factors:

> . . . the traditional expectations for adult female roles; the general attitudes towards women, as less intelligent or less responsible; the values attributed to education, which are incompatible with role expectations; the financial costs of schooling and therefore the socio-economic status of the families concerned.[9]

The limited enrollment of girls at all levels of the educational system has also been a concern of government policy. Reforms to increase access to schooling have been instituted, including a special program to improve the access of women to technical education. NUMEIST was conducted before these reforms were introduced and the effect of limited education

TABLE 2
Initial Capital Investment, by Sex

Level of Investment	Percent of Female Self-Employed	Percent of Male Self-Employed
Less than 50 shs.	66.1	30.0
50–200 shs.	10.7	16.7
200–500 shs.	7.1	8.1
500–1,000 shs.	0.0	10.0
1,000–5,000 shs.	7.1	12.4
5,000–10,000 shs.	3.6	2.4
10,000 shs. or more	5.4	20.5

Source: NUMEIST, 1971.

on women's earnings from self-employment simply underscores the need that led to the educational reforms.

WOMEN AND CAPITAL

Just as women's limited access to education has constrained human capital investments by self-employed women, their limited access to physical and financial capital has reduced their capital investments in economic activities. To understand the major causes of women's lower earnings, we should also consider the factors influencing women's ability to accumulate capital in urban Tanzania.

The relationship of women to capital in urban Tanzania should be considered in terms of the interaction between women's dual roles as producer and reproducer. Reproduction in this sense is not strictly biological, but includes "social reproduction—the perpetuation of social systems" including inheritance systems and the control of sexuality and fertility.[10] Mbilinyi has used this approach in her study of women engaged in agricultural production in the rural areas of Tanzania. One of the difficulties in considering the interaction of both productive and reproductive roles is that such an analysis is based on the legal, economic, and social position of women in a specific society. Mbilinyi recognized the analytical shortcomings of imposing a degree of generality on rural women who were members of societies that were at very different stages of development prior to the introduction of market capitalism into East Africa.[11] Our study of women as self-employed producers in the contemporary urban areas is equally complex since most women are African migrants from rural areas, while others are African town residents of varying permanency, and still others are Asian migrants or local Tanzanian Asians from diverse religious, cultural, and economic backgrounds. Mbilinyi was able to trace a communality of experience for the traditional role of African women in agriculture. On a similar level of abstraction, we can attempt to define the position of women in relationship to the ownership of capital in the urban areas.

The patterns of the gender division of labor and inheritance that were the norm in the rural areas of Tanzania are important for our urban study since 64.2% of the urban residents in the NUMEIST sample are migrants from rural areas.[12] In the traditional rural systems analyzed by Mbilinyi, men own cattle and land or control the rights to land use. Inheritance is usually through the male line, except in the case of matrilineal societies where the nephew inherits from his maternal uncle.[13] Such inheritance laws virtually precluded the inheritance of physical capital by women:

> If a woman's husband dies, she has no basic rights to the house, land, or household properties, other than certain material possessions clearly defined as her own (e.g., her cooking pots). In particular, her children are retained by members of the husband's lineage. Similar results follow divorce.[14]

When the Law of Marriage Act of 1971 was discussed in the Tanzanian legislature, the sections on inheritance aroused intense debate. Some members proclaimed that it was absurd to discuss the inheritance of property by women since women could not hold property.[15] When the Law of Marriage Act was eventually passed, it included several sections related to women's rights to property. Perhaps the most important was Section 56, which provided married women with equal rights in property holding: "A married women shall have the same right to acquire, hold and dispose of property, whether movable or immovable, and the same right to contract, the same right to sue and the same liability to be sued in contract or in tort or otherwise."[16] These rights were not legally protected until 1971, however, and the women who were interviewed by NUMEIST at the same point in history had not benefited from such full equal rights in the previous period. Thus, most women who sought self-employment found their access to capital limited by their gender as well as their relative economic position within a poor nation.

Despite customs and attitudes that limited their access to capital, some women have been able to secure ownership of capital in the urban areas of mainland Tanzania. The sources of this capital range from loans and gifts by relatives and friends to earnings from wage employment. The majority of women in self-employment who have made initial business investments of more than 200 shillings were unmarried women, either single or previously married. Marriage, rather than providing additional access to capital through the husband's earnings or credit, seems to be a hindrance to the access to capital for women's investments in self-employment activities.[17]

Thus, the greatest hindrance to capital accumulation by self-employed women in Tanzania is their low level of initial capital investments. The very small scale of their activities, limited access to credit lines, and limited opportunities for expansion in the types of activities that women are involved in have limited the profits needed for reinvestment and accumulation.

THE ROLE OF ETHNICITY

For African women in self-employment, access to capital and accumulation are further limited by historical developments and government policies that favored the development of Tanzanian Asians as a commercial class. Earnings in self-employment are skewed by both gender and ethnicity, with African women earning an average of only 132 shillings per month, while African men earn 270 shillings and Asian women earn an average of 350 shillings a month. All of these earnings are well below the average of 2,250 shillings a month earned by Asian men. The source of much of this earnings differential is the level of capital investments that characterize the self-employment activities of Asian men. Asian males are the one group for whom high-capital investments predominate; 70.6% of self-employed Asian men are involved in economic activities that required an initial investment of over 10,000 shillings.

Asian dominance in trade is well-documented in a study by H.C.G. Hawkins. Hawkins observes that although two-thirds of the traders licensed in Tanganyika in 1961 were Africans, African traders accounted for only one-third of the value of total business.[18] Most of the African traders were engaged in small-scale, rural retail shops offering a limited choice of goods. Hawkins notes that the problems of African traders began with difficulties in amassing initial capital and extended through a lack of experience and limited access to credit. Asian traders, on the other hand, were usually able to gain early experience in a relative's shop, and obtain goods on credit.[19]

Government policy during the colonial period actively promoted the role of Asians in trade and other types of self-employment. The segregated Asian schools specialized in commercial courses. Although trade licenses were technically available to all, in practice colonial administrators discouraged African applicants. Rweyemamu points out that the most serious obstacle to African success in commercial activities was the regulation forbidding wholesalers from advancing more than 600 shillings worth of merchandise to Africans. As a result, colonial policy "curbed the formation of an African bourgeois class, while breeding an Asian one."[20]

Ironically, the socialist policies that followed the Arusha declaration may have had a similar effect in contemporary Tanzania.[21] Policies that stem the accumulation of capital by nationalizing some forms of private property and limiting ownership of other forms of capital have further inhibited the emergence of an African business class. The government of Tanzania is strongly committed to labor market policies that eliminate discrimination and earnings differentials based on ethnicity and gender. The effect of government policies in the wage sector has been a gradual elimination of such differentials, especially in those sectors that are under direct or indirect government control. In self-employment, however, both history and policy have worked together to exaggerate existing inequalities. By limiting opportunities for individuals to accumulate capital, the existing gender and ethnic inequalities have been exaggerated. Whether or not this is simply a short-run effect that will be replaced by increasing equality in the long run can only be determined by an analysis of subsequent earnings distributions among the self-employed.

CONCLUSION

The self-employed women of urban Tanzania are caught between two worlds. Although they live in the urban areas, they often produce goods and services using techniques learned in the rural traditional sector. Their earnings are lower than those of the male self-employed, partly because they work fewer hours, but mostly because women have fewer skills and work with lower capital investments. The lower investments in both education and capital are related to women's reproductive role. Given this role and the biological constraints that prevented women from having equal access to labor market opportunities, women in Tanzania, as in other parts of the world, invested more in skills related to household production rather than market production. Cain notes that this pattern of human capital investment by women results from the implicit contract for sharing household income within marriages where the male specializes in market skills. The women's skills are "marriage specific," analogous to firm-specific training. When these marriages dissolve, "a common result is a capital loss, particularly for the wives who made the largest investment in marital skills relative to labor market skills."[22] Many of the female self-employed in urban Tanzania are divorced women who have suffered such a loss in income because of divorce. Many more are married women who are working to supplement the earnings of their husbands. It may not be coincidental that for self-employed women, the highest earnings are in bar, hotel, and restaurant work, occupations that use skills closely related to household production and in which women should be relatively more productive than men.

But self-employed women also earn less because they work fewer hours. Self-employed women work an average of 33.4 hours a week in their primary activity while men work an average of 48.7 hours a week. The difference is not devoted to leisure—women are more likely to have multiple roles, combining several self-employment activities or combining a low-paying, part-time wage job with self-employment. Moreover, since almost 90% of self-employed women are either currently or previously married, most have substantial responsibilities in household production.

By 1971, Tanzania had begun reforms in wage employment that would substantially reduce the differentials in earnings related to gender and ethnicity. It is perhaps more difficult to introduce similar reforms for the self-employed, especially at a time when the nation is striving to define the role of the enterpreneur within the evolving system of Tanzanian *ujamaa* or African socialism. Moreover, in wage employment, labor market discrimination takes the form of unequal wages for workers of equal productivity. In self-employment, women earn less mostly because they are less productive. They are less productive because they have fewer skills, less capital to invest, and fewer hours for market work. Tanzania has already made great strides in increasing women's educational opportunities. For self-employment, nonformal education and apprenticeships should also lead to higher earnings. The government is also encouraging informal savings groups to improve access to capital for income-generating activities. But access to childcare facilities and improvements in household production to allow women to work longer hours might also be considered. The appropriate policy mix must be subject to the budgetary constraints of a poor African nation. At the same time, if programs to increase women's productivity in employment are well-designed, they can yield a relatively high return for the women involved and the nation as a whole.

NOTES

This article is based on my dissertation, "The Economic Activities of Women in Urban Tanzania," Columbia University, 1983. I am grateful to members of my dissertation committee and the Women and Development Study Group for helpful comments on previous drafts. William Dickens, Stephanie Wilson, and Samuel Myers were skilled discussants when an earlier version was presented at the Annual Meetings of the National Economic Association in December 1984. Gloria Scott also offered useful comments when this article was presented at the Symposium on Black Women co-sponsored by the Congressional Black Caucus Foundation and *The Review of Black Political Economy* in September 1985. Natalie Ocean and Laurie Knapp provided able secretarial assistance. The views expressed are my own and do not reflect those of the Federal Reserve Bank of New York or the Federal Reserve System.

1. The National Urban Mobility, Employment and Income Survey of Tanzania [NUMEIST, 1971]. The 5,543 individuals surveyed in 1971 represented a random sample of the adult urban population of seven towns in mainland Tanzania. Of those interviewed, 48.1% were women. The survey contains detailed questions on education, migration, and labor force experience. NUMEIST has been a rich source of information on urban labor markets and has been the data base for several studies of rural-urban migration and urban unemployment.

2. Based on a definition of economic activity that includes subsistence production (mostly small-scale agriculture in and around the urban area).

3. W. Arthur Lewis, "Economic Development with Unlimited Supplies of Labour," *The Manchester School of Economic and Social Studies*, vol. 22, 1954, pp. 139-191.

4. R.H. Sabot, "Open Unemployment and the Employed Compound of Urban Surplus Labour," in *Papers in the Political Economy of Tanzania*, ed. Kwan S. Kim, Robert B. Mabele, and Michael J. Schulteis (Nairobi: Heinemann Educational Books, 1979).

5. Sabot, p. 266.

6. At the time of the NUMEIST Survey, the rate of exchange between Tanzanian shillings and the U.S. dollar was 7:1.

7. Paul Bohannan and George Dalton, *Markets in Africa* (Garden City, N.Y.: Doubleday and Company, 1965), p. 16.

8. Willene A. Johnson, "The Economic Activities of Women in Urban Tanzania," Columbia University, unpub. diss. 1983, pp. 118-124.

9. Marjorie Mbilinyi, "The 'New Woman' and Traditional Norms in Tanzania," *Journal of Modern African Studies*, vol. 10 (1972): 57-72.

10. Lourdes Beneria and Gita Sen, "Accumulation, Reproduction, and Women's Role in Economic Development: Boserup Revisited," *Signs*, Special Issue on Development and the Sexual Division of Labor, vol. 7 (1981): 279-298, p. 290fn.

11. Marjorie Mbilinyi, "Women: Producers and Reproducers in Peasant Production," Economic Research Bureau Occasional Paper 77.3 University of Dar es Salaam, 1977, p. 12.

12. In the NUMEIST survey, only individuals who moved to the town of current residence when they were 14 years of age or older are classified as migrants. Thus, the vast majority of urban residents would be considered migrants if we included those who migrated as children.

13. Thus, in matrilineal inheritance "property descends 'homogeneously,' e.g., *between* males, even when it goes *through* females." Jack Goody, *Production and Reproduction: A Comparative Study of the Domestic Domain* (Cambridge: Cambridge University Press, 1976), p. 6.

14. Mbilinyi, 1972, p. 66.

15. Mbilinyi, 1972, p. 67.

16. The United Republic of Tanzania, *Law of Marriage*, Act No. 5, 1971.

17. McCall's study of self-employed women in Ghana concluded that marriage limited women's earnings from self-employment by limiting both mobility and the ability to make independent entrepreneurial decisions. Daniel F. McCall, "The Effect on Family Structure of Changing Economic Activities of Women in a Gold Coast Town," Columbia University, unpub. diss., 1956.

18. H. C. G. Hawkins, *Wholesale and Retail Trade in Tanganyika: A Study of Distribution in East Africa*: (New York: Frederick A. Praeger, Publishers, 1965).

19. Hawkins, pp. 150-52.

20. Justinian Rweyemamu, *Underdevelopment and Industrialization in Tanzania: A Study in Perverse Capitalist Industrial Development* (Nairobi: Oxford University Press, 1973), p. 29.

21. Dharam Ghai and Yash Ghai, "Asians in Tanzania: Problems and Prospects," in *Self-Reliant Tanzania*, ed. by Knud Eric Evendsen and Merete Teisen (Dar es Salaam: Tanzania Publishing House, 1969), p. 107.

22. Glen Cain, "Welfare Economics of Policies Toward Women," *Journal of Labor Economics*, vol. 3 (1985), S375-S396, p. 381.

JAMAICAN WORKING-CLASS WOMEN:
PRODUCERS AND REPRODUCERS

Beverly J. Mason

Jamaica's economy is underdeveloped, creating and maintaining relatively few income-generating opportunities for its population. To survive, working-class women who assume primary economic and social responsibilities for their children must be economically active, whether in the retrenching formal sector or in the growing informal sector. The following article examines how their culture and economy merge to define Jamaican women and their roles.

This article is excerpted from a larger study,[1] conducted in 1982, entitled "The Continuing Modernization of Underdevelopment: Jamaican Women as Producers and Reproducers," which sought to analyze the interplay among culture, economy, and gender in the Third World. These macroissues were addressed by investigating Afro-Jamaican women's work forms, social roles and networks, and kin systems. To this end, 30 female workers in the factory or formal sector[2] were interviewed. Modernists and other economic development theorists have declared that current development strategies will create and expand the formal sector and pull "backward economies" into full participation in the world capitalist economy, in part by creating employment opportunities in the industrial sector for the indigenous population in these countries, thereby ameliorating poverty.[3]

In addition, 25 petty commodity producers (PCPs) were investigated because the reality for so many poor countries, like Jamaica, has been that the formal sector has created limited, capital-intensive employment, often primarily for men; that poverty has increased and indigenous economic forms have been adversely affected; and that petty commodity production in the informal sector is one attempt by the masses to participate in an international economic system that has a very limited role for them.[4]

This article addresses two issues: (1) the impact and implications of capitalist penetration on the economic organization of Jamaican women and (2) women's perception of their social roles and concommitant responsibilities.

WOMEN AND PRODUCTION

Women in Jamaican culture have two primary responsibilities: to be producers or workers and to be reproducers or maintainers of their families. As producers Jamaican women have one of the highest labor force participation rates in the world, with over 60% of them economically active. In the formal sector, they are involved in a host of positions, including entry-level manufacturing jobs. Retrenchment in this sector between 1960 and 1978, however, resulted in a loss of 24,000 manufacturing jobs for women, with their employment plummeting from 43,865 to 19,400. The majority of these jobs were located in the offshore assembly plants or "screwdriver industries."[5] Women's employment in the manufacturing sector continued to suffer, with a 36.8% unemployment rate in 1981; their unemployment across all industries was almost 40%. In the same year (1981), 55% of all female labor force participants were clustered in two occupation groups: the self-employed—that is, seamstresses, bakers, food vendors, craftswomen, and petty producers—and those in service occupations such as domestics, laundresses, and workers at related activities. Of all occupation groups represented in the Jamaican economy, these two, the self-employed and those in service occupations, have experienced dramatic growth during the last few decades.[6] Concurrently, women's employment in the manufacturing sector, just over 5% in 1981, has undergone a steady decline.

Data for this study were gathered from women employed at five different factories—two food-processing concerns; a plastic factory; a bakery; and a textile factory—in 4 of Jamaica's 14 parishes. All of the women worked full-time; 26 had been employed with their current employer at least 5 years; and over 60% had worked with the same concern for over 10 years. They held permanent entry-level, monotonous, and dead-end jobs with little chance of advancement. Skill-building experiences were limited, and movement within the factory, when available, was horizontal, except for a few isolated cases. Women were assigned to positions by gender in the plastics factory, the bakery, and the textile factory. One factory manager explained the segregation by indicating that some jobs entailed frequent lifting of sacks weighing 40 to 50 pounds, something women could not manage. In reality, neither did men; they employed hydraulic lifts and trucks to manipulate the loads. Another, the plastics factory manager, specifically sought women to work the large looms and sewing machines, noting that they were familiar with the machines, that they "knew their way around them." Managers praised the women as workers, describing them as dedicated, industrious, hard working, and exhibiting a lower absenteeism rate than men. Managers attributed these attitudes and practices to the fact that women shouldered the bulk of the family responsibilities and thus had to work.

The 25 petty commodity producers interviewed had to meet the following criteria: produce a product and be intimately involved in the production process; be the primary decision maker; and, preferably, be the sole owner. Although they could be involved in a host of extraeconomic activities, their primary, most consistent source of income had to come as a result of their production activities. Interviews were conducted in nine parishes.

Producers' work periods were dictated by their activity (seamstresses worked longer days and weeks than bakers); customer flow (urban women with potentially larger customer pools and fewer means available for extra, noncommodity-producing activities spent more time involved in their businesses than rural women who supplemented their PCP income by cultivating and animal husbandry); and time of the year (peak seasons for most businesses were holidays and school openings). Women's activities were characterized by small-scale production at home with little or no capital investment and a short turnaround period. They enjoyed no minimum wage or fringe benefits, and vacation or sick days proffered the possible loss both of access to raw materials and of already scarce customers. The majority were bakers and seamstresses; other interviewees engaged in such diverse tasks as shoemaking, basket weaving, straw decorating, food processing, andd needlecraft. All activities were labor intensive, and equipment used in the production process was often rudimentary, thus inreasing the labor time invested.

WOMEN AND REPRODUCTION

The following two statements present an idea of women's familial responsibilities: "a full third of all women are heads of household, 62 percent of whom never marry," and "over 70 percent of all births occur to unmarried women."[7] In this study, 64% of the *PCPs* interviewed were currently married; the remainder were single, divorced, or widowed. All but two were mothers. Of the 21 married with children, 80% had at least one child before marriage. Of the factory workers, on the other hand, 50% were single, and 93% of that number had at least one child; 40% were married and 75% of that number had a child before marrying. Factory women had fewer children that PCPs, who averaged six whereas the former averaged four. For the overwhelming majority of both groups, employment activities began after the birth of their first child, an event that took place while the women were residing at home with their parents. Interviewees, whether single, married, or involved in Jamaica's most popular mating form—common-law relationship—said they worked because their primary responsibility was reproduction or the everyday maintenance of their children. Those single mothers who eventually marry or enter into a long-term, live-in relationship (many not until they are well into their 30s) still considered their children, some fathered by men other than their eventual husbands or mates, as their exclusive responsibility. It is the assumption of these responsibilities by Jamaican women that perpetuates the practices inherent in the ideology of motherhood.

THE IDEOLOGY OF MOTHERHOOD

Many of the cultural, social, and psychological factors that converge to describe working-class Jamaican women's rites of passage to womanhood are inextricably tied to their reproductive roles. The fact that most Jamaican women (70%) begin having children before marriage and the concommitant responsibilities of rearing and maintaining children necessitate that women be involved in income-producing activities. Unlike societies in which childbearing and marital entry are tightly controlled by the family, religion, state, or a host of other social institutions, or by a combination of them all, these institutions, though vitally important and integral parts of Jamaican society, do not curb or control women's and men's reproductive practices. In short, while the value-defining sociocultural tools of Jamaican society—family, church, and state—are firmly against premarital childbearing, the experiences and practices of low-income and working-class Jamaican women are in opposition to these dicta. For example, several studies have documented that the "preferred" familial form of Jamaican working-class women and men is "monogamous marriage."[8] Yet the majority of babies are born outside this relationship. This contradiction between the ideal—husband, wife, and children—and the reality—woman, children, and possibly mate—is a crucial factor in understanding the complexities of women's multiple roles as they are defined by the ideology of motherhood.

The role of mother is pivotal to Jamaican women's definition of womanhood, yet it is also one of the primary reasons for the perpetuation of their poverty. Women support their children emotionally and economically, as well as provide assistance to members of the extended family. Unfortunately this central role includes the perpetuation of the social relationships that provide the impetus for the oppression of the next generation of young women.

Jamaica is a matrifocal society.[9] The primary domestic relationship is between mother and child. Jamaica, at the same time, is a male-dominated society. In the public sphere, decisions are ultimately made by and for males. Women bear the familial, domestic responsibilities that flow from matriarchy but realize little of the social, political, and economic public power necessary to change their conditions.

Women view themselves as mothers first, daughters second, and wives third. No matter what mating form women eventually enter, they declare that their children are their own primary responsibility and focus. This mother-child bond places the onus of being the provider on women and, in the final analysis, renders men almost peripheral to the domestic sphere.[10] When one is seeking to understand why women bear children under such precarious circumstances, the question immediately begs rephrasing: What are the cultural and socioeconomic structures and the historical factors that converge to encourage a woman to have children early, often by different fathers, and to enter unions late?[11] What are the implications of these practices for Jamaican society, family structure, and women and their life options?

An important factor feeding these childbearing patterns is the lack of avenues for self-actualization. This term is employed in this context to describe a host of factors—inadequate and inappropriate schooling;[12] limited, sex-segregated working-class employment opportunities; poverty; and the hardships involved in living in an underdeveloped economy—that result in women perceiving motherhood as one of the few postive life options. When women become mothers, either by design or by accident, they engage in one of the few life acitivities in which they perceive they have some control and in which they realize some self-esteem. Women live vicariously through their children: a good child is a job done well.

Mothering activities may begin for a daughter as early as she demonstrates that she can care for herself. Either the girl's own mother may continue to have children, or a host of circumstances may produce a baby to be cared for. Whereas young boys, depending on the mother's access to a care provider, are expected to join in caring for youngsters, the family assumes young girls will perform domestic responsibilities, which include child care. Since childbearing can begin during the primary school years, girls often move from caring for another's children to caring for their own.

For the majority of Jamaican women, the movement into womanhood is bound to motherhood. That is to say, childbearing constitutes a movement to the social status of "woman." This "promotion" is dubious, since motherhood often arrives without the economic assistance and support of a mate. It is after childbirth that women, while residing at home with their parents, become economically active.

The majority of interviewees indicated that they were not trying to conceive when they became pregnant. The use of contraceptives is intermittent, and so whether planned or not, pregnancies occur. Older women with adult or near adult children described the poor quality or lack of contraceptives when they entered childbearing years. Most teenage pregnancies were described as "accidents." In fact, many mothers indicated that they did not know they were pregnant until well into the term; one interviewee was in her seventh month. Pregnancies in teenagers often came as a result of their first experimentation with sex. Upon finding out, respondents were shocked, angry, and sad. The shock and anger resulted from the feeling of being betrayed by their lovers, who were perceived as being mature because they were employed and often several years older than the girls and who "had promised to take up the responsibility" of pregnancy prevention.

The relationship between the mother and the child's father often ended in one of two ways: desertion by the father upon learning of the pregnancy, or breakup initiated by the mother upon realizing the relationship had no future. Marriage, according to women, was to be engaged in when men had achieved economic and personal stability—in other words, when the man had a job and some form of residence. When mothers did marry, it was usually after being involved in a visiting or a live-in relationship.

Marriage or a stable common-law relationship with a working husband or mate could mean the difference between gnawing poverty and tolerable desperation. Whereas most women described their economic contribution to the household as crucial, women with income-generating mates were far better off than those without. Some married workers produced the only income for the household; others supplemented overtaxed budgets.

Of course, marriage in no way assured women of having an easier, more financially secure life as was the case with Mrs. P., whose husband had been unemployed for three years. She had complete financial responsibility for him and their five young children. A 26-year-old seamstress, Mrs. P. made baby clothes—24 outfits a week—and sold them in front of a nearby hospital three days a week. She not only did all of the cutting out and sewing of the suits but did most of the housework, cooking, and daily care of the children.

Another factor serving to strengthen the acceptance of the roles inherent in the ideology of motherhood is Jamaican women's image of men and of themselves. Their image of men often clashed with their experiences or the experiences of other women in their sphere. The contradictions between image and reality produced the motor to perpetuate women's subordination by men. Women were very critical of men and the manner in which they failed to carry out their familial roles and responsibilities. Yet women defended the "image" of men with comments such as "men should earn more money than women; they have it all [household and family responsibilities on them]." One respondent supporting this thesis was the mother of two adult daughters, whom she had reared without any assistance from her children's father. Her mother, also a single parent, had been deserted by her daughter's father upon his learning of the pregnancy. Married women, who said they deferred to their husbands as the primary household authority, did so because "that was the way it was supposed to be." Their employment or amount of earnings, sometimes more than their husbands, had little impact on who made the major decisions or was the head of the house. Married women in difficult or crisis-laden relationships were as critical of men as single women and relinquished, as women in common-law relationships did, little authority over themselves or their children to mates. But they, too, declared that men should be household heads. Women eloquently explained men's inabilities to assume "their responsibilities" by identifying the lack of jobs and inadequate salaries offered by employers.

Women's perceptions of other women and themselves appeared to evolve in opposition and isolation from these women and their experiences. For example, they were surprised to hear that other Jamaican women had similar, difficult experiences. Women decried relationships and involvements with nonfamily women, chronicling many of the "anti-women" attacks described in Julia Naish's article on Desirade women: that they gossip, betray secrets, and instigate trouble.[13] Several women said they preferred male friends; only two from the sample, though, actually had one. And yet, women survived by helping and supporting one another, as members of an extended family, as church sisters, as co-residents sharing a yard in Kingston, or as fellow workers.

When women were asked if they had a more difficult time finding employment than men, women's attitudes about their roles and responsibilities became obvious. They reasoned that since women would and should engage in a variety of money-making activities including domestic work, laundry, child care, and so on, they were the more employable of the two sexes. When asked why men could not be domestics, women replied that it was just something they did not do. Although women differentiated between typical men's work—such as heavy lifting, managerial employment, mining, and so forth—and women's work—which included domestic activities, nursing, teaching, operating light machinery, baking and sewing—they all agreed women would do anything to earn income for their children's support, including men's work.

In conclusion, Jamaican women perceive that they have primary responsibility for their children and, in fact, they do. Women begin childbearing while residing at home with their parents; it is not unusual for the grandparent to be a single parent. Young mothers, then, faced with the social and economic responsibility of providing for a child, begin movement into the work world as domestics, babysitters, vendors, petty traders, petty commodity producers, or industrial workers. They may or may not intersperse this labor activity with continued births, since marriage often comes latter in their lives and in no way implies an end to work. Some women may move from emoloyment in the formal sector to petty commodity production or vice versa, depending upon the job market, upon support systems available to assist with child care and economic survival and, to some degree, upon which sector women think it most profitable to be involved in while maintaining their host of other responsibilities. They remain locked into these social and economic roles because of the contradictions surrounding perceptions of men's and women's roles and realities and the lack of life options so prevalent in poor, underdeveloped economies.

EXTRA ECONOMIC ACTIVITIES

For working women living in underdeveloped countries, development policies encouraged by foreign governments and investors, international organizations, and their home governments have had adverse impacts. Current data indicate that whether the emphasis has been on "modernizing" the agricultural sector or on creating employment via increased industrialization women are being either left out of development plans or brought into them as a "categorized" (by gender) labor force to occupy specific, low-skill, low-pay positions. Literature on women laboring along the U.S. -Mexico border, on electronics workers in Tawian, Singapore, and Malaysia, on the classic Texas Instrument's case in Curacao, or on Nigerian displaced indigenous workers attests to many of the problems faced by women as they are affected by industrialization attempts, whether directly or indirectly.[14]

The second research statement to be discussed has to do with the implications of current forms of capitalist penetration on the economic organization of Jamaican women. In Jamaica these economic forces have produced a situation in which those few women fortunate enough to have income-producing activities do not earn enough to maintain their families and consequently must engage, whenever possible, in extra economic activities to survive.

The overwhelming majority of industrial workers in the study worked because of economic need; 57% provided the only or primary household income, and a majority of the remainder reported that their households could not function without their incomes. To make ends meet, over 40% of the factory interviewees engaged in extra income-generating activities—such as chicken and goat rearing, sewing, needlework, buying and selling, and food preparation—in addition to their full-time, five-days-a-week, rotating-schedule jobs. Buying and selling was a popular extra money-making activity for urban industrial workers. For example, Ms. Rd. of Kingston, a single mother of two, worked at a bakery but also bought and sold cosmetics and men and women's undergarments. She began her business after selling goods for a friend at the factory in return for a small fee. Once established, she received orders from co-workers and purchased about $100 worth of goods in downtown Kingston. She brought the goods to work on payday, at which time she was reimbursed. She had been operating her business for four years and realized $20 in net income a week. She provided a valuable service to co-workers who had no time to shop. She planned eventually to turn the activity into a full-time business where she would spend most of her energies. Her profits were placed in a savings account for her children's education.

For many Jamaican women, the role of conduit or middle person allows the economic survival of many families while at the same time providing labor- and time-intensive services to customers. It is common practice among workers to purchase large quantities of goods produced at their workplaces for sale to neighbors. Factories sold goods to workers at wholesale prices and deducted the cost from weekly wages. Women, in turn, sold the goods to neighbors at retail prices. Ms. J., mother of 11, was representative of this group. She purchased wholesale baked goods at her workplace at $.70 an item and sold them to neighbors at the retail price of $1.50. This practice benefited both buyer and seller in that for the buyer there was the convenience of goods delivered to the door at retail prices, and for the seller the difference between wholesale and retail price was lunch money for one or two children a week.

Factory workers had long histories of income-generating experiences prior to beginning their employment in the formal sector. In fact, almost 90% of all factory workers in the study had averaged three economic activities each, and 40% had been involved in petty commodity production. Many women continued their petty commodity production after becoming full-time factory employees.

Many extra activities made the difference in the successful continuation of the household, as Mrs. Md. of St. Catherine illustrated. She was married to a disabled man, and because she was the sole support of her family, which included four young adults, she experienced the same financial crises as single parents had. Until after the birth of her second child, Mrs. Md. resided with her great-aunt, who sent her to sewing classes. Before becoming a permanent factory employee 12 years earlier, she had sewed for a living. Although she worked a 40-hour, rotating shift in the factory each week, Mrs. Md. still sewed every day and on weekends, earning from $40 to $60 per week, to add to her salary. Her income was the primary one in the household and had to support the everyday needs of the entire family as well as all of Mr. Md.'s medical needs. Her sewing also enabled her to provide technical training for her four children.

Residence or geographical location had something to do with the type of additional employment chosen, since it was easier to rear goats and chickens in rural settings with open spaces. But a rural residence was not always a requisite, since both kinds of animals were reared in Kingston, albeit illegally, as well as in other urban areas.

A problem not as difficult to surmount for a factory worker as for someone in a less predictable occupation was the difficulty of raising the investment capital necessary for initiating additional income-producing projects. A seamstress had to have an electric sewing machine if the business was to be successful; buying and selling goods had to commence with the buying. These two activities and others demanded start-up capital, and because borrowing from a bank is extremely difficult for working-class people the world over, other methods were devised. All interviewees except three were members of an informal, rotating banking activity, or "partners," operated at work, whereby depending on how many people were involved in the activity and how much they contributed weekly one could ask for the "draw" and receive from $100 to $500. The draw was often used for school expenses in September, or as part of a house down payment, or as mentioned above, to begin additional economic activities.

For example, Ms. G., 34-year-old mother, had been working for a large factory since 1971. She was purchasing a house, for which she used her draw from the partners system as the down payment. She had been laid off the previous year for nine months and had used her extra employment to sustain her family during that period. She purchased soda drinks and beer each week from a local distributor who delivered them to an agreed-upon point in the housing development. She and her daughter carried the cases on their heads to their home, where neighbors purchased the drinks at a 20¢ markup. Ms. G. received additional assistance from her daughter, who earned lunch money, about $3 a day, selling "suc sucs," a colored sugar water, to neighborhood children. She prepared the mixture before leaving for school in the morning, froze it, and sold it along with the drinks during the evenings to neighbors.

Multiple economic activities appear to be engaged in more by single parents than by married women, but not by a wide margin. The involvement had more to do with the sheer precariousness of the family income, and the kinds of training women received before beginning their factory careers. Seamstresses "fell back" on their talents at dressmaking, and since this was something that could be done any time at home it could be integrated with out-of-the-house employment schedules. The same was true with baking and needlepoint. What was especially attractive and aided factory workers immensely was that they had "ready made markets": fellow workers and neighbors.

All women agreed that there was a need for additional household funds. Those engaged in extra activities had not necessarily increased their standard of living but were contributing toward the void caused by a missing or noncontributing mate. Married women subsidized inadequate incomes earned in the formal sector by both themselves and their mates. For single women receiving no financial assistance, save contributions from the extended family, the need to supplement salaries was greater than for others. It was difficult, though, for this group to amass the investment funds needed to begin a business, since each week's salary was barely sufficient to meet basic needs.

In many cases the fact that factory workers could not earn enough to support their families, a common dilemma in many Third World countries, forced them to participate in the informal sector. Women baked puddings and cakes; some engaged in needlecraft and others sewed; and others reared animals to sell to fellow workers or neighbors. Many workers literally held one and a half or even two full-time jobs in addition to being responsible for domestic chores at home.

Petty commodity producers, on the other hand, were even more active in multieconomic activities, all in the informal sector. Actually, 56% of the producers were involved in more than one income-producing activity; 35% of this group engaged in subsistence farming and the balance in other secondary commodity production activities. All were involved in labor-intensive activities that demanded long hours of tedious work. This labor commitment for many women was evidenced in the case of a basket weaver who with the help of two of her children labored 7-10 hours a day to produce eight laundry hampers a week. Mrs. R.'s two children also made small replicas of her larger baskets, items that sold well among tourists. Mrs. R.'s work process was ongoing once the straw was prepared, an activity that by itself took one full day and evening. She worked as many hours as possible from Monday through Friday night to produce the baskets for sale at Saturday's market. Her activity left little time for additional economic activities. And, too, her family economy was so precarious that there were no discretionary funds for investment capital. Mrs. R., to realize some extra funds, supervised higglering activity on her father's property.[15]

Although Mrs. R.'s primary activity was so time consuming that she could hardly engage in any other income-generating work, other PCPs, because they worked at home, were able to integrate a number of short- or long-term activities into their schedules. A good example of this group is Mrs. Bk. When she (then a single woman) desperately needed additional funds for a daughter's school expenses, she shifted her primary informal sector activity, straw work and decorating, to night time and undertook needlework, which she did under contract to a large Kingston department store. During the day, Mrs. Bk. engaged in a full-time job, sifting sand at a new housing development. When this job ended, she expanded her straw work to include making not only multisized bags, but hats, too. In all Mrs. Bk. worked 18-20 hours a day.

A number of women cultivated small kitchen gardens for home use. (Mrs. R., above, grew in her own garden almost all the produce the family ate.) Any excess was sold on the immediate, local market. Some rural

women, either individually or in conjunction with their husbands, cultivated for both local markets and large, urban markets located in Kingston
and in other parish capitals. Producers engaged in animal husbandry—
goat and chicken rearing, both of which required little daily maintenance.
It was not unusual for rural women to sew or work with straw, cultivate,
and rear animals.

Urban producers, some without the luxury of kitchen gardens, tended
to produce more than one commodity or engaged in petty buying and
selling. Mrs. Bn., a representative member of the most successful producers interviewed (30% of the sample) ran a successful bakery business
selling cakes to primary school students during morning and afternoon
sessions. She had earlier tried sewing and needlework but could not identify enough customers to turn a profit. Then she stumbled into the baking
business. She earned about $30 a day, and after expenses of $106 every
two weeks for flour, sugar, spices, fruit, and eggs, netted $244 bimonthly.
She invested money earned from this business into buying and selling
ready-to-eat chickens. On Thursday evenings, a case of frozen chickens
was delivered to Mrs. Bn. that she, in turn, sold to neighbors throughout
the weekend, realizing $20-25 in net earnings a week. She banked as
much of the income earned from selling chickens as possible, saving for
her two children's schooling.

For both rural and urban women, whether in factory or cottage industry, the degree to which women were able to engage in multiple activities
often depended on familial support and involvement. Women rearing
chickens might assign the morning coop cleaning and feeding and water-
ing to children; a daughter or son might assume cooking and household
duties; or a parent or sibling might finance a business start-up.

CONCLUSION

Jamaica is a country struggling to survive in a world economic system
over which it has no control. It began as a slave colony and has remained
in a state of underdevelopment. Against the backdrop of these larger
conflicts, Jamaican women have struggled to define their lives and control
their own destinies as best they could.

Employment opportunities in the formal sector are scarce and precarious for everyone, especially for women, as foreign capital seeking
cheap labor flits in and out of poor countries. Women have to support
their families, and so whether employment is in the formal or the informal sector, they must work. Those engaged in petty commodity produc-

tion subsidize the industrial sector by being highly active in the informal, nonindustrialized sector. Those in the formal sector hold on to dwindling jobs while also engaging in work in the informal sector. The products of both groups allow for the continuation of the economy and society, and so, indirectly, they keep themselves in subservient, oppressive conditions while they struggle to survive.

Petty commodity producers and women involved in other activities in the informal sector sell their wares and services at cheaper prices than those found in the formal sector because their customers cannot afford retail prices. These women thereby subsidize not only their households, but the households of their customers, as well as local and international capital, by supplying needed and sought-after goods. The same argument holds for factory workers in that they do not earn enough to maintain their families, and so they and PCPs must then seek to supplement their meager earnings with extra economic activities.

Women labor under the triple burden of an underdeveloped economy, a sex-segregated labor force, and the ideology of motherhood. Even though women's primary role of mother and nurturer provides increased self-esteem, endearing relations, and a sense of purpose and direction in life, the role has also enslaved them in very narrow definitions, forced them to engage in arduous work forms, and eliminated life options. International and local economic forces continue to change the Jamaican scene and women's lives drastically. The movement of "screwdriver" or assembly industries and other simple industrial forms, all major employers of women, away from the country; the adverse ramifications from the increased competitiveness of other Third World and industrialized countries in the manufacturing sector; the rigors of a cash economy; and the influx of values, tastes, and attitudes from nearby industrial countries all contribute to the maelstrom. Currently, Jamaican women are not in a position of strength to influence these factors, and so must, as they so often say, "do every little *ting*" to ensure their families' continuation.

NOTES

1. This paper is excerpted from my dissertation, "The Continuing Modernization of Underdevelopment: Jamaican Women as Producers and Reproducers," Brandeis University, 1985. My sincere thank you to Jacqui Alexander for her thorough reading of the larger document, as well as Professors Asoka Bandarage, Egon Bittner, and Gila Hayim, in the Sociology Department at Brandeis University, Waltham, Massachusetts, for their suggestions and support.

2. For a discussion of the informal/formal sector debate, see S.V. Sethuraman, "The

Urban Informal Sector in Africa," *International Labour Review*, vol. 116, no. 3 (Nov./ Dec., 1977): Caroline O. Moser, "The Informal Sector Reworked: Viability and Vulnerability in Urban Development" (Paper presented at the seminar on the "Urban Informal Sector in the Center and Periphery," Johns Hopkins University, June 8 - 10, 1984); and Ray Bromley and Chris Gerry, eds., *Casual Work and Poverty in the Third World* (Chichester: John Wiley and Sons, 1979).

3. W.W. Rostow, *Stages in Economic Growth* (London: Cambridge University Press, 1960), outlined the road Third World economies must travel to move from a state of "underdevelopment" to one of being "developed." Also see the collection of articles in Harold Munoz, *From Dependency to Development: Strategy to Overcome Underdevelopment and Equality* (Boulder: Westview Press, 1981).

4. For a critique of modernist theories, see Andre Gunder Frank, *Latin America: Underdevelopment or Revolution* (New York: Monthly Review Press, 1969); Paul Streethen offers a good critique of these theories on his way to positing a similarly faulty basic needs theory in "Growth, Redistribution, and Basic Human Needs," in *Development Strategies and Basic Needs in Latin America: Challenges for the 1980's* Clae Brundenius and Mat Lundahl, (Boulder: Westview Press, 1982); and James L. Dietz, "Imperialism and Underdevelopment: A Theoretical Perspective and a Case Study of Puerto Rico," in *Review of Radical Political Economics*, vol. 4, no. 11 (Winter, 1979).

5. Lynn Bolles, "The Impact of Working Class Women's Employment on Household Organization in Kingston, Jamaica" (Ph.D. diss., Rutgers University, 1979); *Labour Force Report, 1981* (Kingston: Department of Statistics).

6. *Labour Force Report, 1981* (Kingston: Department of Statistics).

7. Joycelin Massiah, "Women Who Head Households," in *Women and the Family*, ed. Joycelin Massiah (Cave Hills, Barbardos: Institute of Social and Economic Research, ISER, University of the West Indies, 1982).

8. Raymond T. Smith, "Economic Features of the Household Group," in *The Negro Family in British Guiana*, Smith (London: Routledge and Kegan Paul, 1956); and Judith Blake, *Family Structure in Jamaica: The Social Context of Reproduction* (New York: The Free Press of Glencoe, Inc., 1961).

9. *Matrifocal* is employed here to describe a system whereby women/mothers are the culturally defined, positive central figure in the domestic unit and the kinship system; their purview is, however, primarily the domestic sphere. See Nancie Solien Gonzalez, "Toward a Definition of Matrifocality," in *Afro-American Anthropology: Contemporary Perspectives*, Norman Whitten and John Szwied, eds. (New York: Free Press, 1970); also see Lucille Mathurin's article entitled "Reluctant Matriarchs," in *Savacou* (Kingston: 1977).

10. See Massiah, "Women Who Head Households," in *Women and the Family*; Erna Brobder, "A Study of Yards in the City of Kingston," Working Paper No. 9 (Kingston: ISER, 1975); and Victoria Durant Gonzalez, "The Realm of Female Familial Responsibility," in *Women and the Family*.

11. Women tend to have five major junctures governing life stages. In early adulthood (15 to 25 years old), childbearing may begin while a woman is residing at home with parents. The young mother's economic involvement also begins after childbirth. Women may or may not be involved in visiting relationships. From 25 to 35, women may continue having children and may enter into a common-law relationship, or marry and continue working. Women 35 to 45 years old often marry and may conntinue having children (though this activity certainly tapers off) and work. Women 45 and older are usually in a stable relationship or just moving out of one, are working, and are beginning nuturing activities over again, as grandmothers. Women 55 years

old, still working, often in home business, are widowed or live alone and are heads of households.

12. Sherry Keith, "An Historical Overview of the State and Educational Policy in Jamaica," in *Latin American Perspectives*, Issue 17, vol. 5, no. 2, Spring 1978.

13. Julia Naish, "Desirade: A Negative Case," in *Women United, Women Divided: Comparative Studies of Ten Contemporary Cultures* (Bloomington: Indiana Press, 1979).

14. See the excellent articles in *Women, Men, and the International Division of Labor*, June Nash and Maria Patricia Fernandez-Kelly, eds. (Albany: State University of New York, 1983); Keziah Awosika, "Nigerian Women in the Informal Labour Market: Planning for Effective Participation" (Paper delivered at the "Women and Development" conference at Wellesley College, Center for Research on Women and the Professions, Wellesley, Massachusetts, June 2-6, 1976); Nici Nelson, "How Women and Men Get By: The Sexual Division of Labour in the Informal Sector of a Nairobi Squatter Settlement," in Bromley and Gerry, *Casual Workers*; and Alison MacEwen Scott, "Who are the Self-Employed?" in *Casual Workers*.

15. Higglers are self-employed workers who pay to harvest or pay for harvested products and then sell them for a profit in the marketplace. See Melvin R. Edwards, *Jamaican Higglers: Their Significance and Potential*, Monograph No. VII (Swansea, United Kingdom: University of Swansea Center for Development Studies, 1980).

REFERENCES

Bandarage, Asoka. "Women in Development: Liberalism, Marxism and Marxist-Feminism." *Development and Change*. Vol. 5. London: Sage, 1984.

Beneria, Lourdes, ed. *Women and Development: The Sexual Division of Labor in Rural Societies*. New York: Praeger, 1982.

"Reproduction, Production and the Sexual Division of Labour." *Cambridge Journal of Economics*, No. 3 (3), 1979.

Black, Naomi, and Cottrell, Ann Baker, eds. *Women and World Change: Equity Issues in Development*. Beverly Hills: Sage Publications, 1981.

Boserup, Ester. *Woman's Role in Economic Development*. London: George Allen and Unwin Ltd., 1970.

Brody, Eugene B. *Sex, Contraception and Motherhood in Jamaica*. Cambridge: Harvard University Press, 1981.

Kuhn, Annette, and Ann Marie Wolpe, eds. *Feminism and Materialism: Women and Modes of Production*. London: Routledge and Kegan Paul, 1978.

Mathurin, Lucille. "The Historical Study of Women in Jamaica from 1655-1844." Ph,D. Diss., University of the West Indies, 1974.

Meillassoux, Claude. "From Reproduction to Production: A Marxist Approach to Economic Anthropology." In Harold Wolpe, Ed., *Articulation of Modes of Production*. London: Rooutledge and Kegan Paul, 1980.

Mintz, Sidney W. *Caribbean Transformations*. Chicago: Aldine Publishing Company, 1974.

Portes, Alejandro, and John Walton. *Labor, Class and the International System*. New York: Academic Press, 1981.

Powell, Dorian L. "Female Labour Force Participation and Fertility: An Exploratory Study of Jamaican Women." *Social and Economic Studies*, Kingston: Institute for Social and Economic Research, September, 1976.

Roberts, George W., and Sonya Sinclair. *Women in Jamaica: Patterns of Reproduction and Family*. Millwood, New York: KTO Press, 1978.

Signs, Journal of Women in Culture and Society, vol. 7, no. 2. Chicago: University of Chicago Press, 1981.

Steady, Filomina Chioma, ed. *The Black Woman Cross-Culturally*. Cambridge: Schenkman Publishing Co., 1981.

YOU HAVE STRUCK A ROCK:
A NOTE ON THE STATUS OF
BLACK WOMEN IN SOUTH AFRICA[1]

Julianne Malveaux

No volume on the status of black women, especially one that includes a discussion of black women in developing countries, would be complete without a discussion on the status of black women under apartheid, in South Africa. This is especially true since the 1984-85 period marked a resurgence of world resistance to apartheid. This resistance included the awarding of the Nobel Peace Prize to South African Anglican Bishop Desmund Tutu, the birth of the "Free South Africa Movement" by the Washington, D.C. lobby TransAfrica, and campus protests for divestment in the spring of 1985. Indeed, by November 1985, more that 20 cities (including San Francisco, New York, Boston, and Pittsburgh), five states, and several universities had begun the divestment process. In addition, national anti-apartheid legislation was proposed in the spring of 1985; the Anti-Apartheid Act of 1985 passed the House of Representatives in September 1985. Though he vowed not to do so, President Reagan issued an executive order that imposed limited sanctions on South Africa in September 1985.

Despite the crescendo of protest against the injustices of apartheid, there may be questions about viewing the black women of South Africa in a section on women in developing countries. After all, the South African economy is perceived as strong, and indeed it is among the strongest of the African economies. It had a gross domestic product, in 1980, of $70 billion. It produces 20% of the goods and services of the African continent, though its population is just a fraction of that. South Africa is responsible for 50% of the African continent's electrical power, 80% of the steel output, 43% of telephones, and 43% of registered automobiles. On the African continent, South Africa boasts one of the higher standards of living (especially for whites).[2]

But although the South African economy may seem to be a "success" story, it is an economy with a myriad of weaknesses. Before a discussion of some of the characteristics of that economy, the reader may find useful an outline of some key weaknesses.

First, South African policymakers have attempted to portray South Africa as the rival of any industrialized country. But, in fact, the World Bank lists this country as a "middle-income developing country," a category that includes Argentina, Brazil, Nigeria, and Spain. As measured by most of the important economic indicators of development, South Africa lags behind other industrialized countries.[3]

Part of the reason for this gap may be that there are two, perhaps three, distinct economic trends in South Africa. There is a white economy, a black urban economy, and a black rural economy. This analysis clearly obscures aspects of Colored and Asian existences, but notes clearly that the data speak of distinct trends. Between black and white, urban and rural, there are disparate incomes, disparate economic lives, distinctions in education, differences in infant mortality. The data on infant mortality provide an example: among whites there are 13 deaths for every 1,000 live births; among Africans, the rate is 90 for every 1,000 live births. Estimates for rural Africans are as high as 320 for every 1,000 live births—higher than infant mortality rates in the poorest countries in the world. There are similar gaps in educational spending—the $1,115 a year spent on each white student rivals spending in many industrialized countries, and indeed in some states of the United States. The $170 a year spent on the average African student, is, in contrast, abysmally low.[4]

Black South African women complete school less frequently than men do. Although school attendance is poor among blacks, it is higher among African girls than among boys. More boys, however, graduate and are better prepared to enter the workplace. The limited educational opportunities available to black South African women, as well as obstacles to training, mean that black South African women have limited employment opportunities. "Most black women are denied the opportunity to rise above menial and/or manual labor."[5]

The differences in economic status may, in fact, account for South Africa's attempt to isolate blacks in "independent" homelands. If these blacks are isolated and their data are interpreted separately, then the economic status of rural blacks has no negative reflection on the economic evaluation of South Africa as a country.

In any case, it is interesting to note that South Africa, despite its imported technology and corporate presence, is viewed as a developing country, just like another country on the African continent, Nigeria.

Second, the South African economy is an open economy. Trading activities are so extensive that imports plus exports make up more than 50% of the gross domestic product, making South Africa particularly vulnerable to global economic fluctuation. In general, when the world economy is booming, so is the South African economy, and vice versa.

Third, South Africa's reliance on gold, combined with fluctuations in gold prices, again renders that economy vulnerable. The price of gold has declined from a high of $850 an ounce in 1980, to just under $400 in 1983, to a current low of about $325. This decline has placed additional pressure on the South African economy.

Fourth, rising internal security costs undermine the South African economy. Although reliable estimates of the costs of internal security are unavailable, it is clear that the State of Emergency (1985) as well as the administration of pass laws, has significant costs. These expenditures make funds unavailable for economic development.

Fifth, shortages of skilled labor in the economy are the direct result of South Africa's failure to provide educational and training opportunities to blacks.

If the weaknesses in the South African economy are considered,[6] then the position of black women in South Africa is seen as more parallel to the position of other women in developing countries. Whereas women in other developing countries have a chance of improving their situation as their economies improve, the particular character of apartheid will prevent the improvement of the status of black women in South Africa.

The fact of apartheid means that of 29 million South Africans, only 4.5 million whites have full citizenship rights. Some 21 million Africans are treated as foreigners. Black South Africans cannot vote, cannot purchase land, cannot choose living or working conditions, and cannot move freely. "They have been stripped of power and deprived of control of their lives by an elaborate network of legislation and custom."[7]

The impacts of apartheid on black South African women are myriad. Although this article focuses on economic and employment impacts, it is important to note that apartheid permeates every fiber of the fabric of black South African life. Mamazane Xulu, a South African social worker who was forced to move to the United States after the Soweto protests, describes the social structure among blacks as "in chaos" because of apartheid. Women who hold jobs are lucky to earn income, but are un-

able to supervise their children properly because of the excessive commutes and other burdens imposed by apartheid. Children are robbed of
their youth by violence in their schools and in their communities—a
violence initiated by the government of South Africa. Families are forbid-
den to live together by the provisions of apartheid—men who work in
mines and factories are usually housed, by law, in single-sex dormitories.
Domestics are usually only allowed one day a week at home and are
forced to live with their employers. The deterioration of the quality of
black family life seems an intentional product of the apartheid system.[8]

There are more than 10 million black women in South Africa, of whom
about 7 million are over the age of 16. Fewer than 1.5 million of these
women work in paid employment, and the majority of them—almost
800,000—work as domestics. Salaries for domestic workers are pitifully
low, ranging from $40 to $80 a month.[9] It is clear that domestic pay is too
low to support a household; the Household Subsistence level ranges between $243 and $268 a month for an African family, yet wages are as low
as $160 per month. Maggie Oweies, head of the Domestic Workers Asso-
ciation, has stated that many domestics work up to 16-hour days, seven
days a week, at rates as low as three cents an hour.[10]

Low wages may be the least of the problems imposed on black South
African women with domestic jobs. The hours for these women are long;
working conditions are frequently horrendous. The play Homeland, by
black South African writer Selaelo Maredi, dramatized the long commutes, low pay, and demeaning work conditions that black women in
domestic service face. Domestic workers usually live in single-room
shacks in their employers' backyards. They are not permitted visits from
their family, and their employers are subject to fines if family members
visit overnight.[11] When not living on the premises, domestic workers face
long commutes. Lelyveld's book Move Your Shadow documents the way
black workers are treated as irresponsible children by their employers,
despite the fact that blacks travel as many as four hours each way to reach
their jobs on time.[12] It is also important to note that the employers of
South African black women in domestic service are not required to
provide health, pension, or maternity benefits for workers.

Some black women who do not work in domestic service are employed
in factories, especially canning and clothing factories. Many of these
women work for the subsidiaries of U.S. corporations and are paid, on
average, 17% of the earnings of their white counterparts. Like domestics,
these women have no benefits from employment—no health benefits, no
pension benefits, and no maternity benefits. According to Mamazane

Xulu, the Sullivan Principles and other U.S. initiatives to improve the terms and conditions of work for black workers have not had an impact on black women in manufacturing.[13]

Hilda Bernstein notes that paid employment in urban areas is higher (37%) than in the homelands. She notes, however, that most workers are domestics, "followed by smaller proportions of manufacturing (8%) and professional (7%) workers."[14] Women in manufacturing are not usually provided with company housing but are forced to live in government-run hostels and under strict regulations. At a hostel outside of Durban, 11,000 women are housed in six buildings, behind locked gates, with 24-hour police patrols.[15]

A few black women are employed in "professional" jobs in South Africa. Most of these professional women have university educations but were constrained by apartheid in their choice of university. Education in South Africa is racially segregated, with "racially differentiated curricula." But not only is education racially segregated; it is also segregated by ethnicity. Zulus attend the University of Zululand; Xhosas attend the University of Fort Hare; and others attend the University of the North.[16] Educational isolation does not lead to occupational segregation but instead perpetuates the concept of tribal differences that the South African government has promoted as a reason for "homelands."

Most professional black South African women work as teachers, nurses, and social workers. By law, they provide their services only to black South Africans in schools, hospitals, or social service agencies. They are paid between 20% and 30% of the salaries of their white counterparts, even though they have comparable educations. Nurses work long hours at low pay and risk forfeiting their jobs if they become pregnant. This means that many black nurses hide their pregnancies and return to work the day after delivery.[17]

A very few black women work as lawyers or doctors in South Africa. Like their professional sisters in teaching, nursing, and social work, their practices are confined, by law, to the black community, and their pay is similarly depressed. A very finite number (fewer than .5%) of working black women are employed in the corporate world in South Africa—some in clerical and some in professional positions. The numbers of these women are so few, and the information about them so sparse, that no analysis of their status is attempted in this article.

Most black South African women do not work for pay. Isolated in homelands or bantustans by the Group Areas Act and the Black (Urban Areas) Consolidation Act,[18] those black women who do not work eke out an existence for themselves and their children in barren land that is frequently without running water, food, or other survival necessities. Lelyveld describes some of the absurdities of homeland settlements. Because of the imposition of homelands provisions, the majority of black South Africans currently live in homelands. A large number were forcibly removed to these areas.[19] As a result of the Lands Acts of 1913 and 1936, 87% of the country's territory has been reserved for whites and just 13% for blacks, who are 72% of the country's population.

Forcible removal of blacks to homelands escalated in 1960. Before the development of homelands policies, black women who did not work in the paid labor force farmed ancestral land for the survival of their families. After being relocated to the most barren land in South Africa, they found farming efforts were futile. Instead, the majority of black South African women take care of their babies and families as best they can.

It is ironic to note that whereas the labor force participation of black women in South Africa is constrained by apartheid, the growth of the South African economy can be maintained only by an increase in the number of skilled workers in the country. Though the South African economy has grown by 4.4% in recent years, the country's own economic projections indicate that it would need a growth rate of 5% to sustain the current standard of living. Growth has been sluggish because there has been a shortage of skilled workers in South Africa. This shortage could be remedied if black workers were afforded educational and training opportunities. But because of institutional barriers, more than a million skilled workers are currently needed, but unavailable. Even if arpartheid were eliminated today, there would not be enough qualified and trained blacks to fill vacant positions.[20]

Ironically, black incomes are another key aspect of projected economic growth. The white population, sated with consumer goods, is growing more slowly than the black population. So blacks not only represent 40% of the consumer market, but also represent more than 50% of the sales base for some merchants. South Africa seems stuck on a self-destructive path by restricting black incomes through apartheid. Without the spending power of increased black income, South African economic growth is likely to remain sluggish.[21]

Although apartheid restricts black societal participation, economic reality dictates participation. Industrialist Harry Oppenheimer argues that continued growth will force social and political modifications in the apartheid system. In simple economic terms, why increase manufacturing when there is a shrinking set of consumers among whom to sell goods?[22]

Whereas Oppenheimer and others advocate economic growth, the apartheid system is a major economic drain on the South African economy. South Africa has the highest per capita prison population in the world, and convicts a black of pass law violations nearly every three minutes. The costs of internal security are conservatively estimated as between 5% and 15% of gross domestic product, or between $3.5 and $10.5 billion.

For black women in South Africa, apartheid has meant not only a restriction of labor market opportunities but also a systematic crippling of dreams for black women, their families, and their children. As black women in the United States examine their status, it is important that they note this linkage with their South African sisters and that they acknowledge their responsibility in the maintenance of apartheid.

Black women in the United States, who fall between the cracks in an analysis of racism and sexism, have much in common with their South African sisters, who fall between the cracks of economic oppression, sexism, and apartheid. The linkages in our life patterns should inspire black American women to work for divestment, for material aid to black South Africans, and ultimately for an end to the U.S. role in the South African economy.

NOTES

1. "You have struck a rock, you have touched a woman" was a slogan coined by black South African women on August 9, 1956, during a protest against the imposition of passes on women. See *Forward to Freedom: Women and Apartheid in South Africa* (San Francisco:AAWO Discussion Papers, July 1985) for discussion of the resistance to apartheid by black South African women.

2. Study Commission on U.S. Policy Toward Southern Africa, *South Africa: Time Running Out* (Berkeley: University of California Press, 1981).

3. Ibid.

4. The Africa Fund, *South Africa Fact Sheet* (New York: American Committee on Africa, 1984).

5. Washington Office on Africa Educational Fund, "Fact Sheet: Education and Employment Opportunities for Women Under Apartheid" (Washington, D.C.: Washington Office on Africa, 1985).

6. See also Sanford Wright, "Struggling Against Apartheid: The Use of Economic Sanctions on South Africa" in *Review of Black Political Economy* 13, no. 3 (Winter 1984-85) for a discussion of the vulnerabilities of the South African economy.

7. The Africa Fund, *South African Fact Sheet.*

8. Mamazane Xulu, ANC Women's Section, Interview, October 1985.

9. The Africa Fund, *South Africa Fact Sheet.*

10. Washington Office On Africa Educational Fund, "Fact Sheet."

11. Ibid.

12. Joseph Lelyveld, *Move Your Shadow: South Africa, Black and White* (New York: New York Times Books, 1985).

13. Mamazane Xulu, interview.

14. Hilda Bernstein, *For Their Triumphs and for Their Tears: Women in Apartheid South Africa* (New York: Africa Fund, 1978).

15. Washington Office on Africa Educational Fund, "Fact Sheet."

16. Mamazane Xulu, interview.

17. Ibid.

18. The Africa Fund, *South Africa Fact Sheet*.

19. Joseph Lelyveld, *Move Your Shadow*.

20. Study Commission on U.S. Policy Toward Southern Africa, *South Africa: Time Running Out*.

21. Ibid.

22. Ibid.

DISCUSSION

Gloria L. Scott

The need for creating employment and income-generating oppor-tunities for a rapidly growing population and labor force, especially in urban areas, is among the most serious development issues—one that is serious in both industrial and developing countries. A particular dimen-sion of the issue relates to the gender and class distinctions in labor force participation and access to means of production. Some of these aspects are discussed in the two articles presented to the panel on international development—Johnson's article on "Women and Self-Employment in Tanzania," and Mason's piece on "Jamaican Working-Class Women: Pro-ducers and Reproducers."

Johnson draws her data from a well-respected and much quoted survey of "National Urban Mobility, Employment, and Income in Tanzania." It is, however, 1971 data and policy planners should by now be using it as a benchmark for measuring changes. It is hoped that focusing attention on women's self-employment—a very overlooked area of study—should sug-gest questions to be raised in future surveys. Mason derives her data from a 1982 survey of 30 factory or industrially employed women and 25 petty commodity producers in Jamaica. The sample is too small to be represen-tative in any sense, but for those women it does reveal some of the features known from other sources, and some of which fit with Johnson's findings.

Possibilities for creating employment are very much tied to global de-velopment issues—the availability of investment funds, trade restrictions, comparative labor costs, etc., which also contribute to the flight of jobs. As increasing numbers of women join the labor force (some 10 million annually in the last decade, estimated to increase to 13 million annually between 1985 and 2000), it is important to examine the gender implica-tions both of new employment opportunities and of retrenchment. Available evidence suggests that in countries like Jamaica where female-employing assembly-type and export processing industries predominate in the manufacturing sector, women—the least protected by international laws and labor legislation—are the first to be affected by economic recession and by relocation of industries. Already, women account for a larger share than men of those unemployed. Mason cites the loss of jobs for women, mainly in screwdriver industries, because of retrenchment in the manufacturing sector in Jamaica.

For growing numbers of women, an economic contribution is essential for the maintenance and survival of their families, either because of the low earnings of the spouse or other family members, or because the women themselves are heads of households. (It should be noted that worldwide women head one-third of all households. Among black U.S. households the proportion is some 40%.) Many of these women have limited access to formal employment and informal sector self-employment is their only hope for obtaining income. It is important to understand better the factors limiting their work choices, and the characteristics of the women themselves and also of their undertakings.

In Tanzania, self-employment described by Johnson comprises a fairly wide range of activities, many using traditional technologies, requiring low skill levels, and most yeilding low returns. Women are usually at the lower end of the earnings curve. Two-thirds of the self-employed women are either in farming or street trading, activities yielding among the lowest self-employment income and rarely integrated with modern economic activities and methods of production. Mason describes similar activities undertaken by nearly half the factory workers in her survey (in addition to their full-time factory employment) in order to supplement their salaries. Her discussion of the trader's mark-up and returns lead me to draw attention to a frequent problem with own-account activities, especially the petty activities of women—namely omitting from the profit and loss equation many costs, such as time and transport, which affect their returns. The notion is perpetuated that women's time has no value and that the time and effort they devote to household maintenance similarly is of no value.

The Tanzania study notes as factors contributing to the low levels of earnings, women's limited education/skill training, and their limited access to investment capital due to customs and attitudes related both to gender and to women's relative economic position. The highest capital investments were made by women not currently married, and for Tanzania (the same is true of Ghana) marriage seems to limit women's earnings from self-employment by limiting both mobility and the ability to make independent entrepreneurial decisions. That is, nondomestic economic activities are defined by the role of wife and mother.

Mason claims that in Jamaica, the role of mother is the principal reason for women's involvement in income-generating activities. The disposal of earnings—saving for children's education, providing lunch money for children, paying for technical training for children—supports this claim. From her discussion of the ideology of motherhood (which I do not find relevant), two points are significant for policy and apply in many parts of the world. The first is early childbearing linked to ignorance and first experimentation with sex. Teenage pregnancy is a worldwide calamity and in some countries (e.g., Tanzania, where it rules out any chance for further education) it is seriously limiting the life choices for numbers of girls. The second is the perception of motherhood as one of life's few positive options for many poor women and its influence in perpetuating high fertility tendencies. This is inadequately appreciated by organizers of family planning programs. Early and frequent childbearing starts a chain of deprivation for both mothers and their offspring, and daughters in large families who start assisting mothers from a very young age get set in their undervalued female role.

I must confess to some frustration with my assignment. Each of the essays touches some issues that are relevant for development policy and I have tried to highlight these. However, the subject is vast, and women's role in, and contribution to, development has been so poorly articulated that we have merely scratched the surface. Among issues that should be further discussed are:

- *The deficiency of the database*: It is deficient on gender/age in general, and on women's labor force or work contribution it is often inaccurate and misleading. The data cloud both the fact of women's occupational multiplicity and the fact that, especially among the poor, women's relative contribution to family income is largest;
- *The importance of functional education for women*: There is need to identify and deal with the constraints on young women's access to education which will prepare them for the labor market, improve the productivity of their own-account enterprises (as well as their household work), and lead to long-run benefits for their families;
- *The interplay of culture and economics:* Attitudes and perceptions of both males and females, and the system of social organizations intervene in policy formulation and implementation and lead to unantici-

pated consequences with economic costs that frequently fall hardest on women. Discrimination against women is harmful not only to women, but affects society at large.

Finally, concern for women must fit into a total development strategy, which for each country is affected by the world economy and by a host of factors outside the control of the particular government. Since this symposium took place in the United States, it would have been useful to identify some specific links between U.S. policy, including that on development assistance, and women's opportunities in the countries being discussed.

Rational consideration of women's role in development must be based on information that permits assessment and comparison of changes over time. These essays indicate lines of inquiry and approaches to providing that information at the macro level for Tanzania and the micro level for Jamaica. Information at both levels is needed and more such studies might be encouraged by governments and supported by development assistance agencies.

SECTION INTRODUCTION

Julianne Malveaux

When *The Review of Black Political Economy* and the Congressional Black Caucus Foundation chose to collaborate on this undertaking, a Symposium on Black Women, California Assemblywoman Maxine Waters was the unanimous choice for opening speaker. Assemblywoman Waters represents the political future of black women—she is an advocate committed to addressing the inequities that are discussed in some of the articles in this volume. Waters has also been a force in developing the political empowerment of black women. She founded the Black Women's Forum in Los Angeles, serves on the Board of Directors of TransAfrica, and is a founder and Political Action Committee chair of the National Political Congress of Black Women.

In her opening comments, Waters noted that the Symposium on Black Women was the first in the 15-year existence of the Congressional Black Caucus. But as she reviewed the statistics that are by now familiar—the number of female-headed households, the levels of black poverty, high unemployment rates of black females, and the status of black children—she made it clear that a focus on black women has been long overdue.

The fact that the status of black women has been so frequently overlooked inspired the theme of this volume: "Slipping Through the Cracks." Indeed, between the cracks of focus on black men and on white women is a realm of underdeveloped information on the status of black women.

A focus on that status raises questions about the politics of race and the politics of gender. As we examine both the role of black women in the economy and ways to improve the status of black women, we are also confronted with questions about the effectiveness of political coalitions designed to improve the status of "women" or of "blacks," even as subgroups of these coalitions reap limited benefits from supporting such efforts.

Will a focus on the status of black women change a legislative agenda focused on the well-being of blacks, or on the well-being of women? Such a question provoked Bella Abzug's statement to President Jimmy Carter, "Every issue is a women's issue." "Black women's issues" include not only welfare and child care, but also peace and U.S. presence in other countries. "Black women's issues" encompass not only budget cuts but also budget composition. But even as "black women's issues" are global and broad, a sensitivity to the presence of black women adds another dimension to policy perspectives.

Proponents of the Women's Economic Equity Act, for example, failed to note that certain provisions of that act focused on the status of upper- and middle-income women while ignoring the status of low-income women, who gain little from insurance reform. A sensitivity to the breadth of the "women's coalition" might have suggested placing more effort on those provisions of the bill that all women could have supported, such as the day care provisions. Similarly, efforts at job creation, which usually have a positive effect on the black community, usually focus on public works jobs. Concern with the status of black women will mean either making public works jobs more available to women or including a broader range of jobs in job creation efforts.

Our symposium on black women was designed to allow researchers the opportunity to address a set of key policy issues—to make suggestions about both the resolution of these issues and an improvement in the status of black women. Although Professor Phyllis Wallace was unable to join us, she has provided us with an outline for future research on the economic status of black women. Wallace asks pointed questions about the status of black female-headed families that must be addressed by researchers in the future.

Wallace raises a series of questions unasked in many of the articles included in this volume. When she asks about the status of workers in low-wage industries, she is raising questions as much about the status of workers as about the characteristics of these industries. Far too many of the policies formulated to "help" black women have been supply-side policies that have assumed that with education, training, or other human capital enhancements black women might better move into the labor market. Wallace suggests that an investigation on the characteristics of industries (and a possible improvement in those characteristics) might equally improve the status of black women.

As many of the writers in this volume have done, Wallace addresses the status of black men and notes that the status of black men and that of black women are intertwined. In fact, as the status of black men has declined, the status of the black community and the status of the black family have declined as well. As Wallace asserts the connection between black men and women, she further asserts the unique status of black women. Thus, although the status of black men is recognized, such recognition does not preclude the focus on black women that is the subject of this volume.

Wallace also raises the question of welfare dependency in the black community and questions the effectiveness of workfare programs. Maxine Waters asked this question during the symposium when she questioned the types of jobs that would be available to black women under California's newly passed workfare law. Whereas the characteristics of public assistance programs are of concern to black women, the acceptability of substitute programs is also at issue. Discussion at the symposium revealed no opponents to the training of black women but much concern for the quality of training and the options workfare poses for women on AFDC.

It is important to note that workfare has developed differently in different states. California's law, passed in 1985, may not take full effect until 1990. Massachusetts, on the other hand, implemented a workfare program in 1983 that is reported to be successful in providing long-term career options to women who have received public assistance.

As in the workfare case, the detail legislators put into formulating the law will be important in determining the impact of law and policy on black women. Recognizing this fact, the Symposium on Black Women closed with a legislative/policy agenda. Several aspects of the legislative agenda will have a positive impact on black women and on the entire black community. However, the legislative agenda represents an attempt to prioritize the needs of black women in employment, affirmative action, community survival, child care, and education.

The research and legislative agendas presented in this section move us past investigation and into activism. Maxine Waters challenged researchers, in her opening remarks, to investigate the problems of black women and to formulate solutions to these problems. The legislative agenda that was the result of much discussion is, perhaps, a challenge to legislators to incorporate proposed solutions into a policy initiative that will plug the cracks black women have so frequently slipped through and improve the status of black women.

A RESEARCH AGENDA ON THE ECONOMIC STATUS OF BLACK WOMEN

Phyllis A. Wallace

In the economic sphere, black and white women share many common concerns, but there are significant differences in their employment, occupation, and income status. Some of those differences are associated with the double burden of differential treatment on account of sex and race; and other differences are attributed to dissimilar endowments of productivity characteristics (education, skills, work experience, etc.). However, some differences derive from the deteriorating economic status of black males. The erosion of the labor force participation of black men, their excessively high rates of unemployment, their incapacitation because of poor health, and their incarceration in disproportionate numbers have left black families at great economic risk. Here are the stark statistics:

- Black female heads accounted for 22% of black family households in 1960, 28% in 1970, and 43% by 1984. Married couple families had declined from 68% of black family households in 1970 to 52% in 1984.
- During the past 15 years black family households increased by about 37% (from 4.8 million to 6.6 million), but black female heads of family households more than doubled (from 1.3 million to 2.9 million).
- Eighty-four percent of the increase in black families during the 1970-1984 period was accounted for by the increase in black female heads of families mainly from single never-married black females.
- These female-headed families have more children under 18 years of age and have available to them significantly less in economic resources than other categories of families, black or white.

Approximately a third of all black families were below the poverty threshold of $10,069 (for an urban family of four) in 1984. Even when the poverty estimates allowed for the value of noncash benefits such as food stamps and Medicaid, there was no significant change in the poverty rate among blacks. Thus, 70% of all black families in poverty have a female head, and nearly half of all black children live in these families. Median income in 1983 was $21,840 for married couple black families, $15,552 for black male head, and $7,999 for black female householders; (no husband present). The emergence of the greatly impoverished black female head of family household as the primary economic support of black families has far-reaching economic and social consequences, not fully comprehended by many social science analysts.

Black women have traditionally made significant contributions to the economic well-being of their families. Black women whether as workers and recipients of wages and salaries, as nonparticipants in the labor force and recipients of welfare payments and noncash benefits, or dual participants in work and welfare, should be the focus of a major assessment of the economic status of the black communtity.

Such an effort would not require costly data collection or elaborate research designs. Since the mid-1960s there has been a voluminous output of studies in which black females have been represented. Unfortunately, these examinations of employment and training programs, welfare, teenage pregnancy and parenting, and workfare have been narrow in scope. Economists, sociologists, social workers, psychologists, and political scientists have pursued their separate perspectives, frequently duplicating the conventional wisdom of another discipline. What is required now is a more *holistic* approach.

We would ask such an interdisciplinary research team to identify the forces that have produced such a dismal present for black families and indicate ways to alter the future. Some of the questions raised would be:

- Given the shifts underway in the national economy toward a knowledge-based and more technical workplace, how realistic is it to assume that AFDC women can attain economic self-sufficiency?
- Can workfare effectively restructure welfare programs, reduce dependency, and enable the participants to make a permanent transition to well-paying jobs in the labor market?
- Do full-time workers in low wage industries have options for enhancing their earnings?
- What would be the impact on incomes in black female-headed fam-

ilies of a major effort to improve the labor market opportunities of black adult males?

- Could incomes in black female-headed families be improved through a more effective program of jobs for black teenagers?
- What complementary strategies in education, housing, and social services are required of black female heads of families who continue to provide the economic support for the family?
- How much will some restructuring of the black family cost and who will share the burden?

A LEGISLATIVE/POLICY AGENDA TO IMPROVE THE STATUS OF BLACK WOMEN

Julianne Malveaux and Margaret C. Simms

Over a two-day period, in five research sessions, 19 researchers addressed the status of black women. Our examinations restated several known aspects of inequity, and in some cases have found new manifestations of inequitable treatment. More than 10 years after the term "double jeopardy" was coined by *Black Scholar* editor Fran Beal, the essays presented during our series of panels on black women reveal continuing double jeopardy—in employment, in education, as single mothers, in health status, and, yes, in developing *countries*.

It is important for us to note that our focus on the status of black women is not at all meant to divert attention from the very drastic problems that face the total black community. Instead, our effort is meant to talk about ways we can *strengthen* the status of the black community, both now and in the future. The majority of black children, at this time, live in families headed by black women. These children share their mother's jeopardy as their future options are limited by the present constraints their mothers face.

The status of black women is connected with the status of black communities—of black men and black children. But a specific look at black women's status is warranted at this time, especially since researchers have, all too frequently, studied men who are black and women who are white, with the status of black women an invisible one.

While our panels have documented some inequity, it is the challenge of legislators and policymakers to shape our research findings into legislation that corrects measured inequities. It is to this end that we offer the following policy agenda.

- The employment panel revealed the need to alter aspects of our economic structure so that full employment at fair wages with adequate benefits is available for everyone. Otherwise, programs that provide training but no jobs, or affirmative action with no employment expansion, merely shift the burden of unemployment from one population to another. From this perspective, we oppose subminimum wage legislation and municipal subcontracting when it leads to low wage employment. We encourage development of legislation that provides all workers with jobs and dignity on the job.

- Our tax structure must be examined so that tax incentives generate positive employment opportunities, especially for black women. Our current tax structure taxes labor, but not capital, encouraging international capital flight and employment loss. As the nation turns its attention to our tax structure and our growing deficit, we must also view tax incentives and write-off provisions to alter their negative impact on employment structure. Neither of the above two points directly address the status of black women. But because black women occupy *the bottom* of the economic and employment structure, improvements in these structures have a necessarily positive effect on the status of black women. This is true of the next policy points as well.

- Preserve affirmative action. Justice Department efforts to dismantle affirmative action systems are misguided, ill-informed attempts to erode limited gains made by black workers in the past 15 years. There is evidence that affirmative action had a positive impact on black educational and employment access. Until equity is attained, affirmative action should be maintained and enforced as a vital tool.

  It should be noted that detractors of affirmative action have indicated that affirmative action "assumes" inferiority. Yet black competence was not invented in the post-1965 period. Affirmative action has been and will continue to be an effective tool to fight institutional racism, but this tool needs legislative help to continue to survive.

- Revise budget choices to more closely reflect the community survival priorities. In other words, excessive military spending can be eliminated to provide more funds for education, training, and social programs. Alternative budget priorities should include urban revitalization; soil, forest, and energy work; and child-care provision, among others.

- Make the area of child-care provision a priority. Available child care makes it easier for women to participate in the labor force, attend school, and receive training; few of the options available to black women will be effective if black women cannot take advantage of these opportunities.

- Improve educational access by increasing financial aid to black students in the form of direct aid and work study aid. Cuts in student aid have had a disproportionate impact on black students, the majority of whom come from families with incomes of less than $12,000. Other initiatives to expand educational access would include removing penalties for decreases in aid for acquiring additional aid. Such provisions severely affect poor women with children who cannot subsist on the current ceiling. Finally, educational access is maintained through Title III support for traditionally black colleges (which educate 27% of black students with a limited resource base). The proposed revisions under the Higher Educational Aid Act of 1985 are important for black women.

- Black women who are self-employed have lower incomes than other groups who are in business for themselves.. But women who are employed by black-owned businesses face less discrimination than in nonblack owned corporate settings. In addition, as long as the domestic economy is unlikely to generate adequate employment opportunities, the development of black businesses committed to a strong black hiring program has a very positive impact on the black community. For both black women business owners and black women employed by black business, set-asides and other public supports for minority-owned businesses are needed.

- Increasing numbers of black women have little access to health systems. The absence of health insurance is common among the unemployed *and* underemployed who are ineligible for Medicaid. Legislation that moves toward national health care while incorporating elements of hospital cost containment is appropriate. At a minimum, catastrophic health insurance should be generally available. The quality of health service delivery in the black community is preserved by providing access in health occupations for black workers.

- When federal funds are made available to developing countries, mention should be made of the special problems of black women in these countries. Where appropriate, a portion of funds should be set aside to specifically address women's status in developing countries.

- Employment and training programs when properly structured, have a significant impact on black women's economic status. Therefore, attention should be given to ensuring that these programs have incentives that promote the access of black women to employment and training activities that will provide upward mobility in jobs. This approach, rather than punitive measures such as workfare or welfare reductions, are more fruitful avenues for policy revisions.

ABOUT THE AUTHORS

Charles L. Betsey, Ph.D., has been study director of the Committee on Youth Employment Programs at the National Academy of Sciences for the past two years.

Lynn C. Burbridge, Ph.D., is a staff economist for the Joint Center for Political Studies.

Bernadette Chachere, Ph.D., is chair of the Department of Economics at Hampton University.

Cecilia A. Conrad, Ph.D., is an assistant professor of economics at Barnard College, Columbia University.

William A. Darity, Jr., Ph.D., is an associate professor in the Department of Economics at the University of North Carolina at Chapel Hill.

Karen Fulbright, Ph.D., is assistant professor of human resources and urban studies at the New School for Social-Research.

Harriett Harper is chief of the Division of Statistical and Economic Analysis at the Women's Bureau of the U.S. Department of Labor.

Alvin E. Headen, Jr, Ph.D., is an economist with the Center for Health Policy Research of the American Medical Association.

Sandra W. Headen, Ph.D., is an assistant professor of psychology at the University of Health Sciences/Chicago Medical School.

Beryl B. Jackson, Ph.D., is an assistant professor of psychiatric and mental health nursing in the School of Nursing, University of Pittsburgh.

John M. Jeffries, Ph.D., is a research associate at the Urban Research Center of New York University.

Willene A. Johnson, Ph.D., is an economist at the Federal Reserve Bank of New York.

Barbara A.P. Jones, Ph.D., is a professor of economics at Clark College.

Ron Law is executive director of the Paul Robeson Health Organization in New York City.

Harriette Pipes McAdoo, Ph.D., is a professor in the School of Social Work at Howard University.

Fred McKinney, Ph.D., is an assistant professor in the Florence Heller School for Advanced Studies in Social Welfare at Brandeis University.

Julianne Malveaux, Ph.D., is a visiting scholar in the Afro-American Studies Department and the Institute for Industrial Relations at the University of California at Berkeley.

Beverly J. Mason, Ph.D., is currently working as a consultant in the Washington, D.C. area.

Samuel L. Myers, Jr., Ph.D., is an associate professor in the Graduate School of Public and International Affairs at the University of Pittsburgh.

Gloria L. Scott is a former advisor on women in development at the World Bank.

Margaret C. Simms, Ph.D., is director of the Minorities and Social Policy Program at the Urban Institute. She is also editor of *The Review of Black Political Economy*.

Phyllis A. Wallace, Ph.D., is professor of management in the Sloan School of Management at Massachusetts Institute of Technology.

Margaret B. Wilkerson, Ph.D., is an associate professor in the Department of Afro-American Studies at the University of California at Berkeley.

Stephanie Y. Wilson, Ph.D., is a senior economist and vice-president for international economic development at Abt Associates.